John Freely was born in New York and joined the US Navy at the age of seventeen, serving with a commando unit in Burma and China during the last years of World War II. He has lived in New York, Boston, London, Athens and Istanbul and has written over forty travel books and guides, most of them about Greece and Turkey. He is author of *The Grand Turk*, *Storm on Horseback*, *The Cyclades*, *The Ionian Islands* (all I.B.Tauris), *Crete*, *The Western Shores of Turkey*, *Strolling Through Athens*, *Strolling Through Venice* and the bestselling *Strolling Through Istanbul* (all Tauris Parke Paperbacks).

In memory of my beloved brother Jim

Children of Achilles

The Greeks in Asia Minor
since the Days of Troy

John Freely

I.B. TAURIS

LONDON · NEW YORK

Published in 2010 by I.B.Tauris & Co. Ltd
6 Salem Road, London W2 4BU
175 Fifth Avenue, New York NY 10010
www.ibtauris.com

Distributed in the United States and Canada Exclusively by Palgrave Macmillan,
175 Fifth Avenue, New York NY 10010

ISBN 978 1 84511 941 6

A full CIP record for this book is available from the British Library
A full CIP record for this book is available from the Library of Congress
Library of Congress catalog card: available

Typeset in Sabon by Dexter Haven Associates Ltd, London
Printed and bound in Great Britain by
CPI Antony Rowe, Chippenham

FSC
Mixed Sources
Product group from well-managed
forests and other controlled sources
Cert no. SGS-COC-2953
www.fsc.org
© 1996 Forest Stewardship Council

Contents

Illustrations

MAPS

ILLUSTRATIONS (BETWEEN PAGES 108–109)

Prologue – The Trojan Plain

I first visited the site of ancient Troy in April 1961, on my spring vacation at Robert College in Istanbul, where I had started teaching the previous September. My wife Dolores and I and our three small children set out from Istanbul aboard a ship of the Turkish Maritime Lines, which brought us to the port of Çanakkale on the Asian shore of the Dardanelles, the Greek Hellespont. We were accompanied by my student Andreas Dimitriadis, an ethnic Greek with Turkish citizenship, who had decided to join us at the last moment, when he learned that we were going to visit Troy.

Tourism had not yet begun in Turkey, and so we had the site of Troy all to ourselves, except for a Turkish gendarme who was guarding the ruins. I had reread Homer in preparation for our visit, as well as the works of the archaeologists who had studied the site, starting with Heinrich Schliemann, who in 1870 began excavating the huge mound on the Trojan plain known as Hisarlık, hoping to find Homeric Troy.

Schliemann excavated the Hisarlık mound in seven major campaigns between 1870 and 1890. He originally thought that the Homeric city was the second stratum from the bottom of the multilayered palimpsest of ruins, which he called Troy II, now dated ca. 2500–2300 BC. This was more than a thousand years too early for it to have been destroyed in the Trojan War, traditionally dated to ca. 1200 BC. During his 1890 campaign he and his assistant Wilhelm Dörpfeld came upon fragments of Mycenaean pottery in the sixth layer like those they had unearthed at Mycenae and Tiryns, which he had dated to the period of the Trojan War. Schliemann died the following year, but Dörpfeld continued the excavations, and in 1893 and 1894 he discovered the massive fortification walls and great houses of Troy VI, along with much Mycenaean pottery. Dörpfeld estimated that Troy VI had lasted from ca. 1500 to 1000 BC, its destruction layer agreeing roughly with the traditional date for the Trojan War. This convinced him, as he wrote in 1902, that 'The long dispute over the existence of Troy and its site is at an end... Schliemann has been vindicated.'

It was a beautiful spring day, and after we explored the ruins we had a picnic under a valonia oak on the peak of the Hisarlık mound, which was still deeply scarred by Schliemann's excavation trenches. The mound commanded a sweeping view to the north-west, the noonday sun glinting on what Homer called the 'fair waters' of the Skamandros river as it meandered through the 'blossoming meadow' of the Trojan plain, on its way to join the 'swift flowing' Hellespont just above the Asian promontory at Kum Kale, where the strait joins the Aegean.

A short way to the south of Kum Kale we could see two conical mounds standing close by one another near the Aegean shore. I realised that these were the tumuli that Schliemann had identified as the tombs of Achilles and Patroclus. Andreas and I decided that we would hike out across the plain to Kum Kale to have a close look at the tumuli, while Dolores watched the children as they played among the ruins on the mound. I estimated from my map that Kum Kale was about six kilometres distant, which shouldn't take us much more that an hour. But it took at least twice as long because our way was blocked by the Scamander, which we finally managed to cross near Kum Kale on a primitive Tarzan-like bridge made from two cables, one to tightrope walk on and the other to grasp hand over hand.

We found the tumuli about a kilometre south of Kum Kale, and we stopped to rest at the one that Schliemann had identified as the Tomb of Achilles, which was surrounded by the turbaned tombstones of an old Turkish graveyard. I recognised the tumulus from an engraving in Schliemann's *Troy and its Remains*, where the caption identifies it as the 'Mound called the Tomb of Achilles'. Schliemann based his identification on a passage that he had translated in Book XXIV of the *Odyssey*, where Agamemnon appears to Achilles in a dream, telling him of how he and Patroclus were buried by their comrades: 'Then we the holy host of Argive warriors piled over them (thy bones) a great and goodly tomb on a jutting headland upon the wide Hellespont, that it might be visible far off from the sea, to men who now are, and to those that shall hereafter be born.'

While we were examining the tumulus we were startled to hear the sound of approaching hoofbeats, and then we saw half-a-dozen horsemen approaching us from the ridge that parallels the Aegean shore between Kum Kale and the Sigaeum promontory, one of the landmarks in the topography of Homeric Troy.

We walked out to the road to meet the horsemen, who bade us welcome and asked us who we were and what we were doing. Andreas told them that I was an American professor and that he was my student, explaining that we were exploring the surroundings of ancient Troy. The oldest of the horsemen, who appeared to be in his seventies, knew that Troy was an ancient Anatolian city that had been conquered by the Greeks, or so he had been told at school. He said that he and his companions were from the village of Yenişehir, which means 'New City', and that in his youth at least half of his neighbours had been Greeks. He told us that he had always gotten along well with his Greek neighbours and had often been invited to join them at *paniyeria*, their religious festivals. But they had all left in 1923, during the population exchange that followed the Turkish War of Independence, in which he himself had fought, as he told us proudly. Pointing toward the Hisarlık mound, he said that 'The Greeks conquered Troy long ago but we drove them away, and now Anatolia is ours.'

The old man then said that they had work to do and would be off, and he wished us well on our way home. After he and his companions left, Andreas and I rested for a while beside the mound before we started back to Hisarlık, reflecting on our encounter.

Andreas said that his father was about the same age as the old man who had just spoken to us, and would have understood him perfectly. The Dimitriadis family had been exempted from the population exchange of 1923, as had the other Greeks of Istanbul and those from the islands of Imbros and Tenedos, which we could see off the Turkish coast near the entrance to the Dardanelles. About one and one-half million Anatolian Greeks had been replaced by 400,000 Muslim Turks who had been expelled from Greece, a double diaspora that included Greek-speaking Turks and Turcophone Greeks, religion being the determining factor without regard to the complexities of language, ethnicity and culture.

I recalled Schliemann writing that he hired 100 Greek workmen from Yenişehir and two other nearby villages to excavate the mound at Hisarlık in 1871, noting that 'Turkish workmen were not to be had, for they were at present occupied with field work.' He complained that the work was often interrupted 'owing to the various Greek festivals, for even the poorest Greek of this district would not work on a festival even if he could earn 1,000 francs in an hour'. Elsewhere he remarked on his amazement that the Greeks, after more than five centuries of Turkish domination, still preserved their national language intact. But now, less than a century later, the Greeks were all gone, though they were still remembered in Yenişehir. Thus at the Tomb of Achilles I felt that I was in touch with the beginning and ending of the Greek presence in Asia Minor, spanning more than three millennia, during which much of Anatolia was Hellenised before the tide of history turned with the Turkish conquest.

I was intrigued by the historic resonances I had felt at the Tomb of Achilles, and I was determined to learn more about the history of the Greeks in Asia Minor. Our visit to Troy proved to be the beginning of a quest that has continued to the present day, and which has taken me to virtually all of the cities that the ancient Greeks founded (or refounded) in Anatolia, and where their descendants continued to dwell until the population exchange of 1923.

Schliemann's excavations at Troy, Mycenae and Tiryns convinced him that the *Iliad* was based on an actual historical event, in which the Mycenaean king Agamemnon had led the Achaians from Greece to besiege and conquer this great city on the Asian shore of the Hellespont at its Aegean end. Carl Blegen, who excavated Troy in the years 1932–1938, wrote in 1963 that 'It can no longer be doubted, when one surveys the state of our knowledge today, that there was an actual historical Trojan War in which a coalition of Achaeans, or Mycenaeans, under a king whose lordship was recognised, fought against the people of Troy and their allies.' The question of the historicity of the Trojan War is still being discussed by scholars, who now generally agree that Homer should be taken seriously. Thus there is some basis for thinking, as I did when I first visited Troy, that the first Greeks to set foot on Asia Minor may have done so here on the Trojan plain.

My book tells the story of the Greeks in Anatolia through three millennia, focusing on how they preserved their identity and culture through the tides of history that swept over them from the Trojan War to the Turkish War of Independence, conflicts that historians from Herodotus onward have seen as part of the unending clash of civilisations East and West. The final chapter looks back at the Greek experience in Anatolia, where they have left the ruins of their ancient cities and the heritage of their culture, along with almost forgotten memories such as those that were revived for me at the Tomb of Achilles.

Map 1a: Ancient districts of Asia Minor (from George Bean, *Aegean Turkey*)

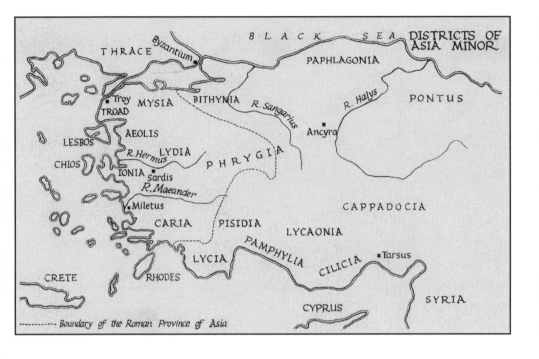

Map 1b: Modern Turkey (from Roderick H. Davison, *Turkey, a Short History*)

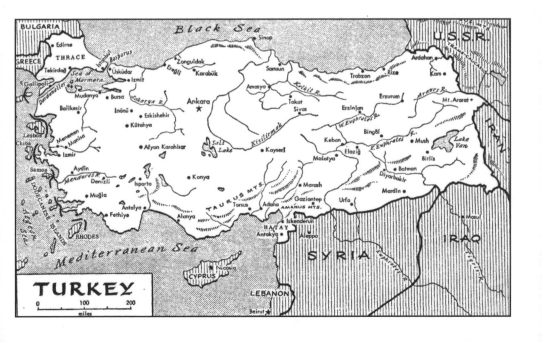

Map 2: Ancient Greek cities on the Aegean coast of Asia Minor
(from J.M. Cook, *The Greeks in Ionia and the East*)

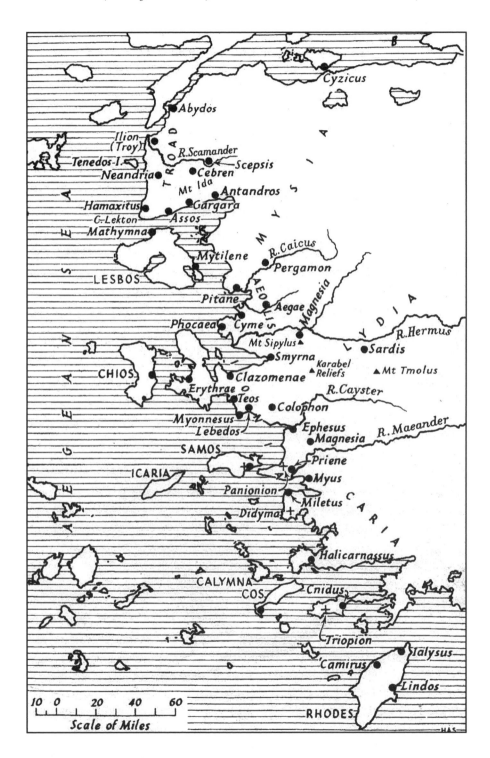

1

The Achaeans in Anatolia

It was the opinion of Thucydides that the Greeks first acted together as a people in the Trojan War, when they besieged the great city of Troy in the north-western corner of Anatolia, as Asia Minor is more generally known today. He writes in Book I of his *History of the Peloponnesian War* that 'we have no record of any action taken by Hellas as a whole before the Trojan War. Indeed my view is that at this time the whole country was not even called "Hellas"... it took a long time before the name ousted all the other names.' He then quotes Homer in support of his argument:

> The best evidence for this can be found in Homer, who, though he was born much later than the time of the Trojan War, nowhere uses the name 'Hellenic' for the whole force. Instead he keeps this name for the followers of Achilles who came from Phthioti and were in fact the original Hellenes. For the rest in his poems he uses the words 'Danaans', 'Argives', and 'Achaeans'... because in his time the Hellenes were not yet known by one name, and so marked off as something separate from the outside world.

And so the history of the Greeks as a people can be said to begin not in Greece itself but in Anatolia, where the birth of their literature comes with Homer's description of the Trojan War.

Anatolia is the Asian part of Turkey, where 93 per cent of the country's land-mass is located, while the European part – Thrace – forms the south-easternmost extension of Europe. The two continents are separated within north-western Turkey by what Petrus Gyllius called the 'strait that surpasses all straits' – the Bosphorus, the Sea of Marmara and the

Dardanelles – which link the Aegean with the Black Sea. The word '*anatoli*' means 'east' in Greek, more literally 'the land of sunrise'. The name 'Asia' may have had the same meaning as this in both the Indo-European and Semitic families of languages, while 'Europe' may have meant 'sunset' or the 'land of darkness'. The distinction would have been evident to the first Greek mariners making their way through the Hellespont from the Aegean, with Asia to the East and Europe to the West, the deep waters of the strait clearly dividing the 'land of sunrise' from the 'land of darkness'.

The greater part of the interior of Anatolia is a vast plateau, ascending eastward from 750 to 1,500 metres in elevation, comprising the regions known in antiquity as Phrygia and Cappadocia. The northern and southern rims of the plateau, which rise to peaks of 2,700 and 3,000 metres respectively, consist of a series of ridges with only a few difficult passes between the interior and the low-lying coastlands along the Black Sea and the Mediterranean. The southern mountain chains – the Taurus and Anti-Taurus – curve inland in south-eastern Anatolia to make way for the Syrian plateau and the great Mesopotomian plain, the easiest pass being the famous Cilician Gates. The northern rim of the plateau is formed by the Pontic range, which runs on into the still higher mountains in north-eastern Anatolia, culminating in Mount Ararat (Turkish Ağrı Dağ), 5,172 metres above sea-level, by far the highest peak in Turkey.

The Mediterranean coast of Anatolia has four distinct regions, which from west to east were known to the Greeks as Caria, Lycia, Pamphylia and Cilicia. The interior mountains descend steeply into the sea in Caria and Lycia, but in Pamphylia they retreat inland to leave a narrow coastal plain, bounded to the north by the highlands of Pisidia. The mountains come down to the sea again in western Cilicia, but in the eastern part of that region they curve sharply inland, leaving a vast alluvial plain created by the silt of the 'Rivers of Paradise', the Sarus and Pyramus (Seyhan and Ceyhan).

The Anatolian coast of the Black Sea, the Greek Pontus Euxinos, is fringed by a narrow coastal strip below the Pontic range. The coastal strip extends outward at its centre in the deltas of two great rivers, the Halys (Kızıl Irmak) and the Iris (Yeşil Irmak), which flow down from the central plateau. The Black Sea coast and highlands are divided into three regions, with Pontus to the east, Paphlagonia in the centre and Bithynia to the west, the latter bounded on its west by the Bosphorus and the Sea of Marmara, the Propontis of antiquity. The region south-west of Bithynia was called Mysia, which extends from the Marmara to the Aegean around the Troad, the country of Troy, which forms the north-western corner of Anatolia. The region south of Mysia was called Lydia, which to its east gives way to Phrygia and on its south to Caria, whose coast curves around from the Aegean to the Mediterranean at the south-west corner of Anatolia.

At its western end the Anatolian plateau descends in what the geographer Max Cary called a veritable 'staircase' that leads 'down to a piedmont country with river valleys shelving gently down to sea level'. The most important of these rivers are, from north to south, the Caicus (Bakır Çayı), the Hermus (Gediz Çayı), the Cayster (Küçük Menderes) and the Maeander (Büyük Menderes), whose valleys have always been the principal corridors between the Aegean coast and the Anatolian plateau.

The chronology of prehistoric Anatolia is divided into periods named for the materials used in tools and weapons, beginning with the Stone Age, further divided into the Old (Palaeolithic) and New (Neolithic) periods, followed by the Copper (Chalcolithic) period and the Bronze Age.

The Neolithic period (7000–5500 BC) saw the beginning of agriculture in Anatolia, as evidenced by the excavations at Hacılar, Can Hasan, Çatal Hüyük and Mersin, the earliest-known towns in what is now Turkey. The Neolithic town of Çatal Hüyük is the most extensive site of its period thus found in the Near East, covering an area of 32 acres, the excavations revealing twelve successive levels of occupation ranging from before 7000 BC until after 5600 BC. The mud-brick dwellings were laid out carefully in grouped blocks around central communal courtyards. Each house had a cult area or shrine with wall-paintings of hunting and religious scenes, including lively depictions of musicians, dancers and acrobats. All of the shrines were decorated with bull heads, the symbol of male procreative power, either carved in relief or sculptured in the round. The cult areas also had figurines of the deity who has come to be known as the Great Mother-Goddess of Anatolia, with the earliest ones representing her as a gross seated figure with huge breasts and thighs, usually in the process of giving birth, sometimes flanked by guardian lions or leopards. The goddess became more slender and virginal in successive cultures, changing in turn to the Phrygian Kubaba, the Lydian Cybele, the Greek Artemis, the Roman Diana, and eventually the Christian Virgin Mary, the

Mother of God, all of whom are represented in the Museum of Anatolian Civilizations in Ankara.

The sites at Can Hasan and Mersin continued to be occupied into the Chalcolithic period (5500–3000 BC), when copper first came into general use in Anatolia to make simple implements. Excavations have revealed other Chalcolithic settlements at Alacahüyük and Alişar, both of which continued in existence into the Bronze Age (3000–1200 BC). Finds from the early Bronze Age at Alacahüyük come principally from a group of thirteen royal graves that belonged to the rulers of the Hatti, the people who dominated north-central Anatolia in the second half of the third millennium BC.

The Hattians are believed to have been the immediate predecessors of the Hittites, an Indo-European people who established themselves in central Anatolia beginning ca. 1700 BC, with their capital at Hattusa (Boğazkale), in the bend of the Halys river. Later Hittite rulers traced their lineage back to the first king of Hattusa – Labarnas – who died ca. 1650 BC. He was succeeded by his son Labarnas II, who changed his name to Hattusilis, 'the Man from Hattusa'. Thus began the period that historians call that of the Old kingdom, when the Hittites expanded to the south and east, capturing Aleppo and Babylon early in the sixteenth century BC. Later in that century an outbreak of civil war caused the Hittites to lose much of the territory they had conquered. Stability was restored when Telipinus came to the throne in 1525 BC, after which he recovered the lost dominions of his ancestors. When he died in 1500 BC, which historians mark as the end of the Old kingdom, the Hittites were the dominant power in Anatolia.

A period of unrest and anarchy followed, until Tudhaliyas II came to the throne in 1560 BC, beginning the dynasty that created the Hittite Empire. This empire reached its greatest extent during the reigns of Suppiluliumas I (r. ca. 1380–1324 BC) and Mursilis II (r. ca. 1323–1295 BC) when it stretched from the Aegean to beyond the Tigris and from the Black Sea to Palestine.

There are several references in Hittite texts to the Land of Assuva, which was probably the region in western Asia Minor known to the Greeks as Lydia. It is generally agreed that the Greek word *Asia* derives from the Hittite *Assuva*. The earliest Greek reference to Asia is in Book II of the *Iliad*, where the poet writes of 'the Asian meadow beside the Kaystrian waters ...', referring to the river Cayster, which flows from Lydia into Ionia. The Hittites penetrated through Lydia into Ionia, as evidenced by rock-carvings, the most notable of which is in the Karabel pass, some 25 kilometres east of Izmir, Greek Smyrna. The Karabel carving is a relief about 2.5 metres tall showing a figure known in Turkish as Eti Baba, or Father Hittite. The relief represents a marching warrior wearing a short tunic or kilt, a short-sleeved vest and a conical headdress, holding a spear in his right hand and in his left hand a bow. There is also a faint hieroglyphic inscription that has been identified as Hittite. The carving is similar to reliefs found in and around Hattusa and may represent the Hittite weather god Teshuba; it is thought to date from the period ca. 1500–1200 BC. The Karabel relief is of particular interest because it is described by Herodotus, who thought it represented the Egyptian pharaoh Sosistris. It has been suggested that the early Greeks in Ionia thought that this kilted figure was an Amazon queen, which gave rise to the legend that some of the cities along the Aegean coast were founded by these mythical women warriors.

Hittite texts mention two place-names – Taruisa and Wilusa – which are believed to be Troy and Ilium, the two names which Homer uses interchangeably in referring to the Trojan capital. Mention is also made of a people called Dardany, which may refer to the Dardanians, the Trojans who were led by Aeneas, the name coming from Dardanos, the legendary ancestor of the Trojan kings. Several references are made to Arzawa, an aggressive independent state that seems to have controlled north-western Anatolia. The most intriguing references are those to the Ahhijava, who have been identified as Achaeans, or Mycenaean Greeks, whom Homer mentions in the first lines of the *Iliad*: 'Sing, goddess, the anger of Peleus' son Achilleus/and its devastation, which put pains thousandfold upon the Achaians ...'

According to the Hattusa archives, the Ahhijava were a powerful seafaring people whose princes corresponded with the Hittite rulers from a western Anatolian coastal city named Millawanda. Millawanda has been tentatively identified as Miletus, on the Aegean coast at the mouth of the Maeander river.

Miletus apparently was first settled ca. 1600 by mariners from Minoan Crete, another of the great civilisations of the Bronze Age, which Thucydides called a *thalassocracy*, or 'empire of the sea'. The Minoan Empire came to an end ca. 1450 BC, when the Mycenaeans took control of Crete. At the end of the fourteenth century the Mycenaeans occupied Miletus and surrounded it with a powerful defence wall. The Miletians traded with cities in Mycenaean Greece and were ruled by an Achaean prince, who in time became a vassal of the Hittite emperor.

The late Bronze Age city at Troy was apparently destroyed around the same time as Hattusa, though the three archaeologists who succeeded Schliemann in excavating the Hisarlık mound differed in their numbering of the layer involved and consequently its date. Wilhelm Dörpfeld believed that Troy VI was the Homeric city, but he was not able to give a precise date since the chronology of Mycenaean pottery was not well established at that time. Carl Blegen believed that the first sub-layer above this, which he called Troy VIIa, represented the city that had been destroyed in the Trojan War, as he wrote in 1963: 'It is Settlement VIIa, then, that must be recognised as the actual Troy, the ill-fated stronghold, the siege and capture of which caught the fancy and imagination of contemporary troubadours and bards who transmitted orally to their successors their songs about the heroes who fought in the war.'

A new excavation project was begun in 1982 by a team from the University of Tübingen under Manfred Korfmann, who in annual campaigns over the next five years excavated sites around Beşika Bay, some eight kilometres south of Kum Kale. Their finds indicated that the ancient harbour of Troy was there rather than at the end of the Hellespont, as previously believed. They also found a Mycenaean burial site dating to the thirteenth century BC, which suggests that this was where the Achaians buried their fallen warriors during the siege of Troy. As Korfmann wrote: 'I can only express an intuitive impression, a feeling I have, that the cemetery we have just laid bare at the harbour of Troy should belong to the very time when the Trojan War ought to have occurred.'

Then in 1988 Korfmann headed an international team of archaeologists who began excavating Troy and the surrounding area, a project that continues to the present day. The layer of the late Bronze Age settlement that might be the Homeric city was labelled by Korfmann as Troy VIIa, dated ca. 1250–1180 BC, evidently destroyed by fire. The later sublevels of Troy VII indicate that this settlement continued in existence up until ca. 1040 BC.

The site was then only sparsely inhabited until shortly before 700 BC, when it was resettled by Aeolian Greeks. The city they founded, identified as Troy VIII (ca. 700–85 BC) was known in Greek as Ilion and in Latin as Ilium. This is the city visited by the Persian king Xerxes before his invasion of Greece and by Alexander the Great when he began his invasion of Asia. Troy IX (ca. 85 BC–AD 500) is identified as the Roman city, visited by Julius Caesar, and which was completely rebuilt during the reign of Augustus (r. 27 BC–AD 14). The emperor Constantine the Great considered making Ilium the new capital of his empire before deciding on Byzantium on the Bosphorus, which in AD 330 was renamed Constantinople. A series of devastating earthquakes ca. AD 500 destroyed the city and led to its virtual abandonment.

Much of Book II of the *Iliad* is taken up by the Catalogue of Ships, a list of the contingents in Agamemnon's expedition against Troy. The catalogue gives a total of 178 places, including Mycenae, 'the strong-founded citadel', one of a group of ten cities that together sent a hundred ships led by 'powerful Agamemnon'. As Michael Wood points out, of the nearly one hundred identifiable places named in the catalogue, '*all* those excavated have revealed Mycenaean occupation…'

The Greeks first appear as a people in what is now Greece around the beginning of the second millennium BC. They would come to call themselves Hellenes and the land in which they lived Hellas. (The word 'Greek' comes from the Roman 'Graeci', stemming from a tribe in Epirus.) Their mythical eponymous ancestor was Hellen, father of Doris, Aeolus and Xuthus, whose sons were Ion and Aechaeus, thus giving a common ancestry to the Dorians, Ionians, Aeolians and Achaeans, the principal ethnic groups of Greeks toward the end of the Bronze Age. Homer refers to Hellas, the Hellenes and the Achaeans in the Catalogue of Ships, where he writes of the contingent led by Achilles:

> Now all those who dwelt about Pelasgian Argos,
> those who lived by Alos and Alope and at Trachis,
> those who held Phthia and Hellas the land of fair women,
> who were called Myrmidons and Hellenes and Achaians,
> of all these and their fifty ship the lord was Achilleus.

The Mycenaean period began about 1550 BC, taking its name from the Bronze Age city of Mycenae in the Argolid. Mycenaean pottery similar to that unearthed at Troy has been found at twenty-four other sites along the Aegean coast of Anatolia or its immediate hinterland. There were Mycenaean coastal settlements at Miletus and Iasus, as well as on the nearby islands of Chios, Samos, Kos and Rhodes, and there is some evidence that the Greeks traded up the two main rivers flowing down from the Anatolian plateau, the Hermus and the Maeander. Mycenaean pottery has also been found at Clazomenae, Ephesus and Sardis, and a Mycenaean burial ground has been unearthed near Bodrum, Greek Halicarnassus.

A few Mycenaean finds have been made on the upper Maeander valley at Beycesultan, where a late Bronze Age palace may have been a centre of the state of Mira, a Hittite ally. Among the Hittite texts mentioning the Ahhijava, or Achaeans, there is one, apparently from a king of Hatti, that refers to 'the towns of the king of the land of Mira'. This and the other Hittite texts mentioning the Achaeans date from the reign of Suppiluliumas (ca. 1380–1324 BC) to that of Arnuvandas III (ca. 1220–1190 BC), the latter being within the period of Troy VII.

The Catalogue of Ships is followed by the Trojan Catalogue, a list of the places that sent contingents to fight in the defence of Troy, each commanded by its own leader The catalogue includes groups from five geographical areas, beginning with the Troad, represented by the Trojans, led by 'Tall Hektor of the shining helm', along with the Dardanians, Zelians and Pelasgians. The second group was made up of three peoples from across the Hellespont, from Thrace westward, namely Thracians, Ciconians and Paeonians. The third group comprised two tribes south of the Black Sea in north-central Anatolia: Paphlagonians and Halizones. The fourth group was made up of two contingents from south-east of the Troad: Mysians and Phrygians, the latter being a people who had migrated from Europe and eventually supplanted the Hittites in central Anatolia. The fifth group included three units from south-western Anatolia: Maeonians, Carians and Lycians. Homer's description of the Carian contingent refers to Miletus, the only one of the Ionian cities mentioned in the *Iliad*.

Mysia, Caria and Lycia have all been at least tentatively identified with regions in western Anatolia mentioned in the Hittite tablets. It appears that the people from these regions, and perhaps the Trojans themselves, spoke an Indo-European language known as Luwian, closely related to Hittite. Günter Neuman, in an article published in 1992, concludes that there were 'indications that the Hittite hieroglyphic script was designed primarily for the Luwian language'.

It has been suggested that in the late third millennium BC, speakers of an early form of Greek moved into north-western Anatolia, and that some of them were still there during the period when the Hittites dominated the central plateau. A suggestion has also been made that the inhabitants of Troy VI spoke an early form of Greek. J. G. Macqueen writes that if these theories are acceptable, they raise the possibility 'that the Trojan War of Greek legend (traditionally dated to ca. 1200 BC) was not a conflict between the alien worlds of Greece and Anatolia, but that, since the inhabitants of Troy at that time were linguistically Greek, it was rather an inter-state conflict within the orbit of the Greek world of the time'. But he goes on to say that more recent research seems to indicate that these theories are without foundation, and that further excavation and study are needed.

Ancient Greek tradition held that after the Trojan War 'mixed multitudes' of people, presumably Hellenes and others, wandered southward to the Mediterranean coast of Anatolia, led by the legendary seers Mopsus, Calchas and Amphilochus, some of them settling in Pamphylia and Cilicia, others continuing farther south to Syria and Phoenicia. According to Strabo, Calchas was the founder of Selge in Pisidia; while Mopsus founded Perge and Mallus in Pamphylia, where he died in a duel with Amphilochus. Mopsus and Calchas were recognised by the Greeks of classical Perge among the founders of their city, as recorded in inscriptions. Mopsus also gave his name to the city of Mopsuestia, literally 'the hearths of Mopsus', in the Cilician plain. The name of Mopsus also appears in a bilingual hieroglyphic inscription, one in Phoenician and the other in Hittite hieroglyphics, of the eighth century BC at Karatepe, in eastern Cilicia. Mopsus appears much earlier than this in the form Muksus, referred to in a Hittite cuneiform tablet dated ca. 1200 BC, which places him in the period of the Trojan War and its immediate aftermath. Mopsus may also be the Muksas of a Hittite text dating from the reign of Arnuwandas III (r. 1220–1190 BC), which again places him in the period of the Trojan War.

These Hittite references give credence to ancient Greek traditions that the first Hellenes in Anatolia were Achaeans of the late Bronze Age, who established settlements along the Aegean coast and fought in a great war in the Troad, after which they formed part of the 'mixed multitudes' that founded cities along the Mediterranean shore. The events that followed are lost to history, shrouded in the several centuries of the Greek Dark Ages that followed the end of the Bronze Age.

2

The Great Migration

Near the beginning of his *History of the Peloponnesian War*, Thucydides remarks that 'the country now called Hellas had no settled population; instead there was a series of migrations, as the various tribes, being under the constant pressure of invaders who were stronger than they were, were always prepared to abandon their own territory'. He goes on to say that 'the period of shifting populations ended' only many years after the Trojan War, followed by the 'period of colonisation', when 'Ionia and most of the islands were colonised by the Athenians'.

The great migration that brought the Hellenes across the Aegean to Ionia and the other regions on the Aegean shore of Anatolia occurred during the Dark Ages of the Greek world, a period of several centuries following the end of the Bronze Age. During a period of some fifty years at the end of the thirteenth and beginning of the twelfth century BC almost every city or stronghold around the eastern Mediterranean and Anatolia was destroyed in some unknown catastrophe, many of them never again to be occupied. A number of alternative explanations of the catastrophe have been proposed, including earthquakes, droughts or other ecological disasters, widespread revolutions, mass migrations such as the invasion by the mysterious 'Sea Peoples' mentioned in Egyptian inscriptions, new methods of warfare, or 'systems collapse' due to one or more of the previously mentioned factors. Whatever the cause, the effect was a drastic depopulation of the Greek world, with many places, particularly the Aegean islands, being totally abandoned, the surviving communities scattered and isolated from one another.

Ancient tradition held that the Greek migration to Anatolia was due to the invasion of Dorians from the north, but modern scholarship has rejected this idea. The Dorians were in any event part of the migration, along with the Aeolians and Ionians, a mass movement which probably began in the eleventh century BC. The Ionians settled in the central sector of the Aegean coast of Anatolia and its offshore islands, with the Aeolians to their north, with some overlapping, and the Dorians to the south. The Aeolian settlements were, with one exception, between the Hellespont and the Hermus river, as well as on the islands of Lesbos and Tenedos. The cities founded by the Ionians were between the valleys of the Hermus and the Maeander, as well as on Chios and Samos. The Dorian colonies were on Kos and Rhodes and in Caria, the south-western corner of Anatolia, where the Aegean merges with the Mediterranean.

According to Herodotus, all three groups of Greek colonists formed political confederations, originally twelve cities each of the Aeolians and Ionians and six of the Dorians. These confederations were loosely knit, and the individual cities were entirely autonomous, as were the other Greek settlements that never joined any of the three leagues.

Tradition held that the Aeolian cities were founded by colonists from eastern Thessaly and Boeotia, who sailed across the northern Aegean to the islands of Lesbos and Tenedos and on to the Anatolian coast, where they established their settlements between the Hellespont and the Gulf of Smyrna. Protogeometric pottery unearthed in Lesbos and Smyrna indicates that the first Aeolian settlers arrived there ca. 1000 BC or even earlier.

The cities of the Aeolian confederation were between the Caicus and Hermus rivers, separated from those of Lesbos, Tenedos and the northern coast by the territory of the Mysians. The Mysians lived between the Caicus river and the Adramyttene Gulf, the deep indentation of the Aegean bounded on its north by the Troad, the huge peninsula formed by Mount Ida, flanked on its north by the Hellespont. The Greek settlements on Lesbos, Tenedos and the Troad never joined the Aeolian confederacy, which seems to have been founded before the end of the eighth century BC.

The members of the Aeolian confederacy, as Herodotus names them, were 'Cyme (also known as Phriconis), Larissa, Neon Tichus, Temnus,

Cilla, Notium, Aegiroessa, Pitane, Aegaea, Myrina, and Grynea'. Notium was an anomaly, since it was far to the south of Aeolis in Ionia, and eventually became the port of Colophon, one of the Ionian cities. Smyrna was originally part of the Aeolian confederacy, but it was later taken by the Ionians, though it did not became a member of their confederation until the third century BC.

Except for Notium, the other cities of the Aeolian confederation were between the Hermus and Caicus rivers. Cyme, Myrina, Grynea and Pitane were on the coast, the others some distance inland. Cyme was the southernmost of the coastal settlements in Aeolis, just to the north of the Hermus, and Pitane was the farthest north, at the mouth of the Caicus.

The original settlers in Aeolis encountered resistance from the local Anatolian people in the region, namely the Mysians to their north and the Leleges and Pelasgians along the coast where they established their colonies. When the first Greek settlers arrived at Pitane they were attacked by the indigeneous people known as the Lelegians, and they had to call on the Ionians in Erythrae to fight them off.

Farther inland in the highlands of Anatolia were the Phrygians, an Indo-European people who supplanted the Hittites in central Asia Minor early in the first millennium BC. The Phrygians are mentioned by Homer in Book X of the *Iliad*, where they are listed along with the Leleges, Pelasgians and Mysians among the Anatolian allies of the Trojans.

Cyme was by far the most important city in the confederation, renowned for its maritime enterprises. Aeolian Cyme, along with the Euboean cities of Chalcis and Eretria, joined together in 757 BC to found Cumae, the first Greek colony on the Italian mainland. The Cymeans on their own later founded Side on the Mediterranean coast of Anatolia. Strabo writes that 'The largest and best of the Aeolian cities is Cyme; and this with Lesbos might be called the metropolis of the rest of the cities, about thirty in number, of which not a few have disappeared.'

Strabo goes on to say that Cyme was the birthplace of Hesiod's father, Dius, who emigrated from there to Boeotia in Greece. Hesiod writes that his father 'settled near Helicon, in a wretched village, Ascre, which is bad in winter, oppressive in summer, and pleasant at no time'. Strabo notes that the Cymeans claimed that their city was the birthplace of Homer, but he says that 'it is not agreed that Homer was from Cyme, for many people lay claim to him'.

Pitane, the northernmost city of the confederation, near the mouth of the Caicus river, also had an important port. Its original settlement appears to have been far earlier than the Greek migration, for pottery sherds have been found in its necropolis dating back to the third millennium BC.

Tradition held that Pitane, along with Smyrna, Cyme, Myrina and Grynea, had been founded by the Amazons, a myth that may have stemmed from the relief of the Hittite warrior that Herodotus saw in the Karabel pass. Myrina was said to have been named for an Amazon queen mentioned by Homer in Book II of the *Iliad*, where he writes of her mythical tomb outside the walls of Troy: 'This men call the Hill of the Thicket, but the immortal/gods have named it the burial ground of the dancing Myrina.'

Grynea, better known by its Latin name of Grynium, is mentioned by Strabo, who says 'that it had an altar of Apollo and an ancient oracle and a costly shrine of white marble'. The shrine is also described by Pausanias, who writes of 'its most beautiful grove of Apollo', in which there 'are cultivated fruit-trees and every wild tree that can give human pleasure by sight or scent'.

Aside from Cyme and Pitane, the settlements of the Aeolian federation made no mark on history, most of them having virtually disappeared without a trace. The Aeolians were noted in antiquity for their sybaritic way of life; Athenaeus of Naucratis says they were much 'given to wine, women and luxurious living'.

There was another Greek settlement in Aeolis named Elaea, which was at the mouth of the Caicus river east of Pitane. According to Strabo, Elaea was the earliest Greek settlement on the Aeolian coast, founded by Menestheus, leader of the Athenian contingent at the siege of Troy. Homer mentions Menestheus in the Catalogue of Ships in Book II of the *Iliad*, where he says that 'Never on earth before had there been a man born like him/for the arrangement in order of horses and shielded fighters.' Elaea never became a member of the Aeolian confederacy, because it was founded by the Ionians and retained its links with their confederation in Ionia. The settlement gave its name to the Eleatic Gulf, the deep indentation of the sea around the mouth of the Caicus that formed the northern boundary of Aeolis.

Herodotus says that the Aeolians also had settlements on Lesbos and Tenedos as well as around Mount Ida on the Troad, but these were not members of the confederation. There were originally six cities on Lesbos, of which the most important were Mytilene, across the stretch of the Anatolian coast occupied by the Mysians, and Methymna, which was just across the strait from Cape Lekton, the south-western promontory of the Troad. Colonists from Methymna founded the city of Assos on the coast of the Adramyttene Gulf west of Cape Lekton, probably by the end of the eighth century BC. An expedition from Mytilene founded a small settlement on the northern coast of the Troad called Achilleion, which Strabo says included the Tomb of Achilles.

There was just one city on Tenedos, but it controlled a number of settlements along the coast of the mainland opposite, the so-called Tenedean Peraea. One of the settlements on the Tenedean Peraea was Chryse, which is mentioned by Strabo in his account of the cult of Sminthian Apollo, in which the god was worshipped in the form of a mouse. It seems that the first colonists on the Troad, the Teucrians, were advised by an oracle to 'stay on the spot where the earth-born should attack them', and on their first night 'a great multitude of field mice swarmed out of the ground and ate up all the leather in their arms and equipment', whereupon they took this as a sign from the god that they should settle there.

Chryse is mentioned by Homer several times in Book I of the *Iliad*, for it was the home of Chryseis, daughter of Chryses, the priest at the shrine of Sminthian Apollo there. Agamemnon had captured Chryseis and made her his mistress, and her father appealed to Apollo, who sent a plague 'which put pains thousandfold upon the Achaians', starting the quarrel between Achilles and Agamemnon which is the opening theme of the *Iliad*.

Other Aeolian colonies were founded in the Troad at sites ranging from the shore of the Adramyttene Gulf to the Hellespont, including Antandros, Polymedion, Lamponia, Hamaxitus, Colonae, Neandria, Cebren, Scepsis, Gergis, Sigeion and Dardanos, while Abydos was founded by Ionians from Miletus. Around 750 BC Aeolian colonists also founded a settlement on the site of ancient Troy called Ilion, the stratum on the Hisarlık mound now known as Troy VIII, perpetuating the name of the Homeric city.

Other Aeolian cities in the Troad also had Homeric associations, the most obvious being Achilleion and Dardanos. Dardanos, on the Hellespont north-east of Troy, is named for the mythical ancestor of the Trojan kings.

Homer writes of him in Book XX of the *Iliad*, where Aeneas tells Achilles of his royal ancestry:

> First of all Zeus who gathers the clouds had a son, Dardanos
> who founded Dardania, since there was as yet no sacred Ilion
> made a city in the plain to be a centre of peoples,
> but they lived yet in the underhills of Ida with all her waters.

Abydos, on the Hellespont north of Dardanos, is mentioned by Homer in Book II of the *Iliad*, in the Trojan Catalogue, where he writes of 'They who dwelt in the places about Perkote and Praktion,/who held Sestos and Abydos and brilliant Arisbe...' Scepsis was said by Strabo to be the residence of Aeneas, who survived the fall of Troy and 'set sail with his father Anchises and his son Ascanius...'

As Virgil tells the tale in the *Aeneid*, Antandros was the place from which Aeneas embarked on his voyage after the fall of Troy, eventually settling in Italy and founding the kingdom that would later have its capital in Rome.

The migration of the Ionian Greeks took them from Attica and Boeotia through the central Aegean, where they established colonies in the Cyclades before settling on the coast of Anatolia between the Hebrus and Maeander rivers as well as on Chios and Samos. By the end of the ninth century the Ionian colonists had formed a league called the Dodekapolis, 'the Twelve Cities', ten of them on the Aegean coast of Anatolia and one each on the islands of Chios and Samos. Herodotus says that the Ionians 'had the good fortune to establish their settlements in a region which enjoys a better climate than any other we know of. It does not resemble what is found either further north, where there is an excess of cold and wet, or further south, where the weather is both too hot and too dry.'

According to Herodotus, the settlers were by no means solely Ionian, nor were their immediate descendants purely Greek, for the colonists took wives from among the local population.

> It is quite absurd to pretend that they are any more Ionian, or of purer blood, than the Ionians generally... Even those who came from the Council House in Athens and believe themselves to be of the purest Ionian blood, took no women with them but married Carian girls, whose parents they had killed. The fact that these women were forced into marriage after the murder of their fathers, husbands, and sons was the origin of the law, established by oath and passed down to their female

descendants, forbidding them to sit at table with their husbands or to address them by name. It was at Miletus that this took place.

The settlements started out as small kingdoms, each ruled by the leader of the original expedition and his descendants. But this gave way in turn to oligarchy, tyranny and eventually, through Athenian influence, to democracy. The various colonies had traditions concerning their founders, who they believed were sons of the mythical King Codrus of Athens. Miletus is supposed to have been founded by Neleus, a son of Codrus. The supposed founder of Ephesus was Androclus, another son of Codrus, who drove out the native Leleges and Lydians who occupied the site.

The twelve cities had their religious centre and meeting-place at the Panionium, at the promontory of Mount Mycale on the mainland opposite Samos, where tradition had it that the first Ionian settlers had landed. Herodotus describes the Panionium in Book I of his *Histories*, where he says that 'it was here that the Ionians gathered from their various cities to keep the festival called the Panionia'. Every fourth year the Ionians also held a festival on the island of Delos in the Cyclades, the mythical birthplace of Apollo, their patron deity. The festival is described in the Homeric Hymn to Delian Apollo, in which the poet addresses the god himself:

> Yet in Delos do you most delight your heart: for the long-robed Ionians gather in your honour with their children and shy wives. Mindful, they delight you with boxing and dancing and song, so often as they hold their gathering. A man would say they are deathless and unageing if he should come upon the Ionians so met together. For he would see the graces of them all, and would be pleased in heart gazing at the well-girded women and the men with their swift ships and great renown.

At some time in the second half of the eighth century BC Ionians from Colophon seized control of Smyrna from the Aeolians. The incident is described by Herodotus in Book I of his *Histories*, noting that 'The people of Smyrna were then distributed amongst the other eleven Aeolian towns, where they were given civil rights.'

Miletus was the most important of the mainland cities in the Dodekapolis, renowned as the oldest of the Ionian settlements and their greatest maritime power. The Milesians proudly called their city 'the first settled in Ionia, and the mother of many and great cities in the Pontus and Egypt, and in various other parts of the world'.

During its early years Miletus founded a far greater number of colonies than any other city-state in the Greek world, including more than thirty around the shores of the Pontus Euxinos (Black Sea) and its approaches in the Hellespont and the Sea of Marmara. The Milesian colonies founded on the Anatolian shore of the Pontus, beginning in the eighth century BC, included Sinope (Sinop), Amisus (Samsun) and Trebizond (Trabzon), which are today the three most important Turkish cities on the Black Sea. Besides its colony of Abydos on the Hellespont, the Milesians also established a settlement at Cyzicus on the western Asian shore of the Sea of Marmara.

At the eastern end of the Marmara several colonies were established by Megara, perhaps with the encouragement of the Milesians. The most important of these was Byzantion, Latin Byzantium, which they founded ca. 660 BC on a peninsula on the European shore at the entrance to the Bosphorus from the Sea of Marmara.

Miletus also had a privileged position at Naucratis, the great emporium on the Nile delta founded by the Greeks ca. 610 BC, in which the Milesians established a fortified trading station known as Milesionteichos. They were joined at Naucratis by eleven other Greek cities, including Ionians from Samos, Chios, Teos, Phocaea and Clazomenae; Dorians from Rhodes, Aegina, Cnidos, Halicarnassus and Phaselis; and Aeolians from Mytilene.

Miletus was rivalled in its maritime ventures by Phocaea, the northernmost of the Ionian cities, founded beyond the Hermus river on the peninsula that forms the northern horn of the Smyrnaic Gulf. It was settled later than the other cities in the Dodekapolis, founded by colonists from the Ionian cities of Erythrae and Teos, probably in the eighth century BC. The site was chosen for its excellent natural harbour, the finest on the Aegean coast of Anatolia.

The Phocaeans took full advantage of their superb location to send colonising expeditions overseas, and in their first venture they joined the Milesians in founding Amisus on the Black Sea coast of Anatolia. Then in 654 BC the Phocaeans on their own founded Lampsacus, on the Asian shore of the Hellespont. Around 600 BC they established Massalia, the present Marseilles, with colonists going on from there to found Nicaea and Antipolis, now known as Nice and Antibes. Then in 560 BC the Phocaeans founded Alalia on Corsica, and at the same time they established a short-lived colony on Sardinia. They even sailed out into the Atlantic and founded a colony at Tartessus, on the present site of Seville.

The Ionian and Aeolian cities traded with the Lydians, whose capital was at Sardis, some fifty miles east of Smyrna in the Hermus valley. Mycenaean pottery found at Sardis indicated that the Hellenes had penetrated into Lydia in the late Bronze Age, though the Ionians and Aeolians do not seem to have reached Sardis until the seventh century BC.

Two settlements named Magnesia were founded somewhat inland of the Ionian colonies. One of them, Magnesia ad Sipylon, was east of Smyrna under Mount Sipylus; the other, Magnesia ad Maeandrum, was south-east of Ephesus in the Maeander valley. The founders of these two cities were said to be Aeolians from Magnesia in northern Greece, the so-called Magnetes, who are supposed to have stayed on in Asia Minor after the Trojan War. An inscription in Magnesia ad Maeandrum states that the founders of the city were the first Greeks to cross into Anatolia.

The migration of the Dorians took them from Lacedaemon in the central Peloponnesos across the Aegean to Crete, Rhodes, Cos and the south-western coast of Anatolia in Caria. The Dorians founded a confederacy, originally called the Hexapolis, or Six Cities, comprising three cities on Rhodes – Lindus, Ialysus and Camirus – one on Kos and two in Caria, namely Halicarnassus and Cnidus. The mainland cities were established on the south-westernmost extensions of Anatolia, Cnidus on the Asian peninsula between Rhodes and Kos, Halicarnassus on the one just north of Cos.

The cities of the Dorian League had their religious centre and meeting-place at the Triopium, on the same peninsula as Cnidus. Halicarnassus eventually came under the influence of the Ionian cities to its north, principally Miletus, which led to its expulsion from the Hexapolis, thereafter called the Pentapolis, or the Five Cities.

Halicarnassus was founded on the southern shore of the Myndus peninsula, named for a settlement on its western promontory. According to Strabo, Myndus and seven other cities in the region were founded by the Leleges, 'who in earlier times were so numerous that they not only took possession of that part of Caria which extends to Myndus and Bargylia, but also cut off for themselves a large portion of Pisidia'. The Leleges eventually became Hellenised, as did the Carians and other Anatolian peoples along the western shores of Anatolia.

There was also a Dorian settlement at Iasus, midway along the coast between Miletus and Halicarnassus. Excavations have revealed that the site was inhabited as early as the third millennium BC. Minoan pottery and houses have been found from the period ca. 1900–1550 BC, as well as Mycenaean pottery dated ca. 1400–1200 BC. According to tradition, the first Dorian settlers were Argives from the Peloponnesos, who arrived in the ninth century BC. The Argives encountered fierce resistance from the local Carian inhabitants and they were forced to call on the Milesians for help, as a result of which Iasus become Ionian rather than Dorian.

The Dorians on Rhodes acquired territory on the Anatolian mainland opposite their island, a region know as the Rhodian Peraea, which extended from Caria into Lycia, the region on the western Mediterranean coast of Anatolia and its hinterland. The Greek tradition concerning the origin of the Lycians is recorded by Herodotus in Book I of his *Histories*: 'The Lycians come originally from Crete, which in ancient times was occupied entirely by non-Greek peoples... In their manners they resemble in some ways the Cretans in other ways the Carians, but in one of their customs, that of taking the mother's name instead of the father's, they are unique...'

Hittite archives of the mid-fourteenth century BC refer to a rebellious people in the general area of south-western Anatolia called the Lukka, who would seem to be the Lycians. Egyptian tablets of the same period refer to a nation of sea-raiders called the Lukki, who are probably the Lycians. This evidence lends support to the tradition recorded by Herodotus, that the Lycians came from Crete, probably in a great population movement that began in the latter half of the second millennium BC, passing through Caria on their way down through Lycia and the Mediterranean coast.

The principal city of Lycia was Xanthus, located at the mouth of the river of the same name. The earliest reference to Xanthus is by Herodotus in connection with the Persian conquest of western Anatolia beginning in 546 BC. Although the Xanthus river in Lycia is mentioned in the *Iliad*, there is no reference to a city of that name. The reference to the river is in the last line of the Trojan Catalogue, where Homer writes that 'Sarpedon with unfaulted Glaukos was lord of the Lykians/from Lykia far away, and the whirling waters of Xanthos.'

The Rhodians also established a settlement at Phaselis, on the eastern coast of Lycia, across the Gulf of Antalya from Pamphylia, where the

Aeolians from Cyme established a colony in the seventh century BC at Side. The Aeolian colony at Side must have been culturally absorbed by the native Pamphylians, according to the testimony of Arrian, biographer of Alexander the Great: 'There is a tradition among them that when the first settlers from Cyme sailed thither and landed from their ships to found a new home, they promptly forgot their native Greek and began to talk in a foreign tongue – not the language spoken by the people of these parts, but in an entirely new dialect of their own ...' George Bean writes that 'This Sidetan language ... can hardly (despite what Arrian says) be other than the original language of Pamphylia.' He goes on to say that the Aeolian colony must have been a weak one, for the Aeolians 'seem to have been unable to impose their own Greek in the new city, but were constrained to adopt the local speech'.

The easternmost of the Rhodian colonies on the Mediterranean coast was at Soli in Cilicia. According to tradition, some of the other settlements along the coast in Pamphylia and Cilicia were founded by veterans and refugees of the Trojan War who had followed the seers Mopsus, Calchas and Amphilocus south across Anatolia. Strabo writes of this migration, quoting Herodotus and the Ephesian poet Callinus:

> Herodotus says that the Pamphylians are the descendants of the people led by Amphilocus and Calchas, a miscellaneous throng who accompanied them from Troy; and that most of them remained here, but that some of them were scattered to numerous places on earth. Callinus says that Calchas died in Clarus, but that the peoples led by Mopsus passed over the Taurus, and that, though some remained in Pamphylia, the others were dispersed in Cilicia, and also in Syria as far as Phoenicia.

And in this way the great Hellenic migration, which had first reached Anatolia on its Aegean shore, spread along the Mediterranean coast through Lycia to Pamphylia and Cilicia, where the 'mixed multitudes' had already founded settlements when they wandered this way after the Trojan War.

3

The Archaic Renaissance

Some three centuries after the great migration the Greek cities on the Aegean coast of Anatolia and its offshore islands emerged from the Dark Ages, the light of dawn coming with the epics of Homer.

Students of the so-called Homeric question now tend to date the composition of the *Iliad* and the *Odyssey* to the period 750–650 BC, some four to five centuries after the traditional date of the Trojan War. This is traditionally taken to be the beginning of the archaic period, which lasted from the mid-eighth century BC to the end of the Persian Wars in 479 BC. Opinions vary about whether the two epics were composed by the same poet, and it has been suggested that 'Homer' is really the personification of a succession of bards, who passed down the story of the Trojan War and its aftermath through the centuries of the Dark Ages to the dawn of the Greek renaissance. Odysseus, in Book VIII of the *Odyssey*, pays tribute to such a bard in the palace of King Alkinoös.

> For with all peoples upon the earth singers are entitled to be cherished and to their share of respect, since the Muse has taught them her own way, and since she loves all the company of singers.

The Homeric question also concerns the *Homeric Hymns*, which have been dated from the eighth to the second century BC, most of them from the archaic period, ca. 650–480 BC. According to Ken Dowden, the *Homeric Hymns* 'cannot, by their language, actually have been composed by Homer'.

21

He goes on to say that 'The poet who composed the *Hymn to Delian Apollo*, alludes to himself in the last line, where he says farewell to the maidens of the chorus: "Whom think ye, girls, is the sweetest singer that comes here, and in whom do you most delight?" Then answer, each and all, with one voice: "He is a blind man, and dwells in rocky Chios: his lays are evermore supreme".

Chios was one of the places that some Hellenistic scholars held to be the birthplace of Homer, others being Colophon and Smyrna. According to the anonymous author of a curious work called *The Contest of Homer and Hesiod*: 'But as for Homer, you might almost say that every city with its inhabitants claims him as her son. Foremost are the men of Smyrna, who say that he was the son of Meles, the river [god] of their town, by a nymph Creitheis.'

During the archaic period the Greek cities on the western coast of Asia Minor and the nearby Aegean isles gave birth to the world's first philosophers of nature, as well as lyric poets, geographers, architects and historians, the flowering of a renaissance that had begun during the previous century with the epics of Homer. The most notable of the historians, Herodotus of Halicarnassus, was born at the very end of the archaic period, during the Persian Wars, which he describes in his *Histories* as a great struggle with the successive Asian conquerors who emerged to confront the Greeks in Anatolia and Hellas.

The dominant power in Anatolia during the first three centuries of the first millennium BC was the Phrygian kingdom, which had its capital at Gordion on the central plateau. According to tradition, the eponymous founder of Gordion was King Gordios, who was succeeded by Midas. Assyrian annals in the reign of Sargon II (r. 722–705 BC) mention a ruler named Mitas of Muski, who has been identified as Midas of Phrygia, though several of the Phrygian kings may have had this name.

Tradition says that the leaders of the expedition that founded the original Aeolian colonies were descendants of Agamemnon, and that an early king of Cyme bore that name. This Cymean king Agamemnon had a daughter Demodike who married 'Midas the Phrygian', who was probably a descendant of the famous 'King Midas of the golden touch'. This story may be apocryphal, but it indicates that Cyme and the other Greek cities on the coast were in contact with the Phrygians, trading with them up the Hermus and Maeander rivers. There was a cultural exchange as well, as evidenced by similarities in the Greek and Lydian alphabets as well as in architecture and metal work.

The Phrygian kingdom came to an end ca. 690 BC, when Gordion was destroyed by the Cimmerians, a warrior people from the Crimea who devastated much of western Anatolia at the time. The Cimmerians destroyed the Aeolian city of Antandros, and they also attacked the Ionian cities in plundering raids.

The Ephesian poet Callinus wrote 'Now there comes upon us the army of the Cimmerians, the dealers in violence', and he prayed to Zeus to protect his city. Ephesus was spared and the Cimmerians went on to destroy Magnesia ad Maeandrum.

After the downfall of the Phrygians the Lydians became the dominant power in western Anatolia. According to Herodotus, the original Lydian kings were the Heraclidae, who were supplanted by a dynasty known as the Mermnadae ca. 687 BC. The founder of the Mermnadae was Gyges, who assassinated Candaules, the last of the Heraclidae, a story told by Herodotus in Book I of his *Histories*. The Mermnadae ruled Lydia for nearly a century and a half from their capital at Sardis, at the foot of Mount Tmolus on the banks of the Pactylus river.

Soon after Gyges usurped the throne he attacked the Ionian cities on the coast. According to Herodotus, 'Once established in power, Gyges sent a military expedition against Miletus and Smyrna and captured the citadel of Colophon.'

After Gyges' victory some of the Colophonians fled to southern Italy, where they founded a city known variously as Polieion or Siris. Those Colophonians who remained in their city became strongly influenced and corrupted by the Lydians. This was the view of Xenophanes of Colophon, a poet, philosopher and historian, writing of his compatriots while living in exile at Elea in southern Italy, a colony founded by Phocaea: 'They had acquired useless luxuries from the Lydians, while still they were not subject to hateful tyranny. They would come to their meeting in purple cloaks – a full thousand of them as a rule, not-less flaunting their comely locks and drenched in scented unguents.'

Gyges was killed ca. 652 BC in fighting against the Cimmerians, who captured the lower town of Sardis. He was succeeded by his son Ardys (r. 652–621 BC), who held out in the citadel of Sardis until the Cimmerians departed. Ardys then resumed his father's invasion of Ionia, capturing Priene and besieging Miletus, which resisted his attacks.

During the reign of Alyattes (609–560 BC) the Lydians minted the world's first coins, using the gold that was washed down from Mount Tmolus by the Pactolus river. The invention of coinage added to the already considerable wealth of the Lydians, allowing them to further develop their widespread trade, which extended from central Anatolia to the Aegean coast and on into the Mediterranean.

Alyattes continued his father's campaign against Miletus, which is described by Herodotus in Book I of his *Histories*:

> Alyattes carried on the war which he had taken over from his father, against the Milesians. His custom each year was to invade Milesian territory when the crops were ripe, marching in to the music of pipes, harps and treble and tenor oboes. On arrival he never destroyed or burned the houses in the country, or pulled their doors off, but left them unmolested. He would merely destroy the trees and crops, and then retire… The Lydians refrained from demolishing houses in order that the Milesians, having somewhere to live, might continue to work the land and sow their seed, with the result that they themselves would have something to plunder each time they invaded their country.

Alyattes also attacked Smyrna, which he captured and destroyed ca. 600 BC. He then went on to attack Clazomenae, where he 'met with disaster', according to Herodotus, after which he returned to Sardis. Archaic Smyrna never recovered from this catastrophe, and for the next four centuries the city was an almost uninhabited ruin, its people dispersed among the villages in the surrounding region.

Tradition, supported by archaeology, indicates that during the last forty years of Alyattes' reign there was peace between the Lydians and the Greeks. It was during this period that the Greek renaissance began on the western shore of Anatolia and its nearby Aegean isles. The Ionian city of Miletus, with its network of colonies and trading stations on the Nile and around the Black Sea and its approaches, was a centre of this renaissance, which was stimulated by the contacts that the eastern Greeks had made with other cultures in Anatolia, Mesopotamia, Phoenicia and Egypt.

Miletus gave birth to the first three philosophers of nature – Thales, Anaximander and Anaximenes – whose successive lives overlapped to span most of the archaic period. Aristotle referred to them as *physikoi*, or physicists, from the Greek *physis*, meaning 'nature' in its widest sense, contrasting them with the earlier *theologoi*, or theologians, for they were the first who tried to explain phenomena on natural rather than supernatural grounds.

Plato listed Thales among the Seven Sages of ancient Greece, while Aristotle considered him to be the 'first founder' of Ionian natural philosophy. There is a tradition that Thales visited Egypt, where he is supposed to have calculated the height of a pyramid by pacing off its shadow, doing this at a time of day when the height of any object is equal to the length of its shadow. Herodotus credits Thales with predicting the total eclipse of the sun on 28 May 585 BC, when King Alyattes of Lydia was at war with the Medes. Given the state of knowledge at the time, it would have been impossible to make such a prediction, but once Thales became enshrined as one of the Seven Sages, all kinds of intellectual accomplishments were attributed to him, including the first geometrical theorems formulated by the Greeks.

The most enduring ideas of the Milesian physicists proved to be their belief that there was an *arche*, or fundamental substance, which endured through all apparent change. Thales thought the *arche* was water, which although liquid under normal conditions, could with changing temperature become a vapor as steam or a solid as ice. Anaximander said that the *arche* was *apeiron*, the 'unlimited', for he believed that the basic substance should be completely undifferentiated in its original state. Anaximenes thought that the *arche* was *pneuma*, or 'air' (it also means 'spirit'), which only manifests itself when it is in motion as in wind or when heated.

Thales apparently left no writings, and all that we know of his ideas are quotes or paraphrases by later writers, particularly Aristotle. Themistius, writing in the fourth century AD, says that Anaximander was 'the first of the Greeks, to our knowledge, who was bold enough to publish a treatise on nature'. Anaximander is also credited with books on astronomy, in which he is said to have used the gnomon, or shadow-stick, to determine 'solstices, times, seasons and equinoxes', as well as a work on geography in which he was the first to draw a map of the *oecumenos*, the inhabited world.

Hecataeus of Miletus, who flourished ca. 500 BC, is credited with following the lead of Anaximander in drawing a map of the world known to the Greeks. As a supplement to his map he also wrote a *Periegesis*, a 'guide' or 'journey around the world', in which he described the lands and peoples to be seen in a coastal voyage around the Mediterranean and the Black Sea, along with some excursions inland, ranging as far as Scythia, Persia and India. The enormous extent of his map, which shows the continents of Europe, Africa and Asia surrounded by Oceanus, is a measure of how far abroad the Greeks, particularly the Milesians and Phocaeans, had travelled in their voyages of colonisation and trade.

Heracleitus of Ephesus, a contemporary of Hecataeus, took a very different view of nature than the Milesian physicists. He believed that the enduring reality in nature is not Being, as in the existence of a fundamental substance, but Becoming, or perpetual change, hence his famous aphorism 'Panta rhei', or 'Everything is in flux'. As Plato comments on this and another Heracleitan aphorism: 'Heracleitus somewhere says that all things are in the process and that nothing stays still, and likening existing things to the stream of a river he says you would not step twice into the same river.'

Heracleitus held that the relative stability of nature was due to what he called the Opposite Tension, a balance of opposing forces producing equilibrium. He believed that the universe was coordinated by Logos, or Reason, which gives unity to the natural world. The evidence of our senses is deceptive and must be used with caution, since it deals with transitory phenomena; in another of his aphorisms he says 'Evil witnesses are eyes and ears for men, if they have souls that do not understand their language.'

Classical Greek writers refer to Heracleitus as a *paradoxolog*, or maker of paradoxes, because of the puzzling nature of his gnomic sayings, which he is said to have collected in a book that he deposited in the temple of Artemis at Ephesus. A probably apocryphal story has it that when Socrates was asked by Euripides what he thought of this book he replied: 'What I understood was fine, and no doubt also what I didn't understand; but it needs a diver to get to the bottom of it.'

The Artemesion of Ephesus was one of the two largest temples ever erected in the Greek world, the other being the Heraion of Samos, both of them founded by the Ionians. The Heraion, erected in the years 580–570 BC, was designed by two Samian architects, Rhoecus and Theodorus, who were also renowned engineers and craftsmen. With them begins the history of Greek architecture, for Theodorus of Samos was the first to write a book on the subject, now lost, but mentioned by Vitruvius in his *De architectura*, known in English as *The Ten Books on Architecture*.

During the third quarter of the sixth century BC the Greek enlightenment spread from Ionia to Magna Graecia, the Greek colonies in Sicily and southern Italy, beginning with the arrival there of Pythagoras, the most enigmatic of the early philosophers.

Pythagoras was born on Samos, one of the two Aegean islands that were part of the Panionic League, along with Chios. He is said to have left Samos during the reign of the tyrant Polycrates, who seized power ca. 540 BC, moving to Croton, a Greek colony in southern Italy. There he founded a society that was both a scientific school and a religious sect, whose beliefs including that of *metempsychosis*, or the transmigration of souls. Otherwise little is known of Pythagoras himself, and it is impossible to distinguish his own ideas from those of his followers.

The Pythagoreans are credited with laying the foundations of Greek mathematics, particularly geometry and the theory of numbers. The most famous of their discoveries is the Pythagorean theorem, which says that in a right triangle the square on the hypotenuse equals the sum of the squares on the other two sides. According to tradition, the Pythagoreans were the first to recognise the numerical relations involved in musical harmony, to which they were led by their experiments with stringed instruments. This made them believe that the cosmos was designed by a divine intelligence according to harmonious principles, and that this harmony could be expressed in terms of number.

The cultural renaissance of the eastern Greeks also included the two great Aeolian poets of the archaic period – Sappho and Alcaeus of Lesbos – who were contemporaries of Thales. They flourished during the reign of King Alyattes of Lydia, whose realm extended through Aeolis and the Troad, putting his cavalry within sight of Lesbos. Some of their poems refer to the Lydians, as in Sappho's 'Invocation to Aphrodite', where she writes of her lost love Anaktoria

> who has gone from me
> and whose lovely walk and the shining pallor
> of her face I would rather see before my
> eyes than Lydia's chariots in all their glory
> armored for battle.

One fragment by Alcaeus refers to a payment made to him and his comrades by the Lydians, who were going to support them in their attack on a city, perhaps Mytilene. 'Father Zeus,' he writes, 'the Lydians, indignant at our misfortunes, gave us two thousand pieces, if we could enter the holy city...' Alcaeus fought as a mercenary in the Troad, serving with the citizens of Achilleion in their war against the Athenian colonists in Sigeum. He tells his friend Melanippus of how he fled from the battlefield to save his life, leaving his shield behind him as a trophy for the Athenians.

> Tell them, Alkaios from the stricken field
> Has come back safe, but not, alas, his shield;
> By now the tough war-hide that he let fall
> Adorns grey-eyed Athena's temple wall.

Alyattes died ca. 560 BC and was buried under an enormous tumulus beside the Gygean Lake, ten miles north of Sardis, where it can still be seen. Herodotus considered the tomb of Alyattes to be 'the greatest work of human hands in the world, apart from the Egyptian and Babylonian,' as he writes in Book I of the *Histories*:

> The base of this monument is made of huge stone blocks; the rest of it is a mound of earth. It was raised by the joint labour of the tradesmen, craftsmen, and prostitutes, and on the top of it there survived to my own day five stone phallic pillars with inscriptions cut in them to show the amount of work done by each class. Calculation revealed that the prostitutes' share was the largest. Working-class girls in Lydia prostitute themselves without exception to collect money for their dowries, and continue the practice until they marry. They choose their own husbands... Apart from the fact that they prostitute their daughters, the Lydian way of life is not unlike the Greek.

Alyattes was succeeded by his son Croesus, the last and most famous of the Mermnadae, under whom the Lydian kingdom reached the pinnacle of his greatness, the golden age of Sardis. According to Herodotus, Croesus began his reign with a renewed invasion of the Greek cities along the Aegean coast, forcing them to pay tribute to him. The terms that Croesus imposed on the Greeks of Ionia and Aeolia were not unduly harsh. Their cities were not occupied by Lydian garrisons nor did they have royal governors, their only obligations being to pay an annual tribute to Croesus and to supply troops to his army when he was on campaign.

Croesus was very generous to the Greeks; he sent fabulous treasures to the shrines of Apollo Pytheos at Delphi and Apollo Branchidae at Didyma, and helped the Ephesians restore their temple of Artemis. The Ionians

crossed the Hellespont into Asia, leaving a large army in Europe under his general Megabazus, who conquered the Samian colony of Perinthus on the Sea of Marmara. Then, according to Herodotus, 'Megabazus marched through Thrace, bringing every city and every people in that country under the control of the Persian king. All this was according to orders; for he had received instructions from Darius to conquer Thrace.' Megabazus then penetrated westward into Europe as far as the frontier of Macedonia, before returning to Sardis with the prisoners he had taken.

After his Scythian campaign Darius appointed his half-brother Artaphernes as satrap in Sardis. As acting-governor of Miletus he appointed the Milesian aristocrat Aristagoras, whose cousin and brother-in-law Histaios, the former governor, Darius took with him to the Persian capital at Sousa as an advisor.

By that time Persian rule had become extremely onerous in Ionia, and during the remaining years of the sixth century BC it became even more unpopular, particularly in Miletus. Thus in 500 BC Aristagoras decided to cast off the Persian yoke, prompted by a secret message he had received from Histaios urging him to revolt. He then gathered together his supporters, who were virtually unanimous in their approval of his plan to break free from Persian rule.

The Ionian Revolt began late in 499 BC when Aristagoras and his party seized control of the Persian fleet, which was wintering in the habour of Myus. Aristagoras then went off to Greece, where he succeeded in gaining support for the rebellion from both Athens, which agreed to send two warships with troops, and from Eretria, which promised to send five ships. Meanwhile agents of Aristagoras had been active throughout the satrapies of Lydia and Phrygia gaining support for the rebellion.

The Athenian and Eretrian ships landed at the port of Ephesus, where they were joined by Ionian troops sent from Miletus by Aristagoras. The allies then marched inland and took the lower city of Sardis, whose acropolis was held by Artaphernes and the Persian garrison. During the fighting the whole of the lower city was destroyed by fire, forcing the Ionians and their allies to return to Ephesus, leaving Sardis a smoking ruin. Persian troops throughout western Anatolia were quickly formed into an army that caught up with the insurgents at Ephesus, where the Ionians were defeated with great loss of life, including the commander of the Eretrian contingent.

The burning of Sardis made a deep impression throughout western Anatolia, and brought widespread support for the Ionian Revolt, though their defeat at Ephesus led the Athenians to abandon the cause.

The fiercest land fighting of the war took place in Caria, where a Persian army defeated the Milesians and Carians in two campaigns during the years 497–496 BC, with both sides suffering heavy losses. This turned the tide of war, and two years later the Ionians made their last stand at Miletus, which had been besieged by the Persians since the beginning of the revolt. The last battle was fought off Lade, then an isle outside the harbour of Miletus, now connected to the mainland because of silt deposited by the Maeander. There in midsummer of 494 BC an armada of 600 Phoenician ships decisively defeated an Ionian fleet of 353 triremes, after which the Persian army captured Miletus and burned it to the ground, enslaving those of its surviving inhabitants who had not escaped.

This catastrophe deeply shocked the Athenians, particularly because they had abandoned the Ionian cause. Herodotus writes of the Athenian distress in Book VI of his *Histories*:

> The Athenians, on the contrary, showed their profound distress at the capture of Miletus in a number of ways, and, in particular, when Phrynicus produced his play, *The Capture of Miletus*, the audience in the theatre burst into tears. The author was fined a thousand drachmas for reminding them of their own evils, and they forbade anyone ever to put the play on stage again.

Exiles from Miletus and the other Ionian cities along the Aegean coast resettled in Greece and Magna Graecia, bringing with them the culture that had given rise to the archaic enlightenment.

The poet Anacreon was born in Teos ca. 560 BC. He left with the other Teans when their city was besieged by Harpagus the Mede and was among those who founded Abdera. After he established his reputation as a poet he was invited by Polycrates of Samos to tutor his son, and became the tyrant's boon companion. When Polycrates was killed by the Persians, ca. 524 BC, Anacreon returned to Abdera, but soon afterwards he was invited to Athens by Hipparchus, eldest son of the tyrant Peisistratus.

Anacreon finally returned to Teos in his last years, and passed away there at the age of eighty-seven, choking on a grape-pit while drinking raisin wine. Pausanias writes that Anacreon was 'the first poet after Sappho of Lesbos to write mostly love poems'. One of his fragments could serve as his epitaph: 'Bring water, lad, bring wine; aye bring them thither, for I would try a bout with love.'

Xenophanes of Colophon was a contemporary of Anacreon, and he too was driven from his home by the Persian invasion, spending the rest of his long life as an exile in Magna Graecia. He became the poet of the Ionic enlightenment in the West, and some of his seminal ideas profoundly influenced the development of natural philosophy in Magna Graecia. Plato conidered him to be the founder of the Eleatic school of philosophy, whose most notable figures were Parmenides and his disciple Zeno.

Xenophanes objected to the anthropomorphic polytheism of Homer and Hesiod, whom he condemned for having 'ascribed to the gods all deeds that are among men a shame and a reproach: thieving, adultery and mutual deception'. He said that men make gods in the image of themselves, so that 'The Ethiopians say their gods are snub-nosed and black, the Thracians that theirs have light blue eyes and fair hair.' His own view was monotheistic and pantheistic, as is evident from one of his fragments: 'God is one, greatest among gods and men, in no way like mortals either in body or mind. He sees as a whole, perceives as a whole, hears as a whole. Always he remains in the same place, not moving at all, nor does it befit him him to go here and there at different times; but without toil he makes all things shiver by the impulse of his mind.'

The Pythagorean notion of the transmigration of souls was ridiculed by Xenophanes, who in one of his poems tells the story of how Pythagoras stopped a man beating a dog, saying to him, 'Stop, do not beat him; it is the soul of a friend, I recognize his voice!'

One of Xenophanes' last poems, written at the age of ninety-two, looks back on his long life of exile: 'Three score and seven years have crossed my careworn soul up and down the land of Hellas, and there were then five and twenty years from my birth.' Another of his late poems reflects on the world that was lost when Harpagus the Mede led the Persian army into Ionia: 'Such things should be said beside the fire in wintertime when a man reclines full-fed on a soft-couch drinking sweet wine and munching chick peas, such things as who and whence art thou? And what age was thou when the Mede appeared?'

4

The Persian Wars

After the end of the Ionian Revolt, Darius set out to restore order in the Phrygian and Lydian satrapies. Then at the beginning of spring in 492 BC Darius appointed his son-in-law Mardonius as commander-in-chief of his army and navy, launching them on an invasion of Europe, his object being to punish Athens and Eretria for the part they had played in the Ionian Revolt.

The campaign was a disaster, for the fleet was caught in a storm off Mount Athos in which some 300 vessels went down with over 20,000 men, according to Herodotus, while the army was attacked by a Thracian tribe and suffered heavy losses, Mardonius himself being wounded. Thus Mardonius was forced to abort the campaign and 'returned to Asia in disgrace'.

Darius launched a new invasion in 490 BC under Datis the Mede, whose second-in-command was Artaphernes, son of the satrap of the same name in Sardis. The two commanders led the army to the Mediterranean shore of Cilicia, where they boarded the transports of the fleet and sailed along the Anatolian coast to Samos. Then they sailed across the Aegean to Naxos, the largest of the Cycladic isles, which they captured, destroying its capital and enslaving the inhabitants.

The Persian fleet then made its way to Eretria, on the island of Euboea, which they captured after a seven-day siege, here again destroying the town and enslaving its populace. Thereupon, as Herodotus writes, 'Having mastered Eretria the Persians waited for a few days and then sailed for

Attica, flushed with victory and confident that they would treat Athens in the same way.'

The Persian fleet landed on the beach at Marathon, 26 miles by road from Athens. By the time their troops had landed they were confronted by the Athenians and their Plataean allies. The Greek allies numbered some 10,000, while the Persian force was probably twice that size. The two armies faced one another for four days before the Athenian general Miltiades led the Greeks against the forces of Datis, who had native Persians in the centre and Greeks from Anatolia on the two flanks. Herodotus says that the battle was 'long drawn out', though it lasted less than a day. But in the end the Greeks were victorious and drove the invaders into the sea, with 6,400 Persians killed, while the Athenian dead numbered only 192, according to Herodotus.

After making a futile attempt to take Athens by sea, Datis withdrew his fleet and sailed off to Asia, eventually returning with his prisoners to the Persian capital at Susa. Herodotus says that when Darius learned of the Persian defeat at Marathon, 'his anger against Athens, already grave enough on account of the assault on Sardis, was even greater, and he was more than ever determined to make war on Greece'. Herodotus goes on to say that Darius sent couriers thoughout his empire with orders to raise an army and launch a fleet much larger than before, 'and all Asia was in an uproar for three years'. But the campaign was aborted when Darius passed away in November 486 BC, with his son Xerxes succeeding to the throne.

Herodotus says that 'Xerxes at first was not at all interested in invading Greece, but began his reign by building up an army for a campaign in Egypt.' Xerxes was strongly advised to renew his father's attempt to take revenge on Athens by Mardonius, who told him, according to Herodotus, that if he did so 'your name will be held in honour all over the world, and people will think twice in future before they invade your country'. Although his uncle Artabanus strongly advised against a new invasion of Greece, Xerxes decided to go ahead with the campaign.

Herodotus says that 'For the four years following the conquest of Egypt the mustering of troops and the provision of stores and equipment continued, and towards the fifth Xerxes, at the head of his enormous force, began his march.'

Xerxes set out from Susa in the spring of 481 BC and proceeded to Cappadocia, where the army was assembling under the overall command of Mardonius. He spent the following winter in Sardis, from where he sent heralds to the Greek cities demanding offerings of earth and water as tokens of their surrender, but not to Athens and Sparta, for he was determined to destroy them.

This led the Athenians and Spartans to convene a congress of all the Greek states which were prepared to resist Persia. The representatives met at Sparta in the autumn of 481 BC and formed an alliance known as the Hellenic League, whose inauguration is described by Herodotus in Book VII of his *Histories*: 'At a conference of the Greek states who were loyal to the general cause guarantees were exchanged and the decision was reached that the first thing to be done was to patch up their own quarrels and stop any fighting which happened to be going on amongst members of the confederacy.'

Herodotus says that the army of Xerxes 'was indeed far greater than any of which we know', with contingents from all over the Persian Empire. He reports that there were 1,700,000 men in the army and 3,000 ships in the fleet, which would add another half million to the size of the Persian force, though a modern estimate puts the total number of troops at about 300,000. Herodotus says that there were 1,207 triremes in the Persian fleet, including 307 from the Greek cities in Anatolia, the nearby Aegean islands and the Hellespontine shores. This included the Dorian contingent from Caria commanded by Queen Artemisia, who had succeeded her husband as ruler of Halicarnassus.

The Persian army began its march in the spring of 480 BC, stopping in Sardis before moving on through Lydia and Phrygia to the Troad. The army paused to drink at the Scamander river in the Trojan plain, whereupon, as Herodotus writes: 'Xerxes had a strong desire to see Troy, the ancient city of Priam. Accordingly, he went up into the citadel, and when he had seen what he wanted to see and heard the story of the place from the people there, he sacrificed a thousand oxen to the Trojan Athene, and the Magi made libations to the heroes.'

The next day the army marched on to Abydos on the Hellespont, where Persian engineers had already built a double bridge of boats across the strait. Before crossing the Hellespont, according to Herodotus, Xerxes decided to hold a review of his forces, seated on 'a throne of white marble that had been prepared for his use by the people of Abydos':

And when he saw the whole Hellespont hidden by ships, and all the beaches and plains of Abydos filled with men, he called himself happy – and the moment after burst into tears. Artabanus, his uncle...was by his side, and when he saw how Xerxes wept, he said to him: 'My lord, surely there is a strange contradiction in what you do now and what you did a moment ago. Then you called yourself a happy man – and now you weep.' 'I was thinking,' Xerxes replied, 'and it came into my mind how pitifully short human life is – for of all these thousands of men not one will be alive in a hundred year's time.'

After crossing the Hellespont, Xerxes led his army through Thrace, 'pressing into his service the men of every nation which lay in his path,' as Herodotus writes, for 'the whole country as far as Thessaly had been forced into subjection and made tributary to Persia by the conquests, first of Megabazus and, later, of Mardonius'. His fleet kept pace along the coast, passing through the narrow neck of the Mount Athos peninsula in a canal that had been dug by his engineers, rounding the other two capes of the Chalkidike to join the army at Therma, later to be the site of Thessalonica.

Xerxes then sent his army southward through Thessaly to the pass at Thermopylae, a fortnight's march. The king gave orders for his navy to wait for eleven days before sailing south to the Gulf of Pagasai, a three-day voyage which would take them past Cape Artemision at the northern tip of Euboea. Meanwhile the Greek fleet had taken up position off Cape Artemision, while a force of some 4,000 Greeks under the Spartan king Leonidas, King of Sparta held the pass at Thermopylae. Leonidas and his troops held the pass for two days against the whole Persian army, fighting valiantly to the death. A monument was later erected in their honour, with this laconic epitaph: 'Stranger, tell the Lacedaemonians that here we lie obedient to their words.'

As the Persian fleet rounded Cape Artemision it was struck by a violent storm that raged for three days. According to Herodotus, at least 400 Persian ships sank or ran aground during the storm, which the Greek fleet rode out without loss in the lee of Euboea. The Greeks then sailed north to engage the Persian navy in two engagements off Cape Artemision, with heavy losses on both sides, leaving half of the Athenians' ships disabled. The Greek commanders, having learned of the fall of Thermopylae, then decided to withdraw their fleet under cover of night and sail to Salamis, the offshore island west of Athens.

After taking Thermopylae, the Persian army marched down through Doris, Phocis and Boeotia into Attica. As the Persians approached Athens, the Areopagus council decided to evacuate the populace to Aegina, Salamis and Troezen. The Persians easily overwhelmed the Greek garrison on the Athenian acropolis and destroyed the temple of Athena Parthenos, whereupon Xerxes sent a messenger to Susa to proclaim his victory.

Xerxes then decided to attack the Greek fleet in the strait between Salamis and the mainland, although he was strongly advised not to by Queen Artemisia of Halicarnassus, commander of the Carian contingent, who had distinguished herself in the battles off Cape Artemision. Nevertheless Xerxes decided to go ahead, but first he had to refit his navy after the damage it had suffered at Cape Artemision.

The Persian fleet finally put to sea in late August from the harbour of Phaleron, and paused between the Piraeus and Salamis, while the army moved westward along the coast. The Greek fleet numbered 380 triremes, while that of the Persians was probably only slightly larger. The Persian ships were arrayed in order of battle off the southern end of the strait, where Xerxes had his golden throne set up on a hill looking over the bay of Salamis, for he expected that the action would take place there.

At dawn the next day Xerxes seated himself on his throne, looking down on the Persian fleet as it prepared to enter the strait. There were some ninety warships in the front line, with the Phoenicians on the left and on the right the Ionians from Anatolia and its offshore isles. As the Persian ships moved forward the Greek triremes rowed swiftly to meet them at the entrance to the strait, the ships of Aegina in the front rank and those of Athens behind, commanded by Themistocles. Aeschylus, who fought in the battle, describes the climax in his play, *The Persians*, in the opening lines of which a messenger describes the action to Xerxes' mother Atossa.

Skillfully the Greeks struck from all sides and capsized the Persian ships. No longer was the sea visible, so full was it of wrecks and slaughtered men. The shores and reefs were covered with corpses as every surviving Persian ship rowed off in disorderly flight, while the Greeks with splintered oars, or stumps of wreckage, struck and hewed at the Persian sailors as if they were a catch of tunny fish. Until dark night stopped the slaughter, shrieks and wailing resounded over all the sea. Never in ten days could I complete the tale, were I to tell it all in proper order. Never did such a multitude of men perish in one day.

Herodotus says that a few of the Ionian ships in the Persian fleet 'deliberately held back in the fighting but most did not'. He then goes on to write of how Queen Artemisia of Halicarnassus distinguished herself in the eyes of Xerxes, who saw all of his other commanders going down to defeat as he watched in dismay from his golden throne above the strait. It seems that Artemisia was being pursued by an Athenian trireme when she rammed and sank a ship from her own contingent. Herodotus writes of how Xerxes, thinking that Artemesia had sunk a Greek ship, was led to remark that 'My men have turned into women, my women into men.'

After the battle Xerxes decided that the season was too far advanced to continue the campaign, and so he sent his fleet back to the Hellespont. He then marched his army to Thessaly, where he left most of the troops under the command of Mardonius, while he continued on with the rest, along with an escort under the command of Artabazus.

When Xerxes reached the Hellespont he found that the pontoon bridge had been destroyed in a storm, and so he had his troops ferried across the strait. He then marched his army back to Sardis, pausing en route to loot and destroy the temple of Apollo Branchidae at Didyma, an oracular shrine founded by the Milesians south of their city. According to Strabo, the priests at the shrine, the Branchidae, turned over to Xerxes the treasure that had been deposited there by Croesus, after which 'they accompanied him in his flight in order to escape punishment for the robbing and betrayal of the temple'.

Mardonius resumed the campaign late in the spring of 479 BC, marching south to occupy Athens, which was once again abandoned by its populace. Meanwhile the Athenians and their allies in the Greek League had assembled an army under the command of Pausanias, the Spartan regent. When Mardonius learned that the Greek allies were marching against him he moved his army up into Boeotia, encamping between the Asopos river and the deserted city of Plataea, which he had burned down before taking Athens.

The army of Pausanias numbered about 110,000, that of Mardonius about 180,000, including the contingents of his Greek collaborators, according to some modern estimates. The two armies met on the plain between the Asopos and Plataea early in September of 479 BC, when the Greek allies utterly defeated the Persians. Mardonius himself was killed along with some 10,000 of his Asian soldiers, the rest making their escape with Artabazus, who eventually led them back to Anatolia. According to Herodotus, the Greek dead numbered 759.

Meanwhile a Greek fleet had assembled at Aegina under the command of Leotychidas, king of Sparta, who led his ships across the Aegean to Cape Mycale, the promontory on the Asian coast between Ephesus and Miletus, where the Persians had their main base in Ionia. Leotychidas sailed his flagship close inshore and had a herald call to the Ionians in the Persian garrison to 'remember freedom', urging them to spread the word to their compatriots. The Persian commander, alarmed by this, disarmed his Samian troops and stationed the Milesians away from the sea on paths leading inland. Leotychidas had his captains run their ships ashore and land their crews and marines, and when all of his forces were assembled he ordered them to attack, first the Athenians and then the Spartans. They soon broke into the stockaded camp at Mycale, whereupon the Ionians in Persian service turned on their masters, those who tried to flee inland being cut down by the Milesians. Then, according to Herodotus, 'When most of the enemy forces had been cut to pieces, either in the battle or during the rout, the Greeks burnt the Persian ships and the fort, having first removed everything of value, including a number of money-chests, to a place of safety on the beach.'

Tradition had it that the battle of Mycale was won on the same day as the Greek victory at Plataea, a double triumph that put an end to the Persian invasion of Greece. Herodotus credited the Anatolian Greeks with playing a significant role in this victory, and he says that 'Thus this day saw the second Ionian revolt from Persian domination.'

Herodotus then writes of the meeting that the victorious allies held on Samos after the battle of Mycale, the subject being 'the future of Ionia'. There they considered the precarious situation of the Ionians in Anatolia, for the Persians, although defeated, were still extremely powerful, and it would be very difficult to protect the Greek cities in Asia against them. The Peloponnesian leaders proposed that the Ionians be resettled in Greece, but the Athenians objected and the proposal was rejected.

The allied fleet then sailed off to remove the pontoon bridges that Xerxes had built across the Hellespont, but when they reached Abydos they found that they had already been destroyed. They then proceeded to besiege the Persian garrison that had been left at Sestos on the European shore of the strait. After the garrison finally surrendered, the Greeks executed the Persian governor of the district, after which they finally set sail for home, as Herodotus writes at the end of the last book of his *Histories*: 'This done, the fleet set sail for Greece with all sorts of stuff on board, including the cables of the bridge, which the Athenians proposed to dedicate as an offering in their temples. And that was all that happened during the course of the year.'

And with that Herodotus ended his *Histories*, for his theme had been the great struggle between the Hellenes and the 'barbarians' that took place during the Persian War, which in his account ended with the simultaneous Greek victories at Plataea and Mycale. But the struggle with Persia continued intermittently for another century and a half, during which time the Greek cities in Anatolia were caught up in the struggle between Athens and Sparta that led to the Peloponnesian War. Thucydides writes of this struggle in the introduction to his *History of the Peloponnesian War*, referring to the Persian invasion:

> It was by a common effort that the foreign invasion was repelled; but not long afterwards the Hellenes – both those who had fought in the war together and those who had revolted from the King of Persia – split into two divisions, one following Athens and the other Sparta ... So from the end of the Persian Wars to the beginning of the Peloponnesian War, though there were some intervals of peace, on the whole these two Powers were either fighting with each other or putting down revolts among their allies.

When the Persian Wars ended, Miletus was still in ruins from its destruction by Darius in 494 BC, but after the victory at Mycale the Milesians began rebuilding their city. The new city was planned by Hippodamos of Miletus, who laid it out on a rectangular grid plan that became the model for Greek cities of the classical and Hellenistic era.

By the middle of the fifth century BC Miletus was once again a flourishing city, but it never again became the great marine power that it had been in the archaic period, for after the Persian War, Athens created a maritime empire that dominated the Greek world. Thenceforth the Greek cities in Anatolia became mere pawns in the power struggle between Athens and Sparta as well as in the continuing conflict between Greece and Persia. Nevertheless the Greek cities in Anatolia continued to produce philosophers, poets and historians, most notably Herodotus of Halicarnassus, who was born during the Persian Wars, the conflict between east and west that became the theme of his *Histories*.

5

Between East and West

The classical era in Greek history begins with the end of the Persian Wars in 479 BC. The first half century of this era is known as Pentecontaetia, the 'period of fifty years' between the Persian and Peloponnesian Wars, when Athens emerged as the leading state in Hellas. The Spartans had led the allies to victory over the Persians, but they were not willing to continue the war in the east to protect the Greeks in Asia Minor. The eastern Greeks thus looked to Athens for protection, and the Athenians took advantage of this to create a *thalassocracy*, or maritime empire.

During the summer of 477 BC heralds were sent out from Athens to the Greek cities in and around the Aegean, including Asia Minor, calling for representatives to be sent to a congress at Delos. There they established an alliance known as 'The Athenians and their Allies', soon to be known as the Delian League, whose formation is described by Thucydides in Book I of his *History of the Peloponnesian War*:

> So Athens took over the leadership, and the allies, because of their dislike of Pausanias [the Spartan regent], were glad to see her do so. Next the Athenians assessed the various contributions to be made for the war against Persia, and decided which states should furnish money and which states should send ships – the object being to compensate themselves for their losses by ravaging the territory of the King of Persia... The treasury of the League was at Delos, and representative meetings were held at the temple there.

The tribute-paying members of the Delian League were originally divided into four districts. The Greek cities on the coasts and offshore islands of Asia Minor were included in three of these: the Ionian, Carian and Hellespontine, the other being the so-called Thraceward district. The cities that had formed the original Aeolian, Ionian and Dorian confederacies in Asia Minor were in the first two of these, with the exception of Smyrna, which was still virtually an uninhabited ruin from its destruction by the Lydians. The tribute assessed by Athens on the Greek cities in Asia Minor appears to be about the same as what they had paid to Darius, as if they had exchanged one master for another.

The Persians still had bases in north-eastern Greece at Eion and Doriscus, and in 477 BC Athens mounted a campaign against them under Cimon, the son of Miltiades. Cimon captured Eion and then went on to take Skyros, where the Athenians established a *clerurchy*, or colony. The Athenians then went to war with the city of Carystus on Euboea, forcing it to join the Delian League. Shortly after this the Naxians tried to secede from the league, whereupon Athens attacked Naxos and forced it rejoin, probably at the cost of its independence.

Ten years later Cimon commanded an allied expedition against the Persians, who had assembled a large army and a fleet of some 350 ships at the mouth of the Eurymedon river in Pamphylia, on the Mediterranean coast of Asia Minor. Cimon's fleet numbered 300 ships, of which 200 were launched and manned by Athens, the rest by her allies in the Delian League. The allied fleet assembled at Cnidus, from where they sailed eastward, attacking the Persian garrisons in Caria and Lycia and bringing the coastal cities into the Delian League. The people of Phaselis in Lycia were at first reluctant to be freed from Persian rule, and agreed only after some persuasion.

Using Phaselis as his base, Cimon then took the fleet across to the mouth of the Eurymedon in Pamphylia, where he defeated the Persian army and navy on the same day. A funerary monument was afterwards erected at the mouth of the Eurymedon to honour the Greek warriors who died there, with this epitaph inscribed upon it: 'These are the men who laid down the splendour of their manhood beside the Eurymedon: on land and on the swift-sailing ships alike they fought with their spears against the foremost of the bow-bearing Medes. They are no more, but they have left the fairest memorial of their valour.'

The war with Persia continued, as Athens and her allies attacked the Phoenician fleet in Cyprus as well as in its home waters off Lebanon and in Egypt. Then in 457 BC, while still engaged in hostilities with Persia, Athens went to war against the Spartan Alliance. The war between Athens and Sparta was suspended by a Five Years' Truce, extending through the period 451–446 BC; then, after fighting began again, a Thirty Years' Truce was negotiated during the winter of 446–445 BC. Meanwhile, in 449 BC the Athenians and their allies came to terms with Persia in the so-called Peace of Callias.

The number of allies paying tribute to Athens in the period 454–449 BC decreased from 208 to 163, resulting in a significant drop in revenue. During this period many of the allied cities in the Aegean isles refused to pay tribute, and the Athenian colony at Sigaeum in the Troad was being threatened by other Greeks encouraged by the Persians. Two of the Ionian cities, Miletus and Erythrae, tried to secede from the alliance ca. 452 BC, but both were subdued and forced to rejoin the league. Athenian garrisons were established in both cities, and officials from Athens supervised their governments. Six years later the Milesians rebelled again, only to be put down once more by the Athenians, who installed a democratic government in Miletus.

Despite these difficulties, by the middle of the fifth century BC the Delian League had become an Athenian empire. This transformation was largely due to the leadership of Pericles, who, according to Plutarch, 'introduced a bill to the effect that all Hellenes wheresoever resident in Europe or in Asia, small and large cities alike, should be invited to send deputies to a council at Athens'. Twenty distinguished envoys were sent to deliver this message, five of them going to cities in Asia Minor and its offshore Aegean islands, 'urging them all to come and take part in the deliberations for the peace and common welfare of Hellas'. Sparta declined the invitation and the congress never met, but the proposal was nevertheless a great propaganda victory for Athens, which could now hold itself up as the moral leader of the Hellenic world, while its rivals were indifferent to the cause.

Soon afterwards the Athenians began to intensify their control of their empire, moving the league treasury from Delos to the acropolis of Athens, where Pericles began to build a new temple of Athena Parthenos in 447 BC. They also tightened up the collection of tribute from the allies and enforced their obedience to Athenian decrees. The Ionian city of Colophon, which had not paid its tribute for some years, was dealt with by the establishment of an Athenian *clerurchy* on its territory and was forced to adopt a democratic government, which swore loyalty to 'the demos of the Athenians and their allies'.

The only three states in the alliance that had their own navies were Samos, Chios and Lesbos, which were thus virtually autonomous and exempt from paying tribute. When a war broke out in 440 BC between Samos and Miletus over control of Priene, the Milesians called on Athens for help since they no longer had a navy. When the Samians refused an offer by Athens to mediate the dispute, Pericles sailed to Samos with a fleet of forty triremes and took control of the island. He replaced the oligarchy with a democratic government, supported by an Athenian garrison and officials, but otherwise he allowed Samos to retain its autonomy and keep its navy. This meant that the Samians did not have to pay tribute, although Pericles imposed an indemnity of eighty talents on them for having rebelled.

Meanwhile the Samian oligarchs raised a force of 700 mercenaries with the help of the Persian satrap of Lydia, Pissuthenes. As soon as Pericles departed the oligarchs seized control of the island, capturing the Athenian garrison and officials, whom they turned over to Pissuthenes. Thus it appeared that Persia was prepared to break its truce with Athens in order to regain its former dominance in western Anatolia. At the same time Byzantium also rebelled against Athens, and the city of Mytilene on Lesbos prepared to revolt as well, hoping for support from Sparta. But neither Persia nor Sparta moved to aid the Samians, and Athens eventually crushed the revolt by the early summer of 439 BC.

During that same year many towns in Caria ceased paying tribute to Athens. This region had always been difficult to control, particularly those places in the remote highlands, where the people were more Carian than Greek, and which were effectively within the Persian Empire. The assessment of these towns was not great, and so Pericles chose not to force them to pay, since the cost of mounting a military expedition against them was not worth the effort nor the risk of provoking the Persians. The assessments for 438 BC shows that forty Carian towns were permanently dropped from the tribute lists, and thereafter Caria was merged with Ionia into a single district.

Athens was heavily dependent on grain from its allies around the shores of the Black Sea. Around 437 BC, Pericles led an expedition to the Black Sea, his purpose being to show Athenian support for the Greek cities around its shores, surrounded as they were by alien peoples. These cities first appear on the Athenian tribute lists in 425 BC, making up the so-called Euxine District, which include three on the Anatolian coast: Heracleia, Carousa and Cerasous, though not the more important cities of Sinope and Trapezus (Trebizond).

Meanwhile the long-standing rivalry between Athens and Sparta erupted in the first phase of the Peloponnesian War, which began in 431 BC. Thucydides, in his introduction to the beginning of the war, writes of how it brought 'unprecedented suffering for Hellas'.

Early in the summer of 430 BC the Peloponnesian army invaded Attica and ravaged the countryside for forty days, forcing the inhabitants to take refuge in Athens. The crowded and unsanitary conditions in which the refugees lived led to the outbreak of plague, which lasted for two years in its first phase and then flared up again in the winter of 427–426 BC and went on for another five years. Some 20,000 Athenians are believed to have died of the plague, about a third of the population, including Pericles, who passed away in the autumn of 429 BC.

The terrible losses suffered by both sides led to the so-called Peace of Nicias in 421 BC, in which Athens on one side and the Spartan Alliance on the other agreed to cease war against one another. The uneasy peace lasted until 415 BC, when the Athenians launched a fleet to Sicily under the command of Nicias, Alcibiades and Lamachus. Alcibiades was the driving force behind the expedition, whose avowed purpose was to aid Segesta, an ally of Athens, in its war against Selinus, a Megarian colony allied to Syracuse.

The Sicilian expedition was a disaster for the Athenians, climaxed by the total defeat of their fleet at Syracuse late in the summer of 413 BC and the enslavement of their surviving soldiers. Thucydides considered this to be the 'greatest action that we know of in Hellenic history – to the victors the most brilliant of successes, to the vanquished the most calamitous of defeats...'

The Spartans then sent a general to help the Syracusans in the defence of their city, and at the same time they began preparations to invade Attica. The Greeks subject to Athens in Asia Minor and its offshore islands were ready to revolt, and the two Persian satraps in western Anatolia – Pharnabazus in Phrygia and Tissaphernes in Ionia – offered to support them. The Spartans sent a squadron of five ships to the Ionian coast under Chalcideus, accompanied by Alcibiades, who incited revolts against Athens by Chios, Erythrae, Clazomenae, Teos, Lebedus, Miletus and Lesbos. The Athenians were able to retake Lesbos and Clazomenae, while they besieged Miletus and landed troops on Chios to surround the city. But at the same time they lost Phocaea and Cnidus to the Spartans as well as the three Dorian cities on Rhodes.

The Spartans then penetrated into the Hellespont, taking Abydos and Lampsacus, which led Byzantium, Chalcedon and Cyzicus to revolt against Athens. The Athenians were able to recapture Lampsacus and Cyzicus, and they put a garrison at Sestos, on the European shore of the strait opposite Abydos, to regain control of the Hellespont. But with the revolt of Byzantium and Chalcedon they had lost control of the Bosphorus, which cut off their access to their grain supplies around the Black Sea.

Tissaphernes, the Persian satrap of Ionia, persuaded King Darius II to form a pact with the Spartan Alliance against Athens. The pact, which was signed in 412 BC, recognised Persian suzerainty over the Greek cities in Asia Minor. Persian support for Sparta proved to be sporadic and ineffective, for they were hoping that both sides would exhaust one another.

The Peloponnesian War finally ended in the spring of 404 BC, when the Athenians accepted the peace terms offered to them by the Spartans and their allies. They were to demolish the Long Walls and the fortifications of the Piraeus, recall their exiles, surrender most of their fleet, give up all of their maritime empire, ally themselves with the Spartans, and accompany them in all expeditions on land and sea. Xenophon describes the scene in Athens when the Spartan terms were accepted.

> Some people spoke in opposition, but many more were in favour, and so it was decided to accept the peace. After this Lysander sailed into the Piraeus, the exiles returned, and the walls were pulled down among scenes of great enthusiasm and to the music of flute girls. It was thought that this day was the beginning of freedom for Greece.

Meanwhile Prince Cyrus had been making preparations to contest the Persian throne with his brother Artaxerxes II. The Spartans agreed to help him, and they sent a fleet to Cilicia, where they prevented the Persian satrap Syennesis from employing his army against Cyrus while he was marching against Artaxerxes. Cyrus mustered an army that included a large force of Greek mercenaries, the so-called Ten Thousand, one of them being the historian Xenophon, who would later write of the Persian expedition in his *Anabasis,* or *The March Upcountry.*

The expedition began in the spring of 401 BC, when Cyrus led his army out of Sardis to march them across Anatolia to Persia. The Persian army, commanded by Artaxerxes and Tissaphernes, met them at Cunaxa, near Babylon. Cyrus came close to victory, personally wounding Artaxerxes, but then he was killed and his Greek mercenaries were left without a leader. The survivors of the Ten Thousand made their way back by marching north to the Black Sea at Trebizond, from where they sailed westward along the coast and eventually arrived at Byzantium in the spring of 399 BC. Xenophon then led the remnants of the Ten Thousand to Pergamum, in the valley of the Caicus in Aeolis, where the Spartan general Thibron added them to the army he had mustered to make war against the Persian satraps Tissaphernes and Pharnabazus.

Thibron's expedition was the beginning of a war between the Spartan Alliance and Persia, much of which was fought along the western coast of Asia Minor. The Spartan king Agesilaus, assisted by Lysander, led a campaign against the Persians in 396 BC with an army of some 20,000 troops, including contingents from the Greek cities in Asia Minor. The following year the Spartans overran Phyrgia and routed the forces under Tissaphernes and Pharnabazus, capturing Sardis, but they were forced to withdraw because the Persian navy controlled the maritime approaches to Asia Minor.

The decisive naval battle of the war was fought off Cnidus in 394 BC, when the Peloponnesian navy was defeated by a Persian fleet commanded by Pharnabazus and the Athenian émigré Conon, who had manned his own squadron with Greek exiles and mercenaries. Conon subsequently helped introduce democracies in some of the Greek cities in Asia Minor, including Ephesus and Erythrae, which had been ruled by oligarchies. This alarmed Artaxerxes, who in 392 BC had Conon executed. Five years later Artaxerxes came to terms with the Spartan Alliance, a treaty known as the King's Peace. The treaty confirmed Spartan ascendancy in Greece, while the Persians regained control of the Greek cities in Asia Minor, including the right to exact tribute from them. An inscription found at Erythrae in 1976 seems to date from just after the King's Peace, for it records a plea from the Erythraeans not to 'be handed over to the barbarian'.

Athens gradually recovered during the quarter century after the end of the Peloponnesian War, and in 377 BC she formed a new anti-Spartan defensive alliance known as the Second Athenian Sea League. The Athenians decisively defeated a Spartan fleet off Naxos in September 376 BC. The following year Athenians defeated the Spartans again in the Ionian Sea, leaving Athens as the dominant sea power in Greece. At this point the Athenians needed a pause to recuperate financially, and in 375 BC they negotiated a treaty with Sparta, which recognised the Athenian Alliance and agreed to a peace on terms of a *status quo*.

The agreement was soon violated, and five more years of war were finally ended by a treaty in 371 BC, also known as the King's Peace. Within three weeks after the signing of the new treaty the Spartans went to war with the Boetians, whose general Epaminondas decisively defeated them at Leuctra, near Thebes. This broke the power of Sparta and began the hegemony of Thebes, which lead the Athenians to ally themselves with the Spartans to maintain a balance of power. The climax of the conflict came at the battle of Mantinea in 362 BC, in which the Boetians were at the point of victory before Epaminondas was killed, allowing the Spartans and Athenians to escape. Xenophon closes his *Hellenica* with an account of this inconclusive struggle, which he says left the future of Greece hanging in the balance.

> Nearly the whole of Greece had been engaged on one side or the other, and everyone imagined that, if a battle was fought, the winner would become the dominant power and the losers would be their subjects... Both sides claimed the victory, but it cannot be said that with regard to the accession of new territory, or cities, or power either side was any better off after the battle than before it. In fact there was even more uncertainty and confusion in Greece after the battle than there had been previously.

Meanwhile the Greek cities in Asia Minor remained under Persian rule, with no apparent hope of liberation now that the leading powers of Greece had just fought one another to a standstill. By then many of the eastern Greeks had gone off into exile in Greece or Magna Graecia, as had some of the leading figures of the archaic renaissance before the Persian Wars, bringing with them the genius of the Ionian enlightenment.

Abdera, which had been founded by colonists from Teos when their city was taken by the Persians in 545 BC, is renowned as the birthplace of Democritus, one of the founders of the atomic theory, along with Leucippus, traditionally said to be his teacher. Little is known of Leucippus, who may have been an exile from Miletus. His lost work, *The Greater World System*, apparently originated the atomic theory, which is usually attributed to his pupil Democritus. The atomic theory of Democritus appeared in a lost work called the *Little World System*, which he may have so called out of deference to the work of his teacher Leucippus.

The atomic theory of Leucippus and Democritus holds that the *arche* exists in the form of atoms, the irreducible minima of all physical substances, which through their ceaseless motion and mutual collisions take on all the various forms observed in nature. The only extant fragment by Leucippus himself says that 'Nothing occurs at random, but everything for a reason and by necessity,' by which he meant that atomic motion is not chaotic but obeys the immutable laws of nature.

An extant fragment by Democritus has him saying that he was a younger contemporary of the philosopher Anaxagoras. Anaxagoras was born ca. 500 BC in the Ionian city of Clazomenae, which he left for Athens at the age of twenty. He was the first philosopher to live in Athens, where he resided for thirty years, becoming the teacher and close friend of Pericles.

Anaxagoras had a very original view of the nature of matter known as the 'seed theory'. 'We must suppose,' he writes, 'that there are many things of all sorts in things that are aggregated, seeds of all things, with all sorts of shapes and colours and tastes… There is a portion of everything in everything.' He also postulated an element called the *aether*, which is in constant rotation and carries with it the celestial bodies. He says that 'The sun, moon and all the stars are red-hot stones which the rotation of the *aether* carries round with it.' The *aether* proved to be a very enduring concept, and it kept reappearing in cosmological theories up until the early twentieth century.

Another idea of Anaxagoras concerned what the Greeks of his time called *Nous*, or Mind, by which he meant the directing intelligence of the cosmos, as opposed to inert matter. This earned for Anaxagoras the nickname of *Nous*, as Plutarch notes in his *Life of Pericles*:

But the man who most consorted with Pericles … was Anaxagoras the Clazomenian, whom men of those days used to call 'Nous' either because they admired that comprehension of his, which proved of such surpassing greatness in the investigation of nature; or because he was the first to enthrone in the universe not Chance, nor yet Necessity, but Mind (*Nous*) pure and simple …

Around 450 BC enemies of Pericles indicted Anaxagoras on charges of impiety and 'medeism', being pro-Persian. Aided by Pericles, Anaxagora escaped to Lampsacus on the Asian shore of the Hellespont, where he founded a school that he directed for the rest of his days. After his death, ca. 428 BC, the people of Lampsacus erected a monument to his memory in their *agora*, dedicating it to mind and truth, which were at the core of his philosophy. Anaxagoras was the last of the Ionian physicists, for even in his own lifetime Athens had replaced Ionia as the common meeting-place for philosophers of nature.

Herodotus, the Father of History, was also forced to leave Asia Minor, not in flight from the Persians but because of civil strife in Halicarnassus. According to his later compatriot, Dionysius of Halicarnassus, Herodotus was born 'a little before the Persian War, and lived to the Peloponnesian War'. He left Halicarnassus for good ca. 447 BC and went to Athens, where he lived for four years before moving to the newly founded Athenian colony of Thurii in southern Italy. He remained in Thurii for the rest of his life, apart from his travels, and died there at some time after 430 BC, as evidenced by several unmistakable references that he makes to the early stages of the Peloponnesian War. The theme of his life's work is set forth in the first sentence of Book I of his *Histories*: 'Herodotus of Halicarnassus here displays his inquiry, so that human achievements may not be forgotten in time, and great and marvelous deeds – some displayed by Greeks, some by barbarians – may not be without their glory; and especially to show how the two peoples fought with each other.'

6

Alexander's Dream

The turmoil in Greece at the time of the battle of Mantinea was paralleled in Asia Minor, where some of the Persian satraps had risen against King Artaxerxes II, a revolt that spread to Phoenicia and Egypt.

Ariobarzanes, the satrap of Phrygia, tried to establish himself as an independent ruler in north-western Asia Minor, but he was defeated by two other satraps, Autophradates of Lydia and Mausolus of Caria. Ariobarzanes was then sent as a prisoner to the Persian court, while his post as satrap of Phrygia was given to Artabazus, son of Pharnabazus. Mausolus himself had been in revolt earlier, but he renewed his loyalty to Artaxerxes in time to help put down Ariobarzanes.

The political stalemate in the Greek world was broken by the sudden rise of Macedon, which began when Philip II was elected king in 357 BC. During the twenty-one years of his reign Philip made Macedon the dominant power in Greece, climaxed by his victory over the Athenians and their Theban and other allies at the battle of Chaeronea, early in August 338 BC.

After his victory Philip negotiated peace settlements with the Greek states that had been opposing him, installing Macedonian garrisons in Thebes and Corinth. Athens was forced to disband her Sea League, but she was allowed to keep the islands of Samos, Skyros, Lemnos and Imbros, while some territory was taken from Sparta and given to other cities.

During the following winter Philip summoned the Greek states to send deputies to a congress at Corinth. This gave rise to the League of

Corinth, also known as the Greek Community, a confederation of the Greek states under the aegis of Macedon. The agreement was ratified by all but one of the Greek states south of Macedon, including many in the islands, the single exception being Sparta. At its first regular meeting, in the summer of 337 BC, the federation formally entered into an alliance with the Macedonian state, defined as 'Philip and his descendants'. Philip was elected by the community as hegemon, or leader, as well as commander of their armed forces, after which they declared war on Persia.

The political situation in the western satrapies of the Persian Empire had changed since Philip came to the throne, beginning in 358 BC with the death of Artaxerxes II and the succession of his son Artaxerxes III Ochus. The new king ordered all of the satraps to disband their armies, because they had become virtually autonomous. The most powerful of them was Artabazus, the satrap of Phrygia, who hired an army of Greek mercenaries led by the Theban general Pammenes and launched a fleet commanded by Memnon of Rhodes. Artaxerxes, who also employed Greek mercenaries in both his army and navy, finally put down the revolt in 353 BC. Artabazus and Memnon took refuge in Philip's court in Pella, but four years later they were pardoned and returned to Persia.

Artaxerxes also set out to regain control of Egypt, using an army of Greek mercenaries commanded by Mentor, Memnon's brother. Mentor was victorious in Egypt, and Artaxerxes then sent him to restore Persian control over the coastal areas of Asia Minor, where local dynasts had set themselves up as independent rulers.

A wealthy banker named Euboulos had established a small state on the coast of Asia Minor opposite Lesbos, extending from Assos around the Adramyttene Gulf to Atarnaeus. Euboulos was succeeded by Hermias, a benevolent despot known as the Tyrant of Atarnaeus. Hermias had been a student at Plato's Academy in Athens along with Aristotle, whose father had been personal physician to King Amyntas III of Macedon. After Plato died in 348 BC, Hermias founded a philosophical school at Assos under Aristotle, who taught there for three years before moving across to Lesbos. The following year Hermias was captured by Mentor and sent as a prisoner to the Persian court, where Artaxerxes had him executed. Left without his patron, Aristotle returned to the Macedonian court at Pella, where he served as tutor to Philip's son and eventual successor, Alexander the Great.

Mausolus had inherited the title of satrap of Caria from his father Hecatomnus, who had his capital at Mylasa. The Hecatomnid dynasty lasted for only two generations, the second of which consisted of three sons of Hecatomnus: Mausolus, Idrieus and Pixodarus, and two of his daughters: Artemisia and Ada. After Mausolus became satrap he married his sister Artemisia and moved his capital to Halicarnassus. He then rebuilt Halicarnassus on a grand scale, for he was expanding his satrapy into a kingdom, eventually extending his rule beyond Caria to parts of Ionia, Lycia, Pamphylia and Pisidia as well as the islands of Rhodes, Cos and Chios.

Mausolus was a philhellenic patron of the arts and science, and he adorned Halicarnassus and the other cities of his kingdom with classical Greek temples, theatres and other public buildings. One of those who received his patronage was the renowned astronomer and mathematician Eudoxus of Cnidus, the ancient Dorian city on the peninsula south of Halicarnassus. Eudoxus built a famous observatory at Cnidus, and the astronomical observations he made there, together with his mathematical theories concerning the motions of the planets, are landmarks in the history of ancient science.

When Mausolus died in 353 BC he was succeeded by Artemisia, who successfully defended Halicarnassus when it was attacked by the Rhodians. She spent her last years completing a magnificent tomb that had been begun by Mausolus – the Mausoleum – one of the Seven Wonders of the Ancient World, and when she died in 350 BC they were laid to rest there together.

Idrieus then became ruler of Caria and married his sister Ada, who succeeded him after his death in 344 BC. Four years later her younger brother Pixodarus deposed Ada, who took refuge at the fortified town of Alinda in the Carian hills. Then in 336 BC Pixodarus sent an envoy to King Philip, offering his eldest daughter as a bride to Alexander's half-brother Philip Arrhidaeus. The offer was rejected, but Alexander secretly sent a messenger to Pixodarus saying that he would accept the satrap's daughter as his bride. Plutarch says that when Philip learned of this he quashed the plan and gave Alexander a tongue-lashing: 'He upbraided his son severely, and bitterly reviled him as ignoble and unworthy of his high estate, in that he desired to become the son-in-law of a barbarian king.' Pixodarus then married off his daughter to the Persian nobleman

Orontobates, who became Persian satrap of Halicarnassus after his father-in-law died.

After the formation of the League of Corinth, Philip began preparing for his war against the Persians, in which he intended to free the Greek cities in Asia Minor. Persia had in the meantime gone through two violent regime changes. The first occurred in August 338 BC, when Artaxerxes III was assassinated and Aratxerxes IV became king. The second took place in the spring of 336 BC, when Artaxerxes IV was murdered and replaced by Darius II.

Philip launched a preliminary expedition into Asia Minor in the spring of 336 BC, putting 10,000 troops under the command of Parmenio, supported by the Macedonian fleet. The fleet captured Lesbos, Chios and Erythrae, while the army under Parmenio took Ephesus, overthrowing pro-Persian tyrants or oligarchies and establishing democratic governments. But then the Macedonians were defeated at Magnesia ad Maeandrum by a Persian force under Memnon. This effectively ended the campaign, for that summer Philip was assassinated at Pella. The Macedonian army at Pella then acclaimed Alexander as king, and Parmenio, who was still in Asia Minor, soon pledged his allegiance as well, on condition that all the leading command posts would be held by his kinsmen.

The League of Corinth elected Alexander to succeed Philip as hegemon, after which they agreed to support him in implementing his father's crusade to liberate the Greeks of Asia Minor from Persian rule. But before beginning his invasion of Asia, Alexander had to stabilise Macedonian rule in Europe. Early in the spring of 335 BC he led a campaign in Thrace and Illyria, and later that year he crushed a revolt in Thebes.

King Darius had been secretly financing the Theban rebellion, and after it failed he raised an army of 5,000 mercenaries under Memnon to deal with the Macedonian advance force commanded by Parmenio in Asia Minor. Parmenio had liberated many of the Greek cities along the coast, including Abydos on the Hellespont, and in July 335 BC he took the town of Gryneum in Aeolis, enslaving its populace because they had not come over to him voluntarily.

Parmenio then went on to besiege the Aeolian town of Pitane, but he broke off the siege when he learned that a Persian force under Memnon was attacking Abydos, at the strategic crossing point of the Hellespont. Parmenio raised the siege of Pitane and managed to relieve Abydos, but in the process he lost many of his earlier conquests to Memnon.

Early in the spring of 334 BC, after appointing Antipater to serve as regent in Macedonia, Alexander set out from Pella at the head of his expeditionary force and headed for the Hellespont. Arrian says the Macedonian force comprised 'not much more than 30,000 infantry, including light troops and archers, and over 5,000 cavalry', but a modern estimate puts it at 43,000 infantry and 6,100 cavalry. The Macedonian fleet, supplied by the League of Corinth, consisted of only 160 ships, a third the size of Persia's Phoenician navy, which was far more efficient.

According to Arrian, Alexander's army took twenty days to reach Sestos, on the European shore of the Hellespont, where Parmenio had the cavalry and most of the infantry ferried across to Abydos. Alexander took the rest of the troops down to Elaeus at the outer end of the Gallipoli peninsula, where there was a shrine dedicated to the hero Protesilaus, 'the first of all the Achaians' to die at Troy, according to Homer. Arrian says that Alexander offered sacrifice at the tomb 'to ensure better luck for himself than Protesilaus had', after which he crossed the Hellespont to the Achaean harbour, where Agamemnon had beached his ships during the siege of Troy.

Once ashore, Alexander travelled inland to Ilion, the Aeolian city that had been founded on the site of ancient Troy, where, according to Arrian, he 'offered sacrifice to Athena, patron goddess of the city; here he made a gift of his armour to the temple, and took in exchange, from where they hung on the temple walls, some weapons which were still preserved from the Trojan War'. Arrian then goes on to tell of how Alexander and his bosom friend Hephaestion made a pilgrimage to the tombs of Patroclus and Achilles, their heroic predecessors. 'One account says that Hephaestion laid a wreath on the tomb of Patroclus; another that Alexander laid one on the tomb of Achilles, calling him a lucky man, in that he had Homer to proclaim his deeds and preserve his memory.'

Alexander and his troops then rejoined Parmenio and the rest of the army at Arisbe, near Abydos. They then marched up the Asian shore of the Hellespont to Lampsacus, which Memnon had captured the year before. As Alexander approached Lampsacus he was met by a delegation of the townspeople who persuaded him to spare the town. Alexander then headed eastward along the shore of the Sea of

Marmara toward Dascylium, headquarters of Arsites, the Persian satrap of Phrygia.

Arsites had in the meanwhile sent out an appeal to the two other Persian governors in Asia Minor: Spithridates, satrap of Ionia and Lydia, and Arsames, satrap of Cilicia, who assembled at Dascylium with their forces, including the Greek mercenaries commanded by Memnon. The Persians set up an entrenched camp just east of the Granicus, which Alexander would have to cross to attack Dascylium.

Parmenio tried to persuade Alexander not to make a direct assault across the river, given the strength of the Persian position. But Alexander ordered his troops across to charge the Persians arrayed on the east bank of the Granicus. He was in the thick of the battle and killed Mithridates, son-in-law of King Darius, after which he himself was unhorsed and narrowly escaped death twice. The Persians finally fled after suffering heavy loss of life, including Spithridates, who was killed when he was on the point of striking down Alexander. Memnon survived and lived to fight again. Arrian says that 'Arsites escaped to Phrygia, where he is said to have died by his own hand, because the Persians held him responsible for the defeat.'

Alexander's next objective was Sardis, where the Persians surrendered the town and its citadel without a struggle. Alexander then headed to Ephesus, where the Persian garrison abandoned the citadel and fled. Arrian says that when Alexander arrived 'he recalled everyone who had been expelled for supporting him, stripped the small governing clique of its power, and restored democratic institutions'.

The archaic temple of Ephesian Artemis had been destroyed in 356 BC, supposedly on the very day that Alexander was born, when a madman named Herostratus set it on fire to gain immortal fame. Alexander offered to endow a new temple of Artemis with the tribute that previously had been paid to Persia, provided that the dedicatory inscription be in his name. But the Ephesians politely declined, saying that it was not proper for one god to dedicate a temple to another.

While Alexander was at Ephesus delegations came from the towns of Tralles and Magnesia ad Maeandrum offering their submission, and so he sent a force under Parmenio to occupy both places He also sent another detachment under Alcimachus to proceed to all the towns in Lydia, Ionia and Phrygia that were still held by the Persians. Both commanders were instructed to replace oligarchical governments with democracies, to remit the tribute that they had been paying to Persia, and to leave local laws and customs unchanged. The liberated towns were then made members of the League of Corinth, requiring that they contribute to Alexander's campaign, which probably cost them as much as they had formerly paid in tribute to the Persians.

While Parmenio and Alcimachus were engaged in their missions Alexander made a brief visit to Smyrna, which was still virtually an uninhabited ruin, having been abandoned after its destruction by Alyattes ca. 600 BC. While there he supposedly had a dream that inspired him to have the city rebuilt on a new site under Mount Pagos, the eminence that rises above the inner end of the Smyrnaic Gulf. The new city was not built until the following century, but, according to Pausanias, when it was refounded it was on the site that had been revealed to Alexander in his dream:

> Alexander founded the modern city from a vision he had in his sleep: he was out hunting on Mount Pagos, and on the way home from his hunt they say he came on the sanctuary of the Vengeances with the spring in front of the sanctuary and a plane tree growing over the water. While he was asleep under the plane tree the Vengeances appeared to him and commanded him to build a city there and bring the people of Smyrna to it, turning them out of the earlier city. So the Smyrnaians sent ambassadors to ask at Klaros what their position was, and the god answered with this prophecy: 'Ye shall live three and four times happy/ At Pagos, across the sacred Meles.'

Alexander also visited Clazomenae, which was originally founded on an islet close to the shore of the hydra-headed peninsula that forms the south side of the Smyrnaic Gulf. According to Pausanias, at the time of his visit Alexander 'was to make Klazomenai a peninsula by piling up the causeway between the mainland and the island'.

Then Alexander received word that the Persian fleet was headed toward Miletus, and so he recalled Parmenio and Alcimachus. He also ordered Nicanor, commander of the Macedonian fleet, to head for Miletus, hoping that he would arrive there before the Persian navy. Despite the urgency, while marching toward Miletus Alexander found time to stop at Priene, where he made a generous donation to the temple of Athena that was being erected there. The dedicatory inscription recording his benefaction is still preserved in the British Museum, stating that 'King Alexander presented this temple to Athena Polias.'

Nicanor reached Miletus three days before the arrival of the Persian navy, and he anchored his fleet of 160 ships on the offshore islet of Lade. When Alexander arrived he put a strong force on Lade to prevent the Persians from landing there. The commanders of the Persian navy were forced to anchor their 400 ships off Cape Mycale, for the maritime approach to Miletus was now blockaded by the Macedonian fleet.

Hegistratus, the commander of the Persian garrison in Miletus, had previously offered to surrender to Alexander, but the arrival of the Persian fleet now emboldened him to hold out in the citadel. The following morning Alexander ordered the assault to begin, bringing up his siege engines to batter the walls of the city, his troops poised to attack as soon as the defences were weakened or breached. The Macedonian fleet then moved in to block the inner harbour of Miletus, the Lion Port. This led some of the defenders to plunge into the sea and swim out to an offshore islet in a futile attempt to escape, for Alexander captured them as soon as he took Miletus.

The Persian navy withdrew after the fall of Miletus, whereupon Alexander decided to disband his fleet except for a score of ships manned by the Athenians, which he retained to use as transports. He sent the other ships home because he could no longer afford a large fleet, besides which he felt he no longer needed one, for by capturing the coastal towns he could render the Persian navy impotent.

Alexander then prepared to head south along the coast into Caria, where the Persians had concentrated their forces at Halicarnassus under the command of Memnon and the Persian satrap Orontobates. But first he made a detour up into the highlands of Caria to see Queen Ada, who had been in exile at Alinda since being driven out of Halicarnassus by her brother Pixodarus. Ada surrendered Alinda to Alexander and adopted him as her son and eventual successor, whereupon, according to Diodorus Siculus, 'all the cities [in Caria] sent missions and presented the king with gold crowns and promised to cooperate with him in everything'.

Alexander reached the coast again at Iasus, north of Halicarnassus, where his squadron of transport ships had anchored. The people of Iasus petitioned Alexander for the return of fishing grounds they had lost under Persian rule, and he immediately granted their request. They then presented to him a local youth who had become famous by befriending a dolphin with whom he had swum in the bay of Iasus. According to Pliny, Alexander was so charmed by the story that he took the youth with him on his campaign, and subsequently he 'made the boy head of the priesthood of Poseidon at Babylon, interpreting the dolphin's affection as a sign of the deity's favour'.

Alexander then marched his army to Halicarnassus, while he sent his fleet to Myndus, ten miles to the west at the end of the peninsula. While he waited for his supplies and siege machinery to arrive with the fleet, Alexander tried to take Myndus by direct assault, but its defences were too strong and he failed. After his fleet landed the supplies and equipment, probably on the south coast of the peninsula, Alexander began the siege of Halicarnassus, the most formidable fortress on the coast of Asia Minor. Aside from the city walls themselves there were three separately walled citadels. One of these was on the ancient acropolis at the north-eastern angle of the land; the second was on the promontory at the western horn of the crescent-shaped port, a place called Salmakis; and the third was on the offshore island of Arconessus.

Alexander's artillery and battering-rams created a breach in the walls, and he sent his troops charging through, but they were driven back by Memnon's Greek mercenaries. Several other assaults followed over the course of the next two months, but all of them were repelled by the defenders. Memnon then sallied forth with his mercenaries to attack the besiegers. The counter-attack almost succeeded, but then the mercenaries were forced to retreat back into the city, about 1,000 of them killed in the battle, while the Macedonians had only forty dead.

The failure of this sortie convinced Memnon and Orontobates that it was not possible to hold out any longer, and so in the middle of the following night they set fire to their armoury and abandoned the main city with their troops, retreating to the citadels of Salmakis and Arconessus. The blaze from the armoury was fanned by the wind and spread rapidly through the town, which was still burning when the Macedonians entered it the following morning.

Alexander thought that it was not worth his while to attack the citadels of Salmakis and Arconessus, so he decided to continue his campaign. He appointed Queen Ada to govern all of Caria, with Ptolemy's force to help her deal with the Persians who were still holding out in Salmakis and

Arconessus. He then sent Parmenio to Sardis with part of the army, including the baggage and siege equipment, with orders to continue on into Phrygia, where Alexander would rejoin him the following spring, along with the men who were given leave to go home over the winter.

Alexander then led the rest of the army eastward along the Mediterranean coast from Caria into Lycia, where all of the towns along the way surrendered to him without a struggle, most notably Telmessus, Pinara, Xanthus, Patara and Phaselis. He then marched on into Pamphylia, where he accepted the surrender of Side. There the Macedonians found the townspeople speaking a strange language they had never heard before, the dialect that the original Aeolian settlers from Cyme had developed in the early days of the colony, surrounded as they were by Pamphylians. As Arrian notes, 'from then on the men of Side had remained foreigners, distinct in speech, as in everything else, from their neighbours'.

Alexander left a garrison in Side and took a force up into the Pisidian highlands to Syllium, which Arrian describes as 'a fortified town garrisoned by mercenaries and native troops'. He found the town too strongly fortified to take without employing siege machinery, and so he went back to the coast and approached Aspendos. The people there had earlier agreed to submit, but they reneged and Alexander prepared to put the town under siege. At that point the townspeople surrendered, whereupon Alexander doubled the annual tribute they would have to pay to Macedon.

Alexander continued on and took the surrender of Perge, one of the cities in Pamphylia that had supposedly been founded by the 'mixed multitudes' of Hellenes and others after the Trojan War. He then led his army back up into the Pisidian highlands to attack Termessus, whose mountain-top fortress proved too difficult for him to capture. He continued on to Sagalassus, another mountain fortress, which he took after a hand-to-hand struggle in which 500 Pisidian solders were killed, the Macedonians losing about twenty men, according to Arrian. Arrian goes on to say that 'Alexander then proceeded against the other Pisidian communities; some of their fortified places he took by assault, others surrendered to him without resistance.'

The next stage of Alexander's expedition took him past the Pisidian Lakes to Celaenae (Dinar), a strategic crossroads town on the Persian Royal Road that led from Sardis to Susa. The Persian garrison agreed to surrender in two months if they received no reinforcements from King Darius, and so Alexander left behind 1,500 troops under Antigonus and continued on to Gordion, the ancient capital of Phrygia, where he was to met Parmenio and the rest of the army.

Early in March 333 BC, Alexander reached Gordion, which surrendered to him without a struggle. A month later he was joined by Parmenio, who brought with him the men who had been home on leave as well as reinforcements, including 3,000 Macedonian infantrymen and 500 cavalry.

While Alexander was in Gordion he visited the ancient palace of Gordius and his son Midas, the founders of the Phrygian kingdom, which seems to have been converted into a shrine dedicated to their memory. According to the founding myth, during a period of internal strife the Phrygians consulted an oracle who told him that a wagon would bring them a wise ruler. Soon afterwards a stranger named Gordius drove into the city in a wooden wagon, as if in fulfilment of the prophecy, and the Phrygians made him king. When Gordius died he was succeeded by his son Midas, who supposedly dedicated his father's wagon in the temple of Zeus Basileus, tied to the yoke with the legendary Gordian Knot. The knot was tied so that its ends could not be seen, and the Phrygians believed that the man who could undo it was 'destined to be the lord of Asia,' according to Arrian, who describes the challenge this posed for Alexander.

> For Alexander, then, how to undo it was indeed a puzzle, though he was none the less unwilling to leave it as it was, as his failure might possibly lead to public disturbances. Accounts of what followed differ: some say that Alexander cut the knot with a stroke of his sword and exclaimed, 'I have undone it!' But Aristobulus thinks that he took out the pin – a sort of wooden peg which was driven through the shaft of the wagon and held the knot together – and thus pulled the yoke away from the shaft. I do not myself presume to dogmatize on this subject. In any case, when he and his attendants left the place where the wagon stood, the general feeling was that the oracle about the untying of the knot had been fulfilled. Moreover, that very night there was lightning and thunder – a further sign from heaven; so Alexander, on the strength of all this, offered sacrifice the following day to the gods who had sent the sign from heaven and proclaimed the Loosing of the Knot.

While Alexander was in Gordion he received word that Darius was assembling a large army to march against him, having made Memnon commander-in-chief of all Persian forces in Asia Minor. The Persian fleet under Memnon had already taken control of Kos, Samos, and Chios, after which he took all of Lesbos except Mytilene, which he put under siege. At the same time Memnon's agents in Greece were subsidising a general revolt against Macedonian rule, for which there was enthusiastic support in Athens and Sparta. Thus Alexander was faced with the danger of being cut off from Greece while in the middle of Anatolia, with the Persian army about to march against him from the east.

The day after cutting the Gordian Knot, Alexander departed with his army for Ancyra (Ankara), a strategic crossroads town on the borders of Galatia and Paphlagonia. There he was met by a delegation of Paphlagonians, who offered their submission but begged him not to march his troops into their territory. Alexander accepted their offer of friendship and told them that thenceforth they should take their orders from Calas, one of his generals whom he had made governor of Phrygia.

While Alexander was in Ancyra he received news that his adversary Memnon had fallen ill and died during his siege of Mytilene. Command then passed to the Persian noblemen Pharnabazus and Autophradates, who soon captured Mytilene and went on to take control of the Cyclades.

After leaving Ancyra, Alexander led his army southward across the great Anatolian plateau into Cappadocia, where, according to Arrian, 'he received the submission of all territory bounded by the river Halys and also of a large tract to the west and north beyond it'. This time Alexander did not leave one of his generals to govern the region, but instead appointed a local chieftain named Sabitas, a policy he would follow more and more often as his campaign went on.

Alexander's route now took him toward the narrow pass known as the Cilician Gates, the only way through the Taurus Mountains down to the Cilician plain. The Persian general Arsames left a small force to guard the pass while he laid waste the Cilician plain and moved down to Tarsus, which he intended to strip of all its wealth, leaving nothing for Alexander. When Alexander reached the pass the Persian guards fled, and the Macedonians made their way down across the Cilician plain without opposition. Arsames abandoned Tarsus at their approach, leading his army eastward to join Darius, who was marching the rest of the Persian army westward across Mesopotamia to Cilicia, heading for a showdown with Alexander.

The showdown came in November 333 BC at the battle of Issus, on the shore of the Cilician Gulf where the coastline curves south toward Syria. The battle began in mid-afternoon when Alexander led the Companion cavalry across the Pinarus river to attack the Persian left wing, which collapsed and retreated in disorder.

Alexander then wheeled left to engage the Persian centre, which was being attacked by the Macedonian phalanx. At that point Darius panicked and fled from the field, followed by many of his cavalrymen, leaving the rest of the Persian army to be slaughtered by the Macedonians. Arrian and other ancient sources put the number of Persian dead at some 100,000, with the Macedonian casualities estimated as 450 killed and 4,500 wounded, the latter including Alexander, who suffered a sword cut on his thigh.

Darius did not cease his flight until he reached Babylon, from where he sent envoys to negotiate a settlement with Alexander, who had captured the royal family along with the imperial treasury. Alexander contemptuously dismissed the envoys, whereupon Darius began planning a new campaign, setting out to raise another army in Asia, while he sponsored rebellions in Greece and kept the Phoenician fleet on the offensive in the Aegean.

The Phoenician fleet ceased to be a factor after Alexander captured their main base at Tyre on 29 July 332 BC. He went on into Egypt, where he was crowned as pharaoh at Memphis, after which he founded the city of Alexandria before returning to Tyre. Then early in the following summer he led his army up through Syria and across Mesopotamia, reaching the Tigris in mid-September. Darius made one last futile attempt to negotiate, after which he led his army north from Babylon to confront Alexander, who utterly defeated him at Gaugamela on 1 October 331 BC.

Once again Darius fled the field, but he was soon killed in a coup led by his grand vezir Nabarzanes and Bessus, satrap of Bactria. Thus ended the Achaemenid dynasty, which had begun in 560 BC with the accession of Cyrus the Great. Meanwhile the victorious Macedonian army had proclaimed Alexander 'lord of Asia', fulfilling the prophecy that had been made at Gordion.

Alexander's march of conquest eventually took him as far as Transoxiania and the Indus valley, from where he returned to Persia at the beginning of 324 BC. Early in February he drafted a proclamation addressed to the League of Corinth, which, among other things, required that the Greek cities publicly acknowledge him as a god. The Greeks mocked his divine pretensions, nevertheless they hastened to send envoys to pay homage to him, as Arrian observes in his account of Alexander's return to Babylon, ending on an ominous note: 'Successive delegations from Greece also presented themselves, and the delegates, wearing ceremonial wreaths, solemnly approached Alexander and placed golden chaplets on his head, as if their coming were a ritual in honour of a god. But, for all that, his end was near.'

The end came on the morning of 10 June 323 BC, about a month before Alexander's thirty-third birthday, when he passed away after having been critically ill for ten days following a night of carousing with his companions.

Arrian reports the ancient stories that Alexander was poisoned by his enemies, remarking that 'I put them down as such and do not expect them to be believed.'

He then concludes his work with an encomium for Alexander, whom he believed to have been more than mortal.

> It is my belief that there was in those days no nation, no city, no single individual beyond the reach of Alexander's name; never in all the world was there another like him, and therefore I cannot but feel that some power more than human was concerned in his birth... Even today, when so many years have passed, there have been oracles, all tending to his glory, delivered to the people of Macedon.

A number of the Greek cities in Asia Minor paid divine honours to Alexander, and the house where he stayed during his brief visit to Priene became a shrine, as evidenced by an inscription recording a cult dedicated to him there, with the injunction 'No admission to this sanctuary, except to the pure, and in white rainment.'

The Greeks of Asia Minor were now free of Persian rule, more than two centuries after they had been conquered by Cyrus the Great, though it would soon be evident that they had again exchanged one master for another. Nonetheless it meant a new life for Smyrna, which would be refounded under Mount Pagos through Alexander's dream.

7

Alexander's Successors

The Hellenistic period begins with the reign of Alexander the Great, when Greek culture spread from the Aegean to the Indus valley. After Alexander's death his vast empire was divided up by his leading generals, the Diadochi, or Successors, most notably Antipater, Antigonus Monopthalmus (One-Eyed), Lysimachus, Seleucus and Ptolemy, who fought one another in an interminable series of wars that were continued by their sons, the Epigoni, turning Asia Minor into an enormous battlefield.

Ptolemy stole a march on his colleagues by hijacking the embalmed corpse of Alexander, whom he buried with divine honours at Memphis while preparing a sufficiently grandiose tomb at Alexandria. The Diadochi soon went to war with one another in expanding their realms, a widespread conflict that lasted for more than forty years, during which time the Greek cities in Asia Minor were mere pawns in the struggle for supremacy. The unity of Alexander's empire was lost forever, but his vision of a Greek *oekoumene* lived on through a mosaic of Hellenistic kingdoms that arose in the lands that he had conquered, from Asia Minor to Central Asia and the borders of India.

Antipater, who had been regent in Macedon, continued to rule all of Greece except for Thrace, and when he died in 319 BC he was succeeded by his son Cassander. Thrace and north-western Asia Minor were under the authority of Lysimachus, Antigonus governed Phrygia and western Asia Minor, Seleucus was satrap of Babylonia, and Ptolemy was satrap in Egypt.

Ptolemy ruled continuously from 323 BC and in 304 BC he was proclaimed king of Egypt, taking the name Soter (Saviour). He ruled until his death in 283/282 BC, when he was succeeded by his son Ptolemy II, who was called Philadelphus, 'His Sister's Lover', because he married his sister Arsinoe. By that time the Ptolemaic kingdom had expanded beyond Egypt to include Libya, Ethiopia, Arabia, Phoenicia, Coele (Southern) Syria, southern Asia Minor and the Aegean isles.

Seleucus declared himself king in 312 BC, under the name Nicator (Victorious). Eventually he allied himself with Lysimachus against Antigonus, who was trying to reunify Alexander's empire under his own rule, aided by his son Demetrius Poliorcetes (Besieger of Cities). The allies defeated and killed Antigonus in 301 BC at the battle of Ipsus, in Phrygia, destroying his empire in Asia Minor, though his son Demetrius later became king of Macedon. Then in 281 BC Seleucus defeated and killed Lysimachus at the battle of Corupedium, near Magnesia ad Maeandrum. This gave Seleucus control of Asia Minor, so that his kingdom now stretched from the Aegean to the Indus river.

Later that same year, when Seleucus invaded Thrace, he was assassinated by Ptolemy Keraunus (Thunderbolt), a half-brother of Ptolemy II Philadelphus. Seleucus was succeeded by his son Antiochus I Soter, who renounced his father's ambitions in the West and focused his attention on Anatolia and Syria.

Meanwhile Demetrius Poliorcetes had been succeeded as king of Macedon by his son Antigonus II Gonatas. Thus by 281 BC, forty-two years after the death of Alexander, his empire was divided mainly into three parts, two of them ruled by Epigoni, sons of the Diadochi, the third by a grandson.

After the death of Antiochus in 301 BC, Lysimachus appointed a Paphlagonian named Philetaerus to be his governor at Pergamum, a hilltop fortress on the lower Caicus river in Mysia, entrusting him with the royal treasury. After the death of Lysimachus in 281 BC, Philetaerus retained control of Pergamum and used the treasure that had been left with him to create an independent principality, adorning the city with temples and other public buildings. When Philetaerus died in 263 BC he was succeeded by his nephew Eumenes, whom he had adopted as his son.

The year after his succession Eumenes defeated Antiochus I in a battle near Sardis, thus preserving the independence of Pergamum from the

Seleucid kingdom. During the next two decades Eumenes enlarged his principality to include the whole of the Caicus valley and the coast of Aeolis. He ruled until his death in 241 BC, when he was succeeded by his adopted son Attalus Soter, a grandnephew of Philetaerus.

Attalus began his reign with a great victory over the Gauls, the Celtic tribespeople who had crossed over from Europe a generation before, terrorising all of western Asia Minor. This broke the power of the Gauls, who settled down in the region of west-central Asia Minor that came to be known as Galatia. His triumph led Attalus to proclaim himself king of Pergamum, the first of the Attalid dynasty to assume that title. Attalus ruled for forty-four years, most of which he spent in warfare with the Seleucids, struggling for supremacy in Asia Minor.

Attalus had established good relations with Rome, and after his death in 197 BC this policy was continued by his son and successor Eumenes II Soter. A Roman army under Scipio Africanus invaded Asia Minor in 190 BC, joining forces with Eumenes in an effort to break the power of the Seleucid kingdom, then ruled by Antiochus III Megas (the Great). Scipio and Eumenes decisively defeated Antiochus the following year in a battle near Magnesia ad Sipylum. The Seleucid forces were commanded by Hannibal, whose elephants were left dead in their hundreds upon the battlefield, a sight that so distressed Antiochus that he decided to sue for peace. The Treaty of Apamea awarded most of the former Seleucid possessions in Asia Minor to Pergamum, whose territory was thus greatly increased, extending along the Aegean coast from the Hellespont to the Maeander valley. As Polybius noted, Eumenes succeeded his father 'in a kingdom reduced to a few petty towns, but this he raised to one of the largest dynasties of his day'.

Eumenes died in 159 BC and was succeeded by his brother Attalus II Philadelphus, who continued the Pergamene alliance with Rome. Attalus fought a long and difficult war against King Nicomedes II of Bithynia, in which Pergamum eventually emerged victorious. During the reign of Attalus II the Pergamene kingdom expanded to include most of western Asia Minor from the Black Sea to the Mediterranean.

Attalus II was succeeded in 138 BC by his weak and eccentric nephew, Attalus III, who neglected affairs of state to dabble in alchemy and botany, allowing his kingdom to be dominated by Rome. By then Roman power had grown so great that there seemed little future for an independent realm in western Asia Minor, and so in his last will and testament Attalus bequeathed his kingdom to Rome. When Attalus died in 133 BC his bequest was quickly accepted by Rome. But then a pretender named Aristonicus appeared, claiming to be a bastard son of Eumenes II, and many Pergamenes enlisted in his cause. A three-year war followed before the Romans finally defeated Aristonicus, who was sent as a prisoner to Rome and executed. The Pergamene kingdom was then incorporated into the Roman province of Asia, which came into being in 129 BC.

Rome had by then become the dominant power in the Hellenistic world. Polybius, at the beginning of his *Histories*, says the purpose of his work is to explain 'how, and under what kind of constitution, almost all inhabited parts of the world, in not as many as fifty-three years, fell under the single rule of the Romans, something that is not found to have happened previously'. The period referred to is 220–167 BC, from the start of the second Punic War, against Hannibal, to the end of the third Macedonian War, in which the Romans defeated Perseus, the last king of Macedon. Macedon became a Roman province in 148 BC, and two years later a Roman army under Mummius defeated the Greek allies of the Achaean League, utterly destroying Corinth.

The kingdom of Bithynia in north-western Asia Minor had a somewhat longer lifetime than that of Pergamum. It began as a coalition of Hellenised Thracian tribes and emerged as a kingdom under Zipoites (r. 297–280 BC), who successfully resisted Lysimachus in three campaigns. Zipoites was succeeded by his son Nicomedes I (r. 280–255 BC). The kingdom reached its peak under Prusias I (r. 228–182 BC), who expanded his realm along the shores of the Sea of Marmara and the Black Sea, capturing the Greek coastal cities and founding new cities of his own. The last of the dynasty was Nicomedes IV (r. 94–74 BC), who bequeathed the Bithynian kingdom to Rome, after which it too became part of the province of Asia.

Cius was one of the independent Greek coastal cities on the Marmara that had been absorbed into the Bithynian kingdom. The city had previously been ruled by a series of Persian tyrants, the last of whom – Mithridates – was executed when Antigonus took Cius in 302 BC. The tyrant's son, also named Mithridates, escaped to the Black Sea coast of Asia Minor, where he founded the independent kingdom of the Pontus, with his capital at Amaseia (Amasya). Although the dynasty was Persian in origin, the Pontic kingdom was completely Hellenised, all of its coastal cities having been founded as Greek colonies.

The Pontic kingdom reached its peak under Mithridates VI Eupator (the Great), who came to the throne in 120 BC when he was only eleven years old. When Mithridates came of age he established his capital at Sinope (Sinop), building the powerful citadel and defence walls that still survive in part today. By that time the Pontic kingdom extended into Paphlagonia, Bithynia, Cappadocia, Galatia and Phrygia, and under Mithridates Eupator it expanded around the Black Sea and became a veritable empire. He fought the Romans in four widespread conflicts that came to be known as the Mithridatic Wars, the first of them beginning in 88 BC and the last ending with his defeat and death twenty-five years later.

At the beginning of his first war against the Romans, Mithridates established his headquarters at Ephesus, where soon afterwards he issued secret orders to have all Italians in Asia Minor put to death on a certain day one month later. His orders were carried out and on a single day some 80,000 Italians were killed, women and children included, the highest toll being in Ephesus, capital of the Roman province of Asia. Mithridates went on to occupy most of Asia Minor, the Aegean isles and Greece, including Athens, generally welcomed as a liberator from Roman rule. He was driven out of Greece by a Roman army under Sulla, who in 84 BC forced him to come to terms and abandon his conquests in Asia Minor.

During the second Mithridatic War, 83–81 BC, the new governor of the Roman province of Asia, Lucullus, launched three offensives into the Pontus before being recalled to Rome. The third war began in 74 BC when a Roman army under Lucullus forced Mithridates to lift his siege of Cyzicus. The war dragged on until 67 BC, when Lucullus was recalled to Rome. The fourth and last conflict began the following year, when a Roman army under Pompey invaded the Pontus and forced Mithridates to flee into the Tauric Chersonnese (the Crimea), where he finally died in 63 BC. He was succeeded by his son Pharnaces II, whom Pompey recognised as ruler of the Bosphorean kingdom in the Crimea.

There were also Hellenised kingdoms in Galatia, Paphlagonia, Cappadocia and Commagene, in south-eastern Anatolia, and after Pompey's final defeat of Mithridates he received the submission of their rulers and recognised them as 'friends and allies of the Roman people'. He also reorganised the cities and provinces of Asia Minor, after which he went on to Syria and deposed Antiochus XII Philadelphus in 63 BC. Pompey thereupon reorganised Syria as a Roman province, bringing the history of the Seleucid dynasty to a close.

Pompey then dealt with the pirates who had been ravaging the Aegean islands and the coastal cities of Asia Minor. He launched an all-out campaign against the pirates in 67 BC, and within three months he had cleared them from the Pamphylian and Cilician coasts of Asia Minor, destroying their fleet in a final battle off Coracesium (Alanya). As Plutarch writes in his life of Pompey: 'He took ninety men of war with brazen beaks; and likewise prisoners of war to the number of no less than twenty thousand.'

By the time the Greek cities of Asia Minor recovered from the Mithridatic Wars they were engulfed in the Roman Civil War, which began when Caesar crossed the Rubicon and invaded Italy on 1 January 49 BC. On 9 August of the following year he won a decisive victory over Pompey at Pharsalus in southern Thessaly. Pompey fled to Alexandria, where he was assassinated a few days before Caesar arrived. Caesar then stayed on in Alexandria with Cleopatra, who had succeeded her father Ptolemy XIII as ruler of Egypt, reigning jointly with her younger brother Ptolemy XIV. By the time Caesar left Alexandria the following summer Cleopatra had borne him a son named Caesarion, whom she made co-ruler after the death of her brother later that year.

Meanwhile Pharnaces II attempted to regain his father's dominions in Asia Minor, and in 48 BC he defeated an army led by Domitius Calvinus, Caesar's commander in Asia Minor. The following year Caesar decisively defeated Pharnaces at Zela, one of the new cities created by Pompey, the victory coming on the fifth day of his campaign and after only four hours of fighting. The rapidity of Caesar's victory was advertised in his triumphal procession through Rome, in which his attendants displayed signs with the laconic legend: '*Veni, vidi, vici!*' – 'I came, I saw, I conquered!'

Caesar was assassinated in Rome in March of 44 BC, and another period of conflict engulfed the Mediterranean world. Brutus and Cassius, the two leaders of the conspiracy against Caesar, were forced to leave Rome for the East, where they raised troops and money to face Caesar's supporters, led by Mark Antony and Octavian. Brutus demanded the equivalent of ten years' taxes from the cities of Asia Minor, and when Xanthus in Lycia failed to pay he put it under siege. Rather than surrender, the Xanthians chose to burn down their city, just as they had done five centuries before when it was besieged by Harpagus the Mede. Brutus was appalled by the holocaust, according to Plutarch, and he did what he could to save some of the Xanthians, but almost all of them perished.

Brutus and Cassius were defeated by Antony the following year and committed suicide. By agreement with Octavian, Antony took responsibility for reorganising the eastern half of the empire, in the course of which he revived the Pontic kingdom under the rule of Darius, son of Pharnaces II, who had been killed by his own people.

Antony sought an alliance with Egypt, and in 41 BC he summoned Cleopatra to Tarsus. They became allies and lovers, and after they spent the winter together in Alexandria she bore Antony twins, a boy and a girl. She bore Antony another son three years later, after joining him in Antioch. Then in 34 BC, while celebrating a triumph in Alexandria, Antony proclaimed that Cleopatra and her children were rulers of the expanded Egyptian kingdom, including Armenia, Syria, Phoenicia, Cilicia, Cyprus and Crete.

Rivalry between Antony and Octavian led them to mobilise in preparation for war against one another. Italy and the western provinces swore allegiance to Octavian in October 32 BC, after which he declared war on Cleopatra. The climax came on 2 September 31 BC when Octavian's navy defeated the combined fleets of Antony and Cleopatra off Actium in north-western Greece. Octavian then pursued Antony and Cleopatra to Alexandria, where both of them committed suicide in August of the following year. The death of Cleopatra brought the Ptolemaic dynasty to an end, and soon afterwards Octavian reorganised Egypt as a province of Rome.

Octavian's victory at Actium made him master of the Roman world, an event that historians generally mark as the end of the Hellenistic period. Then on 16 January 27 BC Octavian received the title 'Augustus' from the Senate, beginning the imperial era in Roman history. Thenceforth the Greek cities in Asia Minor were subject to the emperor in Rome, beginning a new era in their history, once again changing masters as they had so often in the past.

The Greek cities in Asia Minor that had been destroyed or damaged were rebuilt by the Diadochi and Epigoni, sometimes on new sites and with new names, and many new cities were founded, often incorporating older towns in their region.

Seleucus I Nicator seems to have founded more cities by far than any of the other Diadochi, or so it appears from Appian's account:

> He founded cities throughout the length of the whole empire and named sixteen of them Antioch for his father, five Laodokeia for his mother, nine for himself, four after his wives, three Apameias and one Stratonikeia…
> The other cities he gave names from Greece or Macedonia, for his own deeds or in honour of King Alexander. As a result the names of many Greek and Macedonian towns are to be found in Syria and the barbarous regions of upper Asia…

The most famous of the cities that Seleucus named for his father Antiochus was Antioch on the Orontes, which he founded in 300 BC after his victory at Ipsus, making it the capital of his extended empire, which now included much of Asia Minor. At the same time he founded Apameia on the Orontes, as well as Seleucia ad Pieria at the mouth of the river, serving as the port of Antioch. Five years later, when Seleucus came into possession of Cilicia, he founded Seleuceia ad Calycadnus, populating it with the people from a number of surrounding towns.

Around the same time Seleucus began building the temple of Zeus Olbia in the highlands north-east of Seleucia ad Calycadnus. This enormous structure has the distinction of being the earliest known Corinthian temple in Asia Minor, most of those of the archaic and classical periods having been in the Ionic order, a few in the Aolian.

Seleucus I also began rebuilding the archaic temple of Apollo at Didyma, which had been destroyed by Xerxes, but the project was halted when he was killed in 281 BC. The Hellenistic temple, which was five centuries abuilding and never completed, was designed on an even grander scale than its predecessor. It was the third largest temple ever erected in the Greek world, surpassed in size only by the Artemesium at Ephesus and the Heraeum at Samos.

Seleucus I may also have begun rebuilding the archaic temple of Artemis at Sardis, but it too was left uncompleted at the time of his death. Successive projects were undertaken later in the Hellenistic era and again in the imperial Roman era, but when it was finally dedicated in AD 141 it was still not fully completed.

According to Strabo, after his victory at the Granicus, Alexander ordered the rebuilding of Ilion, the Aeolian city that had been founded on the site of Troy, a project carried out after his death by Lysimachus. Although Strabo says the temple of Athena at Ilion was rebuilt by Lysimachus, more probably its reconstruction was started by Antigonus Monopthalmus, as evidenced by inscriptions found at Troy. The inscriptions, dated ca. 306/305 BC, indicate that Antigonus founded a league known as the Federation of the Troad, whose centre was the temple of Athena at Ilion.

Antigonus also founded the city of Antigoneia in the Troad, building it on the site of ancient Sigeium. The new city was a synoecism, a regrouping of various localities into one political unit, which seems to have occurred when the Federation of the Troad was founded. The towns included in the synoecism probably included Kebren, Scepsis, Kolonai, Hamaxitos, Neandria and Larisa. Its territory was quite large, including all of the coastal region south from Ilion to Cape Lekton, and its importance was enhanced by the fact that it had the only real harbour on the west coast of the Troad. After the battle of Ipsos the Troad came under the control of Lysimachus, who changed the city's name to Alexandria. Strabo says that the new name was chosen because 'it was thought to be a pious thing for the successors of Alexander to found cities bearing his name before they founded cities bearing their own'. Since the new city was close to the site of ancient Troy, it eventually came to be known as Alexandria Troas.

Antigonus Monopthalmus founded the city of Antigonea on Lake Ascania in Bithynia. Around 300 BC the city was taken by Lysimachus, who renamed it Nicaea after his deceased first wife, a daughter of Antipater. After the death of Lysimachus in 281 BC, Nicaea was captured by Nicomedes I, who made it capital of Bithynia. Then in 265 BC, Nicomedes built the city of Nicomedia and shifted his capital there.

Around 188 BC, Prusias I founded the city of Prusias ad Olympum, so called because it was under Mount Olympus of Bithynia (Ulu Dağ). Construction of the city may have been supervised by Hannibal, who had fled to Bithynia after his defeat at Magnesia in 189 BC. Pressure from the Romans forced Prusias to end his protection of Hannibal, who took his own life in 183 BC to avoid extradition to Rome.

Smyrna, which had been in ruins for more than three centuries, was refounded by Antigonus on the new site around Mount Pagos that had been revealed in Alexander's dream. After the death of Antigonus the rebuilding of Smyrna was completed by Lysimachus, as Strabo notes in describing the new city, which he considered to be the most beautiful in Ionia.

Lysimachus refounded Ephesus at the same time that he rebuilt Smyrna, soon after his victory over Antigonus. He rebuilt Ephesus on a new site closer to the sea, since its habour had become silted up by the Cayster river, after which he enclosed the city with a circuit of defence walls nearly six miles in circumference. According to Pausanias, Lysimachus repopulated Ephesus with people from the Ionian cities of Lebedus and Colophon, which he then destroyed.

The city of Laodikeia on the Lycus in Lydia was probably founded by Antiochus II Theos (the God), who reigned in the years 261–246 BC. Antiochus named the city for his first wife Laodike, whom he divorced in 253 BC, and so the foundation of Laodikeia would appear to date from the period 261–253 BC.

Sardis, the ancient capital of Lydia, was destroyed in 214/213 BC by Antiochus III Megas (the Great), son of Antiochus II Theos, who subsequently rebuilt it through the intercession of his mother, Queen Laodike. The younger Antiochus subsequently sent 2,000 Babylonian Jews to settle in Lydia and Phrygia, including Sardis and Laodikeia, where they played an important part in the commercial life of the region. Some of the Jews were settled at Tire, in the hills above Sardis, where their descendants continued to live until 1976.

The city of Philadelphia in Caria was founded by Attalus II Philadelphus (r. 159–138 BC), probably on the site of a Macedonian colony established early in the Hellenistic period. Around 158 BC Attalus II founded the city of Attaleia (Antalya) in Pamphylia, giving the Pergamene kingdom a port on the Mediterranean.

According to Strabo, Thyateira in Lydia was also a Macedonian colony, which was refounded by Seleucus I Nicator shortly before his death in 281 BC. Strabo notes that there was another Macedonian colony at Stratonikeia in Caria, which 'was adorned with costly improvements by the kings', probably Seleucus II (r. 246–226/5 BC) and his son and successor Seleucus III (226/5–223 BC).

The cities that were rebuilt in the Hellenistic period were planned according to the model created by Hippodamus of Miletus, with streets laid out in the cardinal directions on a rectangular grid plan, important public buildings grouped at the centre. Priene is a good example of the Hippodamean plan, since it was rebuilt on a new site early in the Hellenistic period and it never grew beyond the limits established at that time.

Pompey's reorganisation of Asia Minor resulted in important changes in the civic and provincial administration of Anatolia. The core of the kingdom that had been ruled by Mithridates VI Eupator was made the new province of Pontus and Bithynia, placed under the command of the Roman governor in Nicaea. The urban centres of the new province of Pontus included its ancient capital at Amaseia, the three ports of Amisus, Sinope and Amastris, and seven new cities founded by Pompey, all of which received Hellenic names. The newly reorganised foundations included Mazaca and Megalopolis, later known as Caesaria (Kayseri) and Sebasteia (Sivas), which over the next two millennia would be the two most important cities in central Anatolia.

The reorganisation created a new province of Cilicia, which included the great Cilician plain as well as districts that were formerly part of the province of Asia. Pompey refounded the Cilician coastal city of Soli, which was renamed Pompeiopolis in his honour, and he resettled there many of the former pirates whom he had subdued in 67 BC.

Despite the numerous wars that followed the death of Alexander, the Greek cities of Asia Minor flourished culturally, giving birth to a number of outstanding scientists and philosophers. So far as we know, all of these thinkers studied in either Athens or Alexandria, which became a great cultural centre under the first two Ptolemies. Ptolemy I (r. 305–283 BC) founded the Museum and Library of Alexandria, which under his son Ptolemy II (r. 283–245 BC) became an institution of higher studies patterned on the famous schools of philosophy in Athens, most notably Plato's Academy and Aristotle's Lyceum.

Heraclides Ponticus (ca. 388–ca. 310 BC) was among the first of the Asia Minor Greeks to gain distinction as a scientist and philosopher during the Hellenistic period. His last name stems from his birthplace, the Bithynian city of Heracleia Pontica (Ereğli) on the Black Sea. He studied in Athens under Plato and perhaps Aristotle, and later returned to Heracleia Pontica to run his own school. Heraclides is renowned in the history of science as being the first to say that the apparent nightly motion of the stars around the celestial pole is actually caused by the rotation of the earth on its own axis.

The physician Herophilus (ca. 330–ca. 260 BC) was born in Chalcedon, on the Asian shore at the mouth of the Bosphorus opposite Byzantium. He went on to study in Alexandria, where he founded a school of medicine that was still flourishing at the end of the first century BC. There was also a celebrated medical school at Cnidus, established early in the fourth century BC by Ctesias, who became royal physician at the Persian court.

The physicist and philosopher Strato was born in Lampsacus, on the Asian shore of the Hellespont. He studied in Athens and served as head of the Aristotlian Lyceum ca. 286–268 BC, after which he went on to direct the Museum in Alexandria. He is credited with more than forty works, all lost except for fragments. One of his lost works is known through a commentary by Simplicius in the sixth century AD, which seems to indicate that Strato was a forerunner of Galileo in his demonstration of the motion of freely falling bodies.

The astronomer and mathematician Autolycus was born in the Aeolian city of Pitane and flourished in the second half of the fourth century BC, but otherwise little is known of his life. He is the author of two books on spherical astronomy, the earliest Greek mathematical works that have survived in their entirety.

The philosopher Arcesilaus of Pitane studied in his home town under Autolycus, whom he followed to Sardis. He went on the study at Aristotle's Lyceum in Athens under Theophrastus. He then transferred to Plato's Academy, where he served as director in the years 268–264 BC. Arcesilaus is credited with being the first philosopher to argue both sides of a question, but because of his open-mindedness he could never write a book, or so it was said of him in his time.

The philosopher Cleanthes (331–232 BC) was born in Assos and went to Athens to study with Zeno, founder of the Stoic school of philosophy. After the death of Zeno in 264 BC, Cleanthes became the head of the Stoic school. Cleanthes is remembered principally because of his opposition to the heliocentric cosmology of his contemporary Aristarchus of Samos, whose theory that the earth and the other planets orbited the sun would be revived eighteen centuries later by Copernicus.

The Cilician city of Soli gave birth to the poet and astronomer Aratus and the philosopher Chrysippus. Aratus (ca. 315–239 BC) became a member of the Stoic school in Athens before moving on to the court of the Macedonian king Antigonus II Gonatas at Pella. His only extant work is the *Phaenomena*, a didactic poem on astronomy and meteorology which served to perpetuate the Greek names of the constellations. Chrysippus (ca. 280–216 BC) studied in Athens and succeeded Cleanthes as head of the Stoic school. His writings were so influential that they became the orthodox version of Stoicism, and it was said that 'Without Chrysippus no Stoa'.

Pergamum emerged as an important cultural centre during the enlightened rule of the Attalids, who saw themselves as the champions of Hellenism in Asia Minor. The magnificent Library of Pergamum was surpassed only by that of the Ptolemies in Alexandria. Pergamum was also renowned for its school of sculpture, particularly the sculptural decoration on the magnificent Altar of Zeus The altar was built by Eumenes II to commemorate his defeat of Antiochus III at Magnesia in 189 BC as well as the earlier victory of Attalus I over the Gauls, both of which he saw as triumphs of Hellenism over barbarism. The Attalids patronised a number of writers, scholars and artists at their court, the most renowned of whom was the mathematician Apollonius.

Apollonius was born ca. 262 BC in the Pamphyllian city of Perge, and in his youth he went on to study in Alexandria during the reigns of Ptolemy III (r. 246–221 BC) and Ptolemy IV (r. 221–204 BC). He was also an honoured guest in the court of Attalus I Soter (241–197 BC) of Pergamum. Apollonius is ranked as one of the the greatest mathematicians in the ancient world, along with Archimedes and Euclid. His only surviving major work is his treatise *On Conics*, and even there the last book is lost. This was the first comprehensive and systematic analysis of the three types of conic section: the ellipse (of which the circle is a special case), parabola and hyperbola. He is also credited with formulating the epicycle and eccentric circle methods for describing planetary motion, theories which would be used by astronomers for the next eighteen centuries.

Hipparchus, the greatest observational astronomer of antiquity, was born ca. 190 BC in the Bithynian city of Nicaea. He is known to have studied at the Library in Alexandria before going to Rhodes, where he built an observatory and made astronomical measurements in the years 141–127 BC. His only surviving work is a commentary on the *Phaenomena* of Aratus of Soli, in which he gives the relative brightness and celestial coordinates of some 850 stars, including those of a 'nova' or 'new star', which suddenly appeared in 134 BC in the constellation Scorpio. He is renowned for his discovery of the precession of the equinoxes, a progressive change in the celestial latitude of the stars, which he detected by comparing his star map with one made 128 years earlier by the astronomer Timocharis.

Hipparchus is also celebrated as a mathematician, his greatest achievement being the development of spherical trigonometry. This and his other theories and measurements appear in the *Almagest*, the comprehensive astronomical treatise written ca. AD 159 by Claudius Ptolemais of Alexandria, who gives Hipparchus due credit.

Theodosius of Bithynia, a younger contemporary of Hipparchus, is known for his *Sphaerica*, a treatise on the application of spherical trigonometry to astronomy, which was translated into Arabic and Latin, remaining in use up to the seventeenth century.

Nicander of Colophon, who flourished in the third to second century BC, was a prolific poet who wrote two didactic poems, the first dealing with poisons and their antidotes, the second concerning poisonous creatures and the cures for their bites and stings. The second-century poet and philosopher Bion was born near Smyrna and studied in Athens, after which he opened a school on Rhodes. He is best known for his *Lament for Adonis*, which is sometimes wrongly attributed to Theocritus.

The architect Pythius of Priene, who flourished in the second half of the fourth century BC, designed the Mausoleum at Halicarnassus and the temple of Athena Polias at Priene. He wrote books describing his works, but these have been lost and are known only through Vitruvius.

The architect Hermogenes, who flourished in the second century BC, may have been from Priene. Hermogenes was the great theoretician of classical architecture, particularly in his codification for the Ionic order. His writings are lost, but they profoundly influenced Vitruvius and, through him, the architecture of Europe from the Renaissance onwards.

Two buildings by Hermogenes survive in part: the temple of Artemis Leucophryne at Magnesia ad Maeander and the temple of Dionysus at Teos. According to Strabo, the temple of Artemis Leucophryne ('of the white brow') was the third largest temple in Asia Minor in his time, surpassed only by those of Artemis at Ephesus and of Apollo at Teos. He also remarks that the temple of Artemis Leucophryne is far superior to that of Artemis Ephesia 'in the harmony and skill shown in the structure of the sacred enclosure'. The temple of Dionysus at Teos was considered by Vitruvius to be the archetype for all subsequent temples in the Ionic order. It was the largest temple of Dionysus ever erected in the ancient world, its platform measuring 18.5 by 30 metres.

The architect and engineer Sostratus of Cnidos is renowned as the designer and builder of the famous Lighthouse of Alexandria, one of the Seven Wonders of the Ancient World, which he erected ca. 280 BC for Ptolemy II Philadelphus. The military engineer Biton of Pergamum, who worked for Attalus I Soter, is noted for his construction of catapults and other engines of war.

Hellenistic Asia Minor also gave birth to a number of historians, some of whom wrote histories of their own cities, such Xenophilus of Lydia and Menecrates of Xanthos. Nymphis of Heracleia on the Black Sea wrote a biography of Alexander as well as a history of his birthplace.

The philosopher and grammarian Agatharachides of Cnidus (ca. 215– after 145 BC) wrote a geographical work called *Circumnavigation of the Erythraian Sea*, which describes places as far afield as Ethiopia, Scythia and India. The navigator Eudoxus of Cyzicus was sent by Ptolemy II to find a sea route around Africa to India, an unsuccessful epic journey described by Strabo.

Strabo in his description of the voyage of Eudoxus, refers to Posidonius of Apamea on the Orontes (ca. 135–ca. 50 BC), saying that 'he suspects that the length of the inhabited world, being about seventy thousand stadia, is half of the entire circle on which it is taken, so that, says he, if you sail from the west in a straight course you will reach India within the seventy thousand stadia'. Posidonius studied philosophy in Athens and then went on to do scientific research in the western provinces and North Africa before settling down in Rhodes, where he wrote a *History* in fifty-two books, picking up where Polybius left off. He is also noted for his work in meteorology, particularly for his explanation of the periodicity of tidal action, which he observed in the Atlantic.

Architects, astronomers, engineers, explorers, geographers, grammarians, historians, mathematicians, philosophers, physicians, physicists and poets, such was the richness of culture among the Greeks of Asia Minor under Alexander's successors, whose grandeur of vision saw Hellenism extending from the Mediterranean to the middle of Asia.

8

Roman Rule and Revelation

The accession of Augustus in 27 BC marked the beginning of a new era for the Greeks of Asia Minor, and for the next two and a half centuries they prospered and became more numerous under the mantle of the *pax Romana*.

Augustus entrusted control of the eastern half of the empire to Marcus Vipsanius Agrippa, who spent the years 24–23 BC in Asia and returned in 16–13 BC. Augustus himself made a tour of Asia Minor in 20 BC and made a point of visiting the site of ancient Troy, where he rebuilt the ancient temple of Athena at Ilium.

The beginning of the Augustan Age was accompanied by a new arrangement regarding the provinces of the empire, which were divided between the Senate and the emperor. The provinces of Asia and Bithynia-Pontus were controlled by the Senate, while the other provinces in Asia Minor – Galatia, Cappadocia, Lycia-Pamphylia, and Cilicia – were directly under the emperor. Nevertheless the people in both of the senatorial provinces of Asia Minor looked upon Augustus as their ruler rather than the Senate, and their communities sought permission to establish sanctuaries in which he would be worshipped as a god, as did those in the other provinces. The people of eastern Paphlagonia, who were included in the province of Galatia, swore obeisance to 'Zeus, the Earth, the Sun, all other gods and goddesses and Augustus himself', an oath of allegiance taken by both native Paphlagonians and resident Romans.

Augustus responded by decreeing that he should be worshipped only in conjunction with the deified Roma, a cult that was already in existence in at least eleven places in Asia. The maintenance of the cult of Roma and Augustus was entrusted to a federation called the Commonalty of the Hellenes, which seems to have existed since the middle of the first century BC as an intermediary for communications between the Greek cities of Asia Minor and Roman officials. The federation was headed by the Chief Priest of Roma and Augusta, also called the Chief Priest of Asia, who was chosen at the annual meeting of the Commonalty from among the delegates of the cities that participated, along with other dignitaries known as Asiarchs.

After the reign of Augustus the cult continued as that of Roma et Sebasta, 'Rome and the Emperor'. The Commonalty organised a festival of Rome and the Emperor called *Romaia Sebasta* held at regular intervals, usually once a year. This soon became one of the principal festivals of the eastern provinces of the Empire, drawing celebrants from all of the Asian cities. Seats of the new cult were established in Pergamum, Nicomedia and Ancyra, the provincial capitals of western Asia Minor, all of which erected temples dedicated to Roma and Augustus.

The temple of Roma and Augustus at Pergamum also celebrated the emperor's birthday, at which the priests offered sacrifice and a hymn was sung in his honour. The singers, known as the 'hymnodists of the Deified Augustus and the Deified Roma', were forty in number and came from all over the province of Asia, their expenses paid by a provincial assessment. The choral society was continued by the descendants of the original hymnodists, and it was still in existence in Pergamum as late as the second century AD, with its own building and officials.

The Gauls who had settled in Galatia after their defeat by Attalus I were organised into three tribes, the Tolistobogians in the west, the Testosage in the centre and the Trocmi in the east. The three tribes formed a triarchy headed by a king, the last of whom was Amyntas, who under the aegis of Rome ruled over a kingdom that comprised Galatia, Lycaonia and parts of Phrygia, Pisidia and Pamphylia. After the death of Amyntas in 25 BC his kingdom was annexed by Augustus and made into the Roman province of Galatia, with its capital at Ancyra.

The Gauls themselves remained a minority of the population in Galatia, where the indigenous people – the Phrygians and Cappadocians

– predominated in the towns and large areas of the countryside. The Gauls in Asia Minor continued to speak Celtic up until at least the end of the fifth century, when they were finally hellenised, along with the Phrygians and Cappadocians and other native peoples.

The Lycians were still a distinct race in the first century AD, according to Strabo, and though they were thoroughly hellenised their language remained in use during the imperial era. Although under Roman rule, they still had considerable national autonomy, settling their own affairs as members of the Lycian League. This confederation was founded in 167 BC, probably the revival of an ancient tribal union of the Lycian people, and it was still functioning in Strabo's day.

The hellenised dynasts of Cappodocia and the Pontus retained some degree of power under the aegis of Rome. Archelaus I had been recognised as king of Cappadocia by Antony and also by Augustus, who declared him a 'friend and ally' of Rome and added part of Cilicia to his realm. Archelaus, who had his capital at Mazaca, expressed his gratitude to Augustus by renaming it Caesareia. Archelaus then married Queen Pythadoris, widow of Polemon I, King of Pontus, who had been recognised by Augustus as the successor to her late husband's throne. This marriage brought under the joint rule of Archelaus and Pythadoris all of Asia Minor from the Black Sea to the Mediterranean. But then in AD 15, a year after Tiberius had succeeded Augustus as emperor, Archelaus was summoned to Rome for trial by the Senate on charges of treason. Archelaus, who was then about eighty, was so weakened by the ordeal that he died in Rome, and soon afterwards Cappadocia became a Roman province. Queen Pythadoris continued to rule the Pontus under the aegis of Rome until her death some time after AD 17. Her grandson Polemon II was recognised as king in AD 38 by the emperor Gaius (Caligula), but his realm was soon taken from him and with that the history of the Pontic kingdom comes to an end.

The kingdom of Commagene in south-eastern Cappadocia was fated to be the last of the hellenised client states of Rome to retain some degree of autonomy. Antiochus III, the last king of Commagene, died in AD 72, during the reign of the emperor Vespasian, whereupon his kingdom was added to the Roman province of Syria.

Some of the ancient Greek cities of Asia Minor became extremely prosperous under Roman rule – particularly Smyrna, Ephesus and

Pergamum – expanding far beyond their original bounds as their populations grew into the hundreds of thousands. The public monuments of the Hellenistic age were replaced with larger and more grandiose structures in the Roman style – temples, theatres, gymnasiums, stadiums, libraries, baths, fountains, market-buildings, granaries and aqueducts – many of them dedicated to deified emperors. Cities competed with one another for imperial honours, one being the title of *metropolis*, or 'chief city', another that of *neokoros*, or 'temple-warden', as evidenced by dedicatory inscriptions recording that one or the other is 'First and greatest metropolis of Asia', or 'Four times temple warden of the emperors'.

Tiberius (r. AD 14–37) won the gratitude of the cities in the province of Asia for his beneficence and even-handed justice, and in AD 24 the Commonalty of the Hellenes decreed a temple dedicated to him, his mother Livia and the Senate. Eleven cities in the province claimed the privilege of erecting the temple, and in AD 26 they sent envoys to Rome to present their claims to the Senate, which voted overwhelmingly in favour of Smyrna. Coins of Smyrna struck under the proconsul P. Petronius (AD 29–35) show the temple of Tiberius, though for some unexplained reason the title of 'Temple-Warden' is omitted.

Domitian (r. 81–96) was reviled as a merciless tyrant by the orator Dio of Prusa, who referred to the emperor as 'violent and overbearing, called Master and God of both Greeks and barbarians, but in reality a spirit of evil'. Nevertheless the provinces of the empire seem to have been justly and honestly administered during his reign, when the historian Tacitus served as governor of Asia and Pliny acted as the emperor's personal representative in Bithynia. A colossal temple was dedicated to the deified Domitian at Ephesus, but when he was assassinated in September of the year 96 the Ephesians toppled his gigantic cult statue and erased his name from all monuments in their city.

Trajan (r. 98–117) administered the provinces with justice and granted favours to many of the cities of Asia Minor, which responded by dedicating temples and other monuments in his name. The greatest of these by far was the Trajaneum in Pergamum, a magnificent Corinthian temple erected on the highest point of the city's acropolis. The temple was completed in 125 during the reign of Hadrian (r. 117–138), who was worshipped there along with Trajan, as evidenced by the remains of their colossal cult statues found on the site.

Hadrian's reign was the golden age of Roman rule in Asia Minor, through which he travelled in two imperial journeys, the first in the years 123–124 and the second in 129–131. The historian Dio Cassius writes of Hadrian that he 'aided the cities, both allied and subject, with the greatest generosity; for he visited many of them, more, in fact than any other emperor, and he assisted practically all of them, giving to some supplies of water and to others harbours or grain or public works or various honours'.

Hadrian's benefactions included a colossal temple dedicated to him at Cyzicus, which thus received the title of Temple-Warden. The temple, whose ruins have now almost disappeared was said to be 'the largest and most beautiful of all', and some later writers listed it among the Seven Wonders of the World. At Smyrna Hadrian endowed a grain market and a gymnasium, reputed to be the largest in Asia, as well as a temple in which he was worshipped as 'Olympian Zeus' and as 'Saviour of the whole human race', The Ephesians also erected a colossal temple dedicated to Hadrian as Olympian Zeus, reputed to be the eighth largest temple in the Graeco-Roman world, but this has disappeared without a trace. Besides this the Ephesians dedicated a small but exquisite temple to the deified Hadrian which is now one of the gems of the archaeological site at Ephesus.

The remains of other structures endowed by Hadrian or erected in his honour can be seen throughout the former Roman provinces of Asia Minor, which were never governed better than during his benevolent reign. After the death of Hadrian in July 138, an orator from Asia Minor paid tribute to the deified emperor by reminding his audience in Rome that 'no longer are the cities in variance, hearkening, some to one man, and others to another, while to one city guards are sent and by another are expelled, but...the whole inhabited world, in more complete accord than any chorus of singers, prays that this Empire, welded together under its single leader, may endure for all time.'

Hadrian was succeeded by Antoninus Pius (r. 138–161), whose generosity to the Greek cities of Asia Minor is attested by numerous inscriptions and the dedication of temples and other monuments in his name. Antoninus appears to have reorganised the provincial boundaries in south-central Anatolia, taking the districts of Lycaonia and Isauria from Galatia and adding them to Cilicia. Thus the province of Cilicia was no longer confined to the Mediterranean coast, but extended far inland north of the Taurus Mountains, greatly increasing its extent and importance.

Antoninus was succeeded by his two adopted sons, Marcus Aurelius (r. 161–180) and Lucius Verus (r. 161–169), who ruled as co-emperors. At the beginning of their reign the Parthian king Volosages III launched a two-pronged attack on the Roman provinces in Asia, one into Armenia and the other into Syria, in both cases decisively defeating the imperial armies sent to halt the invasion. Verus went to the East as nominal commander and his generals eventually defeated Volosages, after which the Roman frontiers were extended into Mesopotamia.

But the victory over the Parthians was followed by a pestilence that seems to have been brought back from Mesopotamia by the returning Roman soldiers, spreading through Asia Minor into Europe as far as Gaul. There was also a widespread crop failure that brought on famine and forced farmers to leave their land in both Asia Minor and Europe. Barbarian tribes crossed the Danube and one of them invaded northern Italy, forcing both emperors to take the field against them. After the death of Verus in 169 Marcus carried on the struggle alone, putting down a revolt in Syria by Avidius Cassius. During the last year of his reign Marcus financed the rebuilding of Smyrna, which had been destroyed by an earthquake in 178, and the grateful Smyrnaeans erected an honorific statue of the emperor in their restored agora, whose ruins can still be seen in the heart of modern Izmir.

Marcus Aurelius was succeeded by his son Commodus (r. 180–192), who in the early years of his reign concluded peace with the German tribes. But then, according to a modern historian, he recreated in Rome 'the worst excesses of the reigns of Gaius and Nero'. Commodus was assassinated in 192, the 'year of the four emperors', when Pertinax, Didius Iulianus and Septimius Severus followed one another to the throne, each killing his predecessor.

Severus was immediately plunged into wars of succession against Pescinnius Niger, who had taken control of Syria and Asia Minor, and Clodinius Albinus, who held Gaul. By the beginning of 197 Severus had eliminated both rivals, and within the two years following he extended the bounds of the empire far beyond the Euphrates. He also punished those who had supported his rivals, including the people of Byzantium, which he captured and sacked in 196 after an eighteen-month siege.

Severus was succeeded by his sons Caracalla (r. 211–217) and Geta (r. 211–212). Caracalla killed Geta the following year in the presence of their mother Julia Domna, whom he left in charge of the government while he went off on campaign, hoping to surpass his father's record of conquest. Emulating Alexander the Great, he led his army across the Hellespont and made a pilgrimage to Troy, where he celebrated funeral rites at the tumuli of Patroclus and Achilles when one of his favourites died. He visited Pergamum, where a temple was dedicated to him as the 'new Dionysius', for which he rewarded the city with the title of 'Thrice Temple-Warden', an honour that he also awarded to Smyrna. After visiting Antioch and Alexandria he set out on a campaign against the Parthians, which was cut short in April 217 when he was assassinated by a group of officers led by Marcus Opellius Macrinus, who was then proclaimed emperor.

Macrinus was assassinated the following year and succeeded by Elagabalus, who met the same fate four years later, to be supplanted by Severus Alexander (r. 222–235). Alexander was only fourteen when he came to the throne, and so his mother Iulia Mamaea served as regent, a position she continued to hold throughout her son's reign, for he showed no inclination to rule independently.

One of the enlightened policies of Alexander's reign was his patronage of scholars, most notably the historian Dio Cassius, a native of Nicaea, who identified himself entirely with Roman society despite the fact that he wrote in Greek. He entered the Senate in the reign of Commodus and twice served as consul, first under Septimius Severus and then under Severus Alexander. His history of Rome describes events from the beginning up to 229, concentrating on politics and war rather than on social and economic conditions.

Dio Cassius marked the death of Marcus Aurelius as the end of a reign of gold and the beginning of an age of iron and rust. During the half century after the reign of Severus Alexander a score of ephemeral emperors succeeded one another to the throne, most of them rising and falling by assassination, others killed in battle as the frontiers of the empire collapsed in both Europe and the East. Asia Minor was overrun in turn by the Goths, by the Sassanid Persian king Shapur I, and by Queen Zenobia of Palmyra. The empire regrouped and fought back, and by the end of the third century the Roman frontiers were restored in both Europe and Asia. But the Greek of Asia were no longer secure, for the *pax Romana* had been shattered forever, and there were signs that the ancient Graeco-Roman world was coming to an end.

During the centuries of peace Smyrna and Ephesus vied with one another for primacy in the province of Asia, particularly with regard to the coveted title of 'Metropolis', bestowed on cities that were either Temple-Wardens or possessed authority over their neighbouring communities. Ephesus, which was effectively the provincial capital, with a population that reached some 400,000 and was surpassed in Asia only by Antioch, called herself 'the first and greatest Metropolis of Asia'. But after Caracalla gave Smyrna the right to erect a temple dedicated to his worship she referred to herself as 'the First of Asia in beauty and size, and most brilliant, and Metropolis of Asia, and thrice Temple-Warden of the Augustii, according to the decrees of the most sacred Senate, and ornament of Ionia'.

The Greeks of Asia Minor continued to flourish intellectually under Roman rule, particularly after the inauguration of the Augustan Age. This is particularly evident in the work of the geographer Strabo (64/63 BC–ca. AD 25), whose lifetime extended from the late Roman republic through the early imperial era. Strabo was born at Amaseia in the Pontus and studied at Nysa in Lydia, after which he continued his studies at Alexandria and then went on to Rome, from where he travelled all over the empire. His *Geography* in seventeen volumes covers the whole of the *oecumenos*, 'the inhabited world', with Books XI through XIV dealing with Asia Minor. He writes in his introduction that 'the utility of geography...is manifold, not only as regards the activities of statesmen and commanders but also as regards knowledge both of the heavens and of things on land and sea, animals, plants, fruits, and everything else to be seen in various regions'.

The physician Dioscorides Pedanus was born at Anazarbus in Cilicia and studied medicine at Alexandria, after which he served as a doctor in the Roman army during the reigns of Claudius (r. AD 41–54) and Nero (r. AD 41–68). He is renowned for his *De Materia Medica*, a beautifully illustrated description of some 1,600 drugs and medicinal plants, which in Arabic and Latin translations became the basic text in pharmacology in the medieval world, both Muslim and Christian.

The philosopher and orator Dio Chrysostomos (ca. AD 40–after 112) was born in the Bithynian city of Prusa and spent much of his career in

Rome. Political intrigues led to his banishment from Rome during the reign of Domitian, after which he wandered through Greece, the Balkans and Asia Minor as an itinerant preacher of Stoic-Cynic philosophy, finally returning to Bithynia in his later years. His extant orations, many of them delivered before the public assembly in Prusa, are the principal source of information concerning life in western Asia Minor in his time.

The Stoic philosopher Epictetus (ca. AD 55–ca. 135) grew up in the Phrygian town of Hierapolis, where he was a slave of Epaphroditus, Nero's freedman and slave, who permitted him to study philosophy and later freed him. Epictetus then went to teach in Rome, but when Domitian banished the philosophers he fled to Nicopolis in Epirus, where he taught for the rest of his days. His lectures were published by Arrian, who had studied with him in Rome, and they deeply influenced Marcus Aurelius, as evidenced by passages in the emperor's famous *Meditations*.

Arrian (ca. AD 87–after 171) was born in Nicomedeia, the capital of Bithynia, and studied in Rome. He was appointed by Hadrian as governor of Cappadocia in 131, and three years later he repelled an invasion of Armenia by the Alans, a nomadic tribe from the Russian steppes. He retired in 138 and moved to Athens, where he devoted the rest of his days to writing, his most famous extant work being *The Campaigns of Alexander*.

The philosopher Theon of Smyrna, who was also a mathematician and astronomer, flourished during the reign of Hadrian. His only extant work is *Aspects of Mathematics Useful for the Reading of Plato*, of which Book 3 is on astronomy. The book on astronomy contains a quasi-heliocentric theory, deriving from an ancient Pythagorean belief that fourteen centuries later would inspire Copernicus.

The geographer and traveller Pausanias was born early in the second century AD in Lydia, probably at Magnesia ad Sipylum. His *Description of Greece* in ten volumes is the principal source for the description of shrines and accounts of myths and religious cults in the ancient Greek world.

The rhetorician and satirist Lucian (ca. 125–after 180) was born in Samosata, in the former kingdom of Commagene in south-eastern Anatolia. He refers to himself as 'Assyrian', which means that his mother-tongue was probably Aramaic, though he wrote in Greek. He moved to Athens when he was about forty, and travelled widely through Asia Minor, Egypt and the European provinces of the empire. His extant writings include collections of essays entitled *Dialogues of the Gods* and *Dialogues of the Dead*; the *Symposium*, a satire on Plato's dialogue in which the diners get drunk and behave disgracefully; *The Passing of Peregrinus*, in which he mocks the naivete of Christians; and a romance called *A True Story*, in which he writes about voyages to the moon and Venus, extraterrestrial life, and wars between the planets, anticipating Jules Verne and H. G. Wells by seventeen centuries.

Galen of Pergamum (ca. 130–after 204) was the most renowned medical writer of antiquity. He was born and did his first studies at Pergamum, where he served his medical apprenticeship at the healing shrine of Asclepios, in which his work in treating wounded gladiators gave him an unrivalled knowledge of human anatomy. After further studies in Alexandria and Corinth he moved to Rome, where he served as physician to the emperors Marcus Aurelius, Lucius Verus and Commodus. His writings, translated from Greek into Latin and Arabic, were the basis for all studies of anatomy and physiology up until the seventeenth century, earning him the title of 'Prince of Physicians'. The philosophical basis for his writing is evident from the title of one of his treatises, *That the Best Doctor is also a Philosopher*, as well as from his work *On Scientific Proof and Introduction to Logic*. He also wrote on psychology, including an imaginative analysis of dreams, seventeen centuries before Freud.

The philosopher Alexander of Aphrodisias was born in Phrygia and began lecturing in Athens at the end of the second century AD. His commentaries on the works of Aristotle were translated into Latin in the thirteenth century and were very influential in the interpretation of Aristotelian philosophy in the early European renaissance.

The orator and man of letters Aelius Aristides (ca. 117–ca. 181) was born in Mysia and went to study in Athens, after which he spent most of the rest of his life in Smyrna. The surviving works of Aristides are of interest principally for the vivid picture they give of life in the Greek cities of Asia Minor at the height of the Roman imperial era.

The Roman senator Pliny (61–ca. 112) spent the last two years of his life serving the emperor Trajan as governor of Bithynia, and apparently died in office. He published ten books of letters, the last of which contains his official correspondence with Trajan concerning the administration of Bithynia. In one of his letters Pliny wrote to Trajan asking about the procedure he should follow in dealing with Christians, for he was concerned about the legality of their activities.

Christianity first came to Asia Minor through the missionary journeys made by Paul of Tarus, described in *Acts of the Apostles*. Paul's first mission was with Barnabas in Antioch, where, according to *Acts* 11:26, 'they were to live together in that church a whole year. It was at Antioch that the disciples were first called "Christians".'

After leaving Antioch, Paul and his companions sailed from Seleucia Pieria to Cyprus and then back to Perge in Pamphylia, from where they travelled inland through the Taurus Mountains to Antioch in Pisidia. There Paul addressed the congregation in the synagogue on the sabbath, saying 'Men of Israel and fearers of God, listen!', and then a week later almost the whole town, pagans and Jews alike, 'assembled to hear the word of God'.

Paul and his companions went next to Iconium (Konya) in Lycaonia, where 'they spoke so effectively that many Jews and Christians became believers'. After being driven out of Iconium by hostile Jews, they went on to preach in Lystra and Derbe before returning to Pamphylia, whence they 'sailed for Antioch, where they had originally been commended to the grace of God for the work they had now completed'.

Paul's second and third missionary journeys took him through Asia Minor, the Aegean islands and Greece. On both journeys he stopped in Ephesus, his second visit lasting for more than two years, ca. 56–57. Paul bade farewell to his Ephesian friends in April of the year 57, when he stopped at Miletus on his way to Jerusalem, a moving scene described in *Acts* 20: 17–38:

> 'I now feel sure that none of you among whom I have gone about proclaiming the kingdom will ever see my face again. And so here and now I swear that my conscience is clear as far as all of you are concerned, for I have without faltering put before you the whole of God's purpose...'
> When he had finished he knelt down with them all and prayed. By now they were all in tears; they put their arms around Paul's neck and kissed him; what saddened them most was his saying they would never see his face again. Then they escorted him to the ship.

Tradition, dating back to the second century, has it that the Apostle John lived out his last years in Ephesus, and it was there that he wrote his Gospel. The first explicit reference to this is by Eirenaios, Bishop of Lugdunum (Lyon), who was born in Smyrna ca. 130: 'Last of all John, too, the disciple of the Lord who leant against his breast, himself brought out a gospel while he was in Ephesus.'

Eirenaios believed that John the Apostle also wrote *The Book of Revelation*, but current opinion generally identifies the author as St John the Theologian of Patmos, whoever he may be. The author of *Revelation*, which is dated to ca. 95, identifies himself in telling of his apocalyptic vision.

> My name is John and through our union in Jesus I am your brother and share your sufferings, and all you endure. I was on the island of Patmos for having preached God's word and witnessed for Jesus; it was the Lord's day and the Spirit possessed me, and I heard a voice behind me, shouting like a trumpet, 'Write down all that you see in a book, and send it to the seven churches of Ephesus, Smyrna, Pergamum, Thyatira, Sardis, Philadelphia and Laodicea...

One of the first bishops of the church in Smyrna was St Polycarp, who is said to have been consecrated by St John the Apostle in the last years of the first Christian century. Eirenaios reflects on how Polycarp 'used to describe his intercourse with John and the others who had seen the Lord: and...he remembered their words, and what were the things he had heard from them about the Lord and about His miracles and about his teaching...' Polycarp served as Bishop of Smyrna for more than half a century until his martyrdom on 22 February 153, when he was burned at the stake on orders of the Roman proconsul, L. Statius Quadratus.

Otherwise the Christians of Asia Minor were left in peace until the reign of the emperor Decius (r. 249–251), who ordered the execution of all of his subjects who would not offer sacrifice to the gods and the genius of the emperor. There were further persecutions of Christians under Valerian (r. 253–260) and in the latter years of the reign of Diocletian (r. 284–305), when far more were martyred for their faith than in all previous massacres combined. Christians, particularly among the Seven Churches of Asia Minor, took an apocalytic view of the oppressions, envisioning the destruction of Rome predicted in chapter 18 of *Revelation*, where 'an angel announces the fall of Babylon'.

A new world was about to be created, and the Greeks of Asia Minor were destined to inherit the empire of the east that emerged in the changed order of things, acquiring a new identity in the process.

9

New Rome

The emperor Gallienus was assassinated in 268 and succeeded by Claudius II, one of his murderers. The following year the barbarian Goths set out in a huge fleet across the Black Sea and sailed down the Bosphorus, making a futile attempt to take Byzantium before they continued through the straits to attack Greece and the Balkans. Later that year the Goths were crushed by Claudius at Niş, leaving 50,000 dead upon the field. The emperor then assumed the title of Claudius Gothicus, honoured by a commemorative column at Byzantium, but shortly afterwards he contracted the plague and died in January 270.

During the next fourteen years eight emperors succeeded one another to the throne violently, the last one standing being Diocletian, an Illyrian general, probably of Greek origin, who was proclaimed emperor in 284 at Nicomedia. Diocletian killed his imperial rival Carius in battle the following year, thus beginning a reign that lasted as long as Hadrian's, giving the empire its first period of stability in more than a century.

The year after his accession Diocletian adopted his comrade in arms Maximian as his son, giving him the rank of Caesar. Maximian was to defend the western provinces, while Diocletian himself took control of his native Illyricum and all of the provinces to its east. The following year, faced with a rival to the throne in Britain, Diocletian gave Maximian the title of Augustus, though he himself retained formal precedence as senior emperor. Each emperor maintained his own court and had his own army and administration, with a separate praetorian prefect as his second in command.

Diocletian built a palace in Nicomedia as his principal residence, probably because Bithynia was midway between the Balkan and Mesopotamian frontiers. His decision may also have been based on the fact that he was equally fluent in Greek and Latin, besides which he seems to have believed that the heart of the empire was Greek-speaking Asia Minor.

Then in 293 Diocletian instituted his famous tetrarchy, or 'rule of four', designed to further divide imperial responsibility and regularise succession to the throne. Diocletian now ruled as Augustus of the East, with his son-in-law Galerius as Caesar; Maximian was Augustus of the West, while his son-in-law and praetorian prefect Constantius Chlorus was Caesar. The four Tetrarchs formed a collegium, or board of rulers, in which the Caesars, who had their own praetorian prefects, were designated heirs to the Augusti.

Diocletian and his colleagues reorganised the provincial administration of the empire, which had changed little since the Augustan Age. Wheras there had been fewer than fifty provinces varying greatly in area, in the new arrangement there were about a hundred of fairly uniform size, population and resources, eighteen of them in Asia Minor and its borderlands in the south-east. The new provinces were further grouped into twelve large dioceses, of which most of Asia Minor was included in Asiana and Pontica, while its south-eastern borderlands were in the diocese called the East.

Maximian and Constantius crushed an invasion by the Alamanni in Gaul, while Diocletian signed a peace in 284 with the Persian king Bahram, who ceded Armenia and Mesopotamia to the Romans. Then in 296 the new Persian king Narses attacked the Romans, only to be destroyed by Galerius, after which the upper Tigris basin was added to the province of Mesopotamia.

Diocletian, who was married to a Christian, was tolerant toward Christians during the early years of his reign, even allowing them in the civil service of the empire. But then on 23 February 303, after consultation with Galerius, he issued an edict against the Christians, dismissing them from their positions and ordering the destruction of their churches and sacred scriptures. The edict officially applied throughout the empire, but Maximian and Constantius did little to enforce the decree and it took full effect only in the East.

When the imperial palace in Nicomedia was badly damaged by fire the following year the Christians were blamed, leading Diocletian and Galerius to arrest the Christian clergy and force everyone in the East, except Jews, to sacrifice to the gods of Rome. The cathedral in Nicomedia was demolished, Christians were imprisoned and tortured, and several hundred suffered martyrdom, including the Bishop of Nicomedia, beginning what came to be called the Great Persecution.

The Great Persecution continued until 311, when the edict against Christianity was finally rescinded by Galerius shortly before his death, Diocletian having retired six years before along with Maximian, ending the first tetrarchy.

The second tetrarchy that emerged in 305 had Constantius as Augustus of the West with Severus as his Caesar, while Galerius ruled as Augustus of the East with Maximinus as his Caesar. Constantius died in 306, whereupon the army in Britain proclaimed his son Constantine Augustus of the West. Later that year Maxentius, son of Maximian, seized power in Italy and recalled his father as Augustus, beginning a multilateral war of succession. By the spring of 311 the Roman world was split between four emperors: Maximinus, Licinius, Maxentius and Constantine, a fractious tetrarchy that eventually would be reduced to three, two and then one.

Constantine defeated Maxentius on 28 October 312 north of Rome at the Ponte Milvio, and on the following day he entered the city in triumph, his rival's severed head skewered on a lance held before him. The day after his victory the Senate formally conferred upon Constantine the title of senior Augustus. By that time Constantine had in some sense converted to Christianity, probably through the influence of his mother Helena, who was a devout Christian. During the winter of 312–313 he wrote three letters in which he revealed his new attitude toward Christianity, not just tolerating the Church but actively favouring it with subsidies and other measures.

Constantine's defeat of Maxentius left him sole ruler of the West, while Licinius and Maximinus still contended for the East. Constantine and Licinius met at Milan in February 313, where Licinius married Constantine's half-sister Constantia. The two emperors conferred on their policies, particularly on religious issues, but their discussions were interrupted by the news that Maximinus had invested Byzantium and invaded Europe. Licinius quickly marched his forces eastward and decisively defeated Maximinus near Adrianople. Maximinus retreated into Asia Minor as far as Tarsus, where he realised his situation was hopeless and committed suicide. Licinius then made his triumphal entry into Nicomedia, the ancient capital of Bithynia, where he now ruled unopposed as Augustus of the East. Then on 15 June 313 he issued a joint proclamation with Constantine, the so-called Edict of Milan, granting full toleration to all religions, including Christianity, and restoring all Christian property that had been confiscated during the Great Persecution.

Then in 316 Constantine invaded the territory of Licinius in Pannonia, beginning a conflict for supremacy between the two Augusti that was to continue for the next eight years. The last phase of this conflict began on 3 July 324 at Adrianople in Thrace, where Constantine routed Licinius and forced him to retreat to Byzantium. The final battle was fought on the Asian side of the Bosphorus near Chrysopolis on 18 September of that same year, when Constantine once again defeated Licinius. Byzantium and Chalcedon immediately opened their gates to Constantine, while Licinius fled to Nicomedia.

Soon afterwards Licinius surrendered to Constantine and was confined in Thessalonika, where he was executed later that year. Constantine then occupied the imperial palace at Nicomedia, from where he now reigned as the unchallenged Augustus of the whole Roman Empire.

Soon after his victory over Licinius, Constantine decided to establish his principal residence near Troy, but then he changed his mind and chose Byzantium. This momentus decision is recorded in the *Historia Nova* of Zosimus, who says that Constantine was 'seeking after a city to counterbalance Rome in which to build his own palace'.

While the reconstruction of Byzantium was underway Constantine lived in Diocletian's palace at Nicomedia. His first order of business there was to establish unity in the Christian Church, which led him to convene an Ecumenical Council of bishops in the nearby city of Nicaea. The council met between 20 May and 19 June 325, with more than 300 bishops in attendance, most of them from the eastern provinces of the empire.

Constantine's main purpose in convening the council was to settle a bitter controversy between Alexander, bishop of Alexandria, and Arius, one of his dissident priests, who maintained that Christ was not the immortal son of God, nor of the same substance, a doctrine that came to be called Arianism. The council almost unanimously condemned Arianism, all but two of the bishops signing a document of orthodox dogma that became known as the Nicene Creed, after which Arius was sent into exile along with his supporters. The council then settled other matters, establishing a common date for Easter and confirming the primacy of the bishop of Alexandria throughout Egypt and of the bishop of Antioch in Syria.

The reconstruction of Byzantium was completed early in 330, when Constantine took up residence in the city in preparation for its formal dedication on 11 May of that year. The imperial edict of foundation was engraved on a stele and publicly set up in the Strategicon, recording that thenceforth Byzantium was to be called NOVA ROMA CONSTANTINOPOLITANA, New Rome, the City of Constantine.

Constantinople was protected on its landward side by a line of defence walls that stretched from the Golden Horn to the Sea of Marmara, enclosing an area four times larger than that of the ancient city of Byzantium. The population of the new city can be estimated from the fact that Constantine supplied daily rations for 80,000 people. According to Zosimus, besides the city walls, the structures erected by Constantine included a forum, a hippodrome, a palace, several temples and 'homes for certain Senators who had followed him from Rome'. The forum bore the emperor's name and at its centre there was a huge porphyry column surmounted by a statue of Constantine. The statue has long since vanished, but the column still stands, along with the remains of the hippodrome and the Great Palace of Byzantium, both of which were enlarged and embellished by later emperors.

Byzantine sources credit Constantine with founding or rebuilding a number of churches in his new capital, most notably Haghia Sophia and Haghia Eirene, dedicated to the Divine Wisdom and the Divine Peace, respectively, and the church of the Holy Apostles. But the most reliable of these sources, the fifth-century historian Socrates, credits Constantine only with building the Holy Apostles and restoring Haghia Eirene, and he says that Haghia Sophia was completed by Constantine's son Constantius.

The circumstances of Constantine's final days are narrated by Eusebius of Caesarea in his *Vita Constantini*, where he writes that the emperor's last illness came upon him in 336. Constantine sought to cure his illness in the hot baths of Constantinople, but when this failed he went to his mother's native village on the Gulf of Nicomedia, where there were thermal springs renowned for their therapeutic power. When he found no relief there Constantine moved to Diocletian's palace in Nicomedia, where he summoned the local clergy and made a confession of faith. Bishop Eusebius of Nicomedia then baptised Constantine and received him into the Christian faith. According to the *Vita Constantini*, when the sacraments were administered to Constantine he exclaimed, 'Now I know in very truth that I am blessed, for I am a partaker of divine light.'

Constantine passed away a few days later, on Whitsunday, 22 May 337. His embalmed body was brought back to Constantinople and lay in state in the Great Palace for three months before being entombed in the church of the Holy Apostles.

The long delay in burying Constantine was due to the uncertainty regarding his succession, for the previous year he had made plans for dividing the empire among his sons Constantine, Constantius and Constans, all of whom had been raised to the rank of Caesar. The hiatus ended on 9 September 337 when Constantine's sons gave themselves the title of Augustus and then had their actions confirmed by the Senate in Rome. The three Augusti then disposed of possible rivals in the imperial family, instigating an uprising among the garrison at Constantinople that led to the slaughter of two of their uncles and seven cousins. The only male survivors in the imperial family were two young sons of Julius Constantius, a half-brother of the late emperor Constantine; these were Gallus and Julian, who at the time were eleven and five years old, respectively, the two of them spared because of their youth. The two young princes were thereafter kept under close surveillance, first in Constantinople and later in Cappadocia.

The three Augusti met early in the summer of 338 to divide up the empire, retaining essentially the same regions over which they had ruled as Caesars. Constantius ruled over the eastern parts of the empire, while the western provinces were ruled by Constantine and Constans. This division of the empire inevitably led to a protracted three-sided struggle, in which Constantine and Constans were killed, and in 353 Constantius II emerged as sole ruler of the empire, with his capital in Constantinople.

Constantius continued the pro-Christian policy of his father, and in 356 he issued an edict closing all pagan temples in the empire and banning all pagan practices. He also completed the great church of Haghia Sophia, dedicated to the Divine Wisdom, which would thenceforth be the cathedral of Constantinople.

Constantius had released Gallus from his long captivity in 351, raising him to the rank of Caesar and giving him command of the army on the Persian frontier. Three years later Constantius was convinced that Gallus was plotting to usurp the throne, so he had him arrested and beheaded.

The following year Constantius promoted Julian to the rank of Caesar, sending him to command the army in Gaul, despite the fact that he had absolutely no military experience, having devoted his time solely to scholarship. Despite his inexperience, Julian proved to be an outstanding general, and within five years he won four notable victories over the Gauls, becoming extremely popular with his troops. Though Julian had been a devout Christian in his early youth, his studies in classical Greek philosophy had led him to reject Christianity in favour of the gods of the ancient Graeco-Roman world, though for obvious reasons he kept his apostasy a secret.

Constantius died on 3 November 361 while on campaign against the Persians. Julian had already been proclaimed emperor by his troops and was en route to Constantinople, which he reached on 11 December. He was greeted enthusiastically by the populace as the first emperor to have been born in their city.

Julian openly professed his paganism as soon as he became emperor. A few days after his arrival in Byzantium he issued decrees that permitted public performances of all religious ceremonies, pagan as well as Christian and Jewish. When he reorganised the government he excluded Christians in his appointments, influencing many to renounce their faith, which led his enemies to call him Julian the Apostate, the name by which he is known to history.

Julian spent only five months in Constantinople, leaving the city in June 362 for Antioch and the Persian frontier. He never returned, for he was mortally wounded in a battle against the Persians and died on 26 June 363, after which he was buried in Tarsus. The army chose Jovian as his successor, after which they began the long march back to Constantinople. But Jovian never reached the capital, for on the last stage of the march he became ill, passing away on 17 February 364.

At Nicaea the army chose Valentinian as his successor, and on 26 February he was acclaimed as Augustus. The army demanded that Valentinian name a co-emperor, so as to ensure a suitable successor, and so he nominated his brother Valens, who was acclaimed Augustus on 28

March. The arrangement they agreed upon made Valentinian Emperor of the West, with his capital at Milan, while, Valens was to rule the East from Constantinople. Both brothers were devout Christians; nevertheless they kept an open mind on religious matters, continuing Julian's policy of toleration to pagans and all sects of Christianity.

Valentinian died of a stroke on 17 November 375 and was succeeded by his sixteen-year-old son Gratian, whose younger brother Valentinian II was made co-emperor. Valens continued to rule as Emperor of the East until 9 August 378, when he was killed near Adrianople fighting against the Goths, who destroyed two-thirds of his army.

Gratian appointed the Spanish general Theodosius as co-emperor on 19 January 379, his rule extending over the eastern provinces of the empire. The new Emperor of the East finally reached his capital on 24 November 380, according to Zosimus, who says that 'the Emperor Theodosius entered Constantinople in splendor, as if in celebration of a glorious victory'.

Theodosius had been baptised in 380, and on 27 February of that year he issued an edict declaring that all his subjects should adhere to the Christian faith. The following year Theodosius convened an Ecumenical Council at Constantinople, which confirmed the Nicene Creed and established the dogma that the Father, the Son and the Holy Spirit were three persons of a single Godhead, the Holy Trinity. The council also maintained that 'The Bishop of Constantinople ought to have precedence of honour after the Bishop of Rome, for this city is the second Rome', claiming primacy for the patriarchate of Constantinople over those of Antioch and Alexandria.

Theodosius was determined to stamp out heresies, and during his reign he issued a total of eighteen edicts against schismatic sects. He was totally opposed to paganism and in 391 he enacted laws closing pagan temples throughout the empire, forbidding worship of the old Graeco-Roman gods, even in private, under the pain of severe penalties.

Gratian was assassinated in 383 and Valentinian II suffered the same fate nine years later. Theodosius avenged both of their deaths, putting down and killing those who had overthrown them, his efforts culminating in 392 with his victory over the usurper Maximus in northern Italy. He then marched on to Milan, where he began to make plans for his succession. He decided to divide the empire between his two sons, the East to be ruled by Arcadius, who was then seventeen or eighteen, and the West by Honorius, who was only ten. Both sons were at that time in Constantinople, and Theodosius summoned Honorius to Milan, where he arrived in mid-January 395. By that time Theodosius had become seriously ill, and he died the day after Honorius arrived.

The death of Theodosius left the Roman Empire divided once again, with the East ruled by Arcadius (r. 395–408), and the West under Honorius (r. 395–423). Both of them proved to be weak and ineffective rulers even after they came of age, leaving the control of the empire to others.

Three years after Arcadius came to the throne John Chrysostom became patriarch of Constantinople. The eloquent and often fiery sermons of Chrysostom, which included diatribes against Jews, heresy and paganism, made him a hero to the ordinary people of Constantinople. Despite the edict of Theodosius I in 391, many still worshipped the ancient Graeco-Roman gods, and Chrysostom called for the destruction of their sanctuaries, particularly that of Ephesian Artemis. His words incited a mob of Christians to destroy the temple of Artemis at Ephesus in 401, which Chrysostom saw as the final victory of Christianity over paganism. By that time a Roman basilica in Ephesus had been converted into a church dedicated to the Virgin Mary, and thenceforth her cult supplanted that of Artemis, although many pagans continued to worship the virgin huntress secretly at her most ancient shrine in Asia Minor.

Chrysostom was particularly critical of the loose morals and extravagance of the imperial court, and in one of his sermons he compared the empress Eudoxia to Jezebel. The empress was furious and persuaded Arcadius to exile Chrysostom, but the patriarch's supporters protested so forcefully that he was restored. But Chrysostom renewed his diatribes against the empress and on 20 June he was exiled again by Arcadius, this time for good. When the populace learned that their beloved patriarch had been banished they stormed the gates of the Great Palace, and in the ensuing riot the church of Haghia Sophia was destroyed by fire along with the meeting-place of the senate.

Arcadius died the following year and was succeeded by his son Theodosius II, who was only seven when he came to the throne. Anthemius, Prefect of the East, was appointed regent, a position he would hold until his death in 414. After the death of Anthemius the role of regent passed to the princess Pulcheria, elder sister of Theodosius. Pulcheria, who thereupon received the title of Augusta, acted as regent until her brother reached his majority two years later, but even then she continued to be the power behind the throne for another decade.

During the time that Anthemius was regent he supervised the reconstruction of Haghia Sophia, which was reconsecrated by Theodosius in 415. The year before his death Anthemius also completed a new circuit of fortifications a mile outside the Constantinian walls, stretching for four miles between the Golden Horn and the Sea of Marmara. The fortifications were badly damaged by an earthquake in 447, but within two months they were rebuilt as a double line of walls under the direction of the new Prefect of the East, Constantine.

The new Theodosian walls, as they came to be called, enclosed seven hills, the same as in Rome, a fact mentioned in the *Notitia urbis Constantinopolitanae*, a description of the city written in the years 447–450. The *Notitia* records that the city of Theodosius II was divided into fourteen regions, again the same as in Rome. These regions defined the limits of Constantinople for the next thousand years, during which the Theodosian walls stood as the bulwark of the 'God-Guarded City' through repeated attacks by enemy forces from both Europe and Asia.

Theodosius founded the University of Constantinople on 27 February 425. The charter established thirty-one endowed chairs, including fifteen in Greek, thirteen in Latin, two in jurisprudence and one in philosophy. The fact that there were more chairs in Greek than in Latin reflects the growing hellenisation of the empire. Latin remained the official language of the empire, but Greek was more widely spoken in Constantinople and through the East and eventually it predominated in the imperial court and administration.

Theodosius was determined to regularise the laws of the empire, and in 429 he entrusted the task to a committee headed by Apelles, professor of jurisprudence at the new university. Nine years later the committee produced the document known as the *Codex Theodosianus*, which Theodosius described as a collection of all the constitutions issued by the 'renowned Constantine, the divine Emperors who succeeded him, and ourselves'. The new code came into force the following year under the names of both Theodosius II and the Emperor of the West Valentinian III, his cousin and son-in-law, reasserting the unity of the empire.

Theological disputes continued to trouble the empire during the reign of Theodosius, particularly a controversy concerning the nature of Christ. Nestorius, the patriarch of Constantinople, held that two separate natures, human and divine, coexisted in Christ. According to the chronicler Theophanes Confessor, Nestorius also said: 'No one is to call Mary the Mother of God. For Mary was human and it is not possible for God to have been born from a human being.' The Third Ecumenical Council, convened at Ephesus on 7 June 431, condemned Nestorianism as heretical, whereupon Theodosius deposed Nestorius and exiled him to Egypt.

The army of Theodosius was dominated by foreign mercenaries of the Arian faith, particularly Goths and the people of south-east Russia known as the Alans. The post of *magister milium*, the highest ranking general, was held by Aspar the Alan, who put down a rebellion in Italy in 423, commanded a fleet against the Vandals in 431, and led a campaign against Attila the Hun in 441. Aspar became an ally of Pulcheria, and during the latter years of her brother's reign the two of them held the balance of power in the court at Constantinople.

Theodosius II died on 28 July 450, leaving no son or designated successor. The senate offered the throne to Aspar, but he declined and put forward his aide-de-camp, a Thracian general named Marcian, who was made Augustus after going through a nominal marriage with Pulcheria.

The year after his accession Marcian convened the Fourth Ecumenical Council, which met across the Bosphorus from Constantinople at Chalcedon in the church of St Euphemia. The council set forth the Orthodox doctrine in what came to be known as the Definition of Chalcedon, which held that the two natures of Christ, human and divine, were amalgamated in one person. Those who opposed this doctrine were known as Monophysites, from their belief that Christ had but a single nature, which was divine. This led to a schism in which the Monophysites established separate and independent churches, principally the Armenians, the Jacobites in Syria and Mesopotamia, and the Copts in Egypt.

Pulcheria died in July 453, and was buried in the church of the Holy Apostles beside her brother Theodosius II. Two years later a military coup in Rome overthrew and killed Valentinian III, Emperor of the West, who died without leaving a son, thus ending the dynasty that had begun with Theodosius I.

The empire in the West had already suffered irrevocable damage when Rome was captured and sacked by the Visigoths in 410, and in 452 it was further weakened when Attila the Hun ravaged northern Italy. Valentinian III was succeeded in turn by a series of eight ephemeral emperors over the next two decades, all but one of them Romanised barbarian generals, who now ruled both East and West. The western empire finally came to an end in 480 with the death of Julius Nepos, the last Augustus of the West, who was assassinated in Dalmatia, the last remnant of his domain. Thenceforth the emperor in Constantinople was sole ruler of what remained of the empire.

The shift of the capital to the East brought Asia Minor to the centre of the Graeco-Roman world, revivifying its intellectual life, with Constantinople and Antioch as its bipolar focal points. During the period from Constantine to Theodosius II, Greek scholars in Constantinople, Antioch and Asia Minor produced major works of both secular and religious history, all but one of them writing in Greek. The exception was Ammianus Marcellinus (ca. 330–395) of Antioch, the last great Roman historian, who, though a native Greek-speaker, wrote in Latin, which he would have acquired in his service as a high-ranking army officer under both Constantius and Julian.

The rhetorician Libanius (314–393) was born in Antioch and was educated there and in Athens before going on to teach at Constantinople and Nicomedia. His students, pagan and Christian, included John Chrysostom, probably Basil of Caesarea and Gregory of Nazianzus, and possibly Ammianus Marcellinus. He corresponded with Julian the Apostate, whom he deeply influenced, and the emperor's premature death was a severe blow to him. During his latter years he was a renowned literary figure throughout the Greek world, gaining considerable influence under Theodosius I, who gave him the honourary title of praetorian prefect.

The philosopher and rhetorician Themistius (ca. 317–ca. 388) was born in Paphlagonia and studied in Constantinople, where he opened a school ca. 345. His orations won him the patronage of every emperor from Constantius to Theodosius I, who appointed him prefect of Constantinople and entrusted him with the education of the future emperor Arcadius. His extant orations are an important source for the history and political ideology of his time, particularly because he was a pagan in an officially Christian empire.

Gregory of Nazianzus (ca. 329–389) and his friend Basil of Caesarea (ca. 330–395), the 'Cappadocian Fathers', were educated in Athens, where they were fellow students with Julian the Apostate. Both were appointed to bishoprics in their native Cappadocia, and Gregory served briefly as patriarch of Constantinople. Their orations and letters are among the classics of patristic literature, and Gregory's eulogy for Basil has been described 'as probably the greatest piece of Greek rhetoric since the death of Demosthenes'.

The period of the Theodosian dynasty gave birth to three Christian historians of the Church: Socrates, Sozomen and Theodoret, all of whom wrote their works in the period 439–450. The following half century brought forth the pagan secular historian Zosimus, whose *New History* is largely a summary of the lost works of earlier writers, most notably the history of Eunapius, who was also used by Ammianus Marcellinus. The contrast between the Christian and pagan historians is most evident in their treatment of Julian the Apostate. Socrates, in writing of Julian, says that 'the emperor's speedy death was beneficial to Christianity', while Ammianus, in concluding his account of Julian's reign, writes that 'He was a man truly to be numbered with the heroic spirits, distinguished for his illustrious deeds and his inborn majesty.'

Julian's own writings were voluminous, including speeches, letters and satires. The most famous of his satires is *Misopogon* (Beard-Hater), addressed to the people of Antioch, who had made fun of him for growing a beard in emulation of ancient Greek philosophers. He tells the Antiochenes that he grew his beard as goats do, 'and if you would like to learn something that is usually a secret, my chest is shaggy and covered with hair, like the breasts of lions who are kings among beasts... Why, in the name of the gods are you ungrateful to me?'

During Julian's brief reign he tried to restore the pagan shrines that had been closed by Constantius, including the temple at Jerusalem and the oracular spring at Daphne south of Antioch. But his untimely death cut short his efforts, and within the following century all of the pagan sanctuaries were not only closed but utterly destroyed, including the temple of Ephesian Artemis and the oracular shrines of Apollo at Delphi and at Didyma in Ionia. The last prophecy of the Delphic oracle is said to have been delivered to Julian himself, and its closing is mourned in a threnody preserved in the *Vita S. Artemii*, translated thus by Swinburne:

Tell the king on earth has fallen the glorious dwelling,
And the water springs that spake are quenched and dead.
Not a cell is left to the god, no roof, no cover;
In his hand the prophet laurel flowers no more.

The old order had passed away, and the great goddess at Ephesus was no longer worshipped in her ancient shrine, where the cult-statues of Artemis were buried by her eunuch-priests, sleeping in the Ionian earth until they were uncovered by archaeologists fifteen centuries later.

10

The Age of Justinian

By the end of the fifth century the Roman Empire had been reduced to the predominately Greek-speaking East, where Christianity was rapidly supplanting the worship of the ancient Graeco-Roman deities. The heart of the empire was now Asia Minor, where a Greek was more likely to be called a *Rhomaios*, or Roman, rather than a Hellene, which had come to mean a pagan, while the people of Constantinople referred to themselves as *Byzantini*, or Byzantines. Modern historians consider the end of the fifth century as a watershed in the history of the empire, which thenceforth is generally referred to as Byzantine rather than Roman. As the great churchman Gennadius was to write nearly a thousand years later, in the twilight of the Byzantine Empire:

> Though I am a Hellene by speech yet I would never say that I was a Hellene, for I do not believe as Hellenes believe. I should like to take my name from my faith, and if anyone asks me what I am I answer, 'A Christian.' Though my father dwelt in Thessaly I do not call myself a Thessalian, but a Byzantine, for I am of Byzantium.

The demise of the Theodosian dynasty left the empire without a hereditary succession, and so when Marcian died on 7 February 457 the senate again offered the throne to Aspar. But once more Aspar declined, nominating one of his lieutenants, a Thracian general from Dacia named Leo, who was crowned on 7 February of that year by Anatolis, the patriarch of Constantinople.

Leo remained subservient to Aspar for the first six or seven years of his reign, during which time foreign mercenaries continued to dominate the imperial army. Leo sought to counteract Aspar's power by enlisting the services of the Isaurians, a wild tribal people from the Taurus Mountains, enrolling them in the imperial army under their chieftain Tarasicodissa, who changed his name to Zeno. Soon afterwards Zeno was made commander of the army in Thrace and married the princess Ariadne, eldest daughter of Leo and the empress Verina. The following year Ariadne bore Zeno a son, the future Leo II, who succeeded to the throne when his grandfather died in 474.

Leo II was only seven when he came to the throne, and so his father Zeno was made co-emperor. Nine months later young Leo died and Zeno became sole emperor, beginning a reign that would last for seventeen years. During that time Roman dominion in the West came to an end, leaving Zeno sole ruler of what remained of the empire.

Zeno died on 9 April 491 and was succeeded by Anastasius, a sixty-year old court official who soon afterwards married the empress Ariadne. The populace at first welcomed Anastasius, for he was a Greek-speaker from Dyrracium in Albania rather than a barbarian general, but soon afterwards the factions of the Hippodrome rioted against him because of his puritanical laws and Monophysite beliefs, the first of a series of insurrections and civil wars that would trouble his long reign.

Two years after Anastasius came to the throne the empire was invaded by the Bulgars, who devastated Thrace right up to the suburbs of Constantinople, destroying the aqueducts that brought water into the city and cutting off its food supplies. The Bulgars invaded twice more within the next decade, before Anastasius finally succeeded in halting their incursions by building a line of fortifications forty miles outside the city, the so-called Long Walls, stretching from the Black Sea to the Marmara.

Anastasius had no sooner secured his Balkan frontier than war erupted in the East, where the Persians ended a long truce by invading Armenia in August 502. The imperial armies eventually halted the invasion, and in 505 Anastasius came to terms with the Persians, beginning a peace that would last for more than two decades.

Anastasius died on 8 July 518 at the age of eighty-eight, older than any emperor before or after him, leaving no heir to the throne other than his three nephews, Probus, Pompeius and Hypatius. But the army

1a. The tomb of Achilles on the Trojan plain (from Choisseul-Gouffier)

1b. Yenişehir village above the Trojan plain (from Choisseul-Gouffier)

2a. The walls of Troy VI and the South Gate (Anthony E. Baker)

2b. Doric collonade of the temple of Athena at Assos (Anthony E. Baker)

3a. The theatre at Miletus (Anthony E. Baker)

3b. Ionic stoa of Capito Baths at Miletus (Anthony E. Baker)

4a. Ruins of the Hellenistic Artemesium at Ephesus (Anthony E. Baker)

4b. Partially reconstructed church of St John the
Theologian at Ephesus (Anthony E. Baker)

5a. Temple of Athena at Priene (Anthony E. Baker)

5b. Temple of Artemis at Sardis (Anthony E. Baker)

6. Temple of Apollo at Side (Anthony E. Baker)

7. Head of Alexander the Great from Pergamum, Istanbul
Archaeological Museum (Anthony E. Baker)

8a. Temple of Apollo at Didyma (Anthony E. Baker)

8b. Temple of Zeus at Euromus (Anthony E. Baker)

9a. Theatre at Perge (Anthony E. Baker)

9b. Outer and inner gates at Perge (Anthony E. Baker)

10a. Baths of Herodes Atticus at Alexandria Troas (Anthony E. Baker)

10b. Castle of St Peter at Halicarnassus (Bodrum) (Anthony E. Baker)

11a. The Trajaneum at Pergamon (Anthony E. Baker)

11b. The acropolis at Pergamon (from Thomas Allom)

12a. View from the port at Smyrna (from Thomas Allom)

12b. The citadel at Smyrna (Izmir) from the caravan bridge (from Thomas Allom)

13. A street in Smyrna (Izmir) (from Thomas Allom)

14a. Church of St Theodore at Pergamon (Bergama) (from Thomas Allom)

14b. A church in Magnesia-ad-Sipylum (Manisa) (from Thomas Allom)

15a. 'Dance of the Maidens', relief from the Temple of Zeus on Samothrace, ca. 340 BC, Samothrace Museum

15b. Greek women dancing at a festival in Ottoman Turkey, late eighteenth century (from M. d'Ohsson, Benaki Museum, Athens)

16a. Musicians at a Greek festival in Smyrna
(Izmir), 1900 (Pan. Kounadhis Archives)

16b. Greek refugees from Asia Minor at an encampment
on Chios, 1922 (Pan. Kounadhis Archives)

rejected them in favour of the Illyrian general Justin, who was then sixty-six. Justin's succession was due largely to the astuteness of his nephew Justinian, a young officer in the élite imperial guards, who had been the first choice of the army, but declined so that his uncle could succeed to the throne.

Although Justin was illiterate he governed effectively with the help of Justinian, who was made consul in 521 and then elevated to the rank of Caesar four years later. When Justin became seriously ill early in 527 he named Justinian as his successor. Justinian became co-emperor on 4 April of that year, when he was crowned in a chapel of the Great Palace along with his wife Theodora, a former courtesan and actress whom he had wed three years before. Justin passed away on 1 August 527, whereupon Justinian succeeded him as emperor, with Theodora named as Augusta.

Justinian was about forty-two when he became emperor, fully prepared to rule after the decade he had spent advising his late uncle. Apparently he was already dedicated to the dream of regaining the lost provinces of the empire, an ambition that he first expressed after the Byzantine conquest of Sicily: 'We have good hopes that God will grant us to restore our authority over the remaining countries which the ancient Romans possessed to the limits of both oceans and lost by subsequent neglect.'

The principal source for Justinian's reign is Procopius of Palestinian Caesarea, who has been called 'the last great historian of antiquity'. Procopius is first heard of in 527, when he was appointed to the staff of Justinian's brilliant young general Belisarius. He accompanied Belisarius on campaigns in Persia, North Africa and Italy, after which he returned to Constantinople and began to write his *History of the Wars*, published ca. 541. During the next four years he composed the *Edifices*, a description of all the buildings that Justinian had erected up to that time throughout the empire.

A year after he came to the throne Justinian appointed a commission to reform the laws of the empire. This gave rise to the *Codex Justinianus*, the final version of which was published on 16 November 534. This code, together with the later laws of Justinian, formed the basis for the *Corpus Juris Civilis*, on which the law of most countries in Europe was based up until the beginning of modern times.

Justinian was also determined to enforce religious orthodoxy as established by the Council of Chalcedon. His efforts to impose religious unity also included stamping out the remaining traces of paganism in the empire. One of his laws banned pagans from holding academic chairs, and another made it illegal for anyone 'infected with the madness of the unholy Hellenes' to teach any subject. As a result the ancient Platonic Academy in Athens was closed, ending an existence of more than nine centuries, as its professors of pagan philosophy went off into exile or retired, severing one of the last living links with the classic Hellenic world.

Damascius, the last director of the Academy, was one of those who went into exile, along with Isidorus of Miletus and Simplicius of Cilicia, two of the greatest scholars of late antiquity. They and four other professors from the Academy were given refuge by the Persian king Chosroes I, who in 531 appointed them to the faculty of the medical school at Jundishapur. The following year they all decided to come back from their exile, six of them returning to Athens, while Isidorus took up residence in Constantinople.

The eastern frontier had been quiet during the whole of Justin's reign, but in the last year of his life the Persians invaded Armenia. After Justinian came to the throne he appointed Belisarius as commander of the Army in the East with instructions to march toward the frontier. This began a war with Persia that would last until 531, when the new king Chosroes I agreed to the terms of a treaty known as the Endless Peace.

Five years after his accession Justinian was faced with the most serious insurrection of his reign, which began on 10 January 532 as a riot among the contending factions in the Hippodrome. This erupted into a full-scale revolt three days later, when the factions joined together to storm the gates of the Great Palace, shouting 'Nika!' (Conquer), the rallying cry that would give its name to the insurrection, during which the churches of Haghia Sophia and Haghia Eirene were destroyed by fire.

The imperial council advised Justinian to flee to Thrace, where he could reorganise his forces to recapture the city, but a stirring speech by Theodora convinced him that he should stay and fight for his throne. Belisarius then led forth his barbarian troops and trapped the mob inside the Hippodrome, slaughtering 30,000 of them there, according to Procopius.

Forty days after the end of the revolt Justinian began rebuilding Haghia Sophia on the ruins of the Theodosian church. Procopius writes that 'the Emperor, disregarding all questions of expense, eagerly pressed on to begin the work of construction, and began to gather all the artisans from the whole world'. Justinian appointed Anthemius of Tralles as his chief architect, assisted by Isidorus of Miletus, who the year before had returned from Jundishapur. The building was completed within six years, and on 26 December 537 Justinian and Theodora joined the patriarch Menas in rededicating the church to Haghia Sophia, the Divine Wisdom. During the same period Justinian also completely rebuilt Haghia Eirene as well as the church of the Holy Apostles, where he erected a new and larger imperial mausoleum.

Meanwhile, in the summer of 533, Justinian sent an army under Belisarius against the Vandals in North Africa, whom he decisively defeated in a battle near Carthage. Carthage opened its gates to the imperial army shortly afterwards, and the following spring the Vandal king Gelimer surrendered along with 3,000 of his men.

Two years later Justinian sent Belisarius off on an expedition to reconquer Italy from the Ostrogoths. Belisarius took Rome in 536, but an Ostrogoth army under Vitigis besieged him there and he was forced to appeal to Justinian for more men and supplies. After reinforcements arrived under the eunuch Narses, Belisarius broke the siege of Rome and continued his campaign against the Ostrogoths, who made a last stand at Ravenna before surrendering in May 540.

The Persian king Chosroes took advantage of Justinian's preoccupation with the war in Italy, and in the spring of 540 he broke the Endless Peace and invaded Syria, sacking Antioch and enslaving its inhabitants. Justinian sent Belisarius to lead the Army of the East against Persia, beginning a war that would drag on for two decades. Meanwhile the Visigoths had resumed the struggle in Italy under their new king Totila, who recaptured Rome in 546. Belisarius was sent back to command the army in Italy, and in 547 he occupied Rome after Totila left the city to reconquer southern Italy. Belisarius was then recalled and Narses took command of the army in Italy, renewing the war against the Ostrogoths, whom he defeated in two decisive battles in 552. During the next two years Narses reduced the remaining Ostrogoth garrisons, completing the conquest of Italy.

The following year Justinian took advantage of a war of succession among the Visigoths to land troops at Cartagena to reinforce his army there. Justinian was unable to muster the forces necessary to conquer the rest of Spain, and so eventually he made peace with the Visigoths, retaining the south-western corner of the Iberian peninsula as a new province of the empire.

Thus Justinian would seem to have realised his imperial dream, for his empire now extended almost entirely around the Mediterranean, including all of Italy, the southern Balkans and Asia Minor. Procopius, in his *Edifices*, catalogues the 'innumerable' fortresses that Justinian built or restored to defend his vast realm, as well as the many churches that he founded or rebuilt in Constantinople and other cities of the empire. The most notable of Justinian's churches in Asia Minor was the basilica of St John the Theologian in Ephesus, which Procopius says was patterned on the new church of the Holy Apostles in Constantinople.

The second Persian war finally came to an end in 562, when Justinian and Chosroes signed a treaty agreeing to fifty years of peace. During that time the Persians were to be paid an annual subsidy, in return for which they gave up Lazica, the region beyond Armenia at the eastern end of the Black Sea.

Thus ended the last of Justinian's wars, and during the remaining years of his life he concentrated on rebuilding Haghia Sophia, which had been damaged by a series of earthquakes during the previous decade. The restored church was rededicated by Justinian on Christmas Eve 563, the last noteworthy occasion of his reign. He continued to carry out his imperial duties until the last day of his life, 14 November 565, when he dropped dead from a stroke or heart attack. Two days later he was borne to the new mausoleum he had built in the church of the Holy Apostles, where he was buried in a porphyry sarcophagus next to that of Theodora.

Justinian was eighty-three when he died, after a reign of more than thirty-eight years, which some consider to be the most illustrious period in the history of the Byzantine Empire. Yet the chronicler Evagrius took a darker view, as he writes in recording the passing of Justinian: 'Thus died this prince, after having filled the whole world with noise and troubles; and having since the end of his life received the wages of his misdeeds, he has gone to seek the justice which was his due before the judgement-seat of hell.'

During the age of Justinian a number of distinguished scholars emerged from Asia Minor, and almost all of them at one point or another were drawn to the emperor's court in Constantinople. Among them were Anthemius of Tralles and Isidorus of Miletus, the architects of Haghia

Sophia, two distinguished mathematical physicists from western Asia Minor who had previously worked for Justinian on an engineering project in Mesopotamia.

Anthemius was the son of a physician in the Phrygian town of Tralles. He went on to become a professor of geometry in Constantinople, where, according to Agathius of Myrina, he was renowned as one of those scientists 'who apply geometrical speculation to material objects to make models or imitations of the natural world'. Some of his work on applied geometry survives in a fragmentary treatise *On Burning Mirrors*, that is, using sunlight reflected from a curved mirror to burn objects placed at its focal point, an invention of Archimedes. His other extant work on applied geometry is a treatise *On Remarkable Mechanical Devices*. One of the inventions described in this work was apparently a device to simulate earthquakes, thunder and lightning using steam pressure and an array of mirrors, which he used to frighten his troublesome upstairs neighbour, the rhetorician Zeno.

Isidorus was born in the ancient Ionian city of Miletus, which a thousand and more years before had given birth to the first three philosophers of nature, Thales, Anaximander and Anaximenes. He was educated at the Platonic Academy in Athens, where he was the third but last director before it was closed by Justinian, who invited him to Constantinople after he returned from exile in Jundishapur. Isidorus was apparently responsible for the first collected edition of the works of Archimedes, which included three treatises – *On the Sphere and Cylinder*, *On the Measurement of the Circle* and *On the Equilibrium of Planes* – which might otherwise have been lost. He also wrote a commentary of a treatise *On Vaulting* by the Alexandrian physicist and inventor Hero, which would have influenced his design of the great dome of Haghia Sophia, which Procopius says seems to be 'suspended from Heaven'.

The historian and poet Agathius was born in the ancient Aeolian town of Myrina and studied in both Athens and Constantinople, where he practiced law during the reign of Justinian. His *History* was meant to bring up to date the narrative of Procopius' *History of the Wars*, but he covered only the years 553–559 before his death. The work is of particular interest to historians of architecture because it contains a description of the rebuilding of Haghia Sophia after it was damaged by earthquakes in 553 and 557. He also published a collection of contemporary epigrams which survive in the *Greek Anthology* as the *Cycle of Agathius*. Among them are a hundred or so of his own epigrams, including one giving advice on matters of love.

Other epigrams in the *Cycle of Agathius* are by Paul the Silentiary, who may be his father-in-law. Paul's title came from his position as a gentleman usher in Haghia Sophia, where his duty was to silence those in the congregation who conversed during the liturgy. Aside from his epigrams in the *Cycle of Agathius*, Paul also wrote a lengthy poem that he recited in front of Justinian on Christmas Eve 563, when Haghia Sophia was rededicated after its restoration. The poem praises the beauties of the church, which he describes in exquisite detail, including the circlet of windows below its great dome, whose glow he likens to that of the famous Lighthouse of Alexandria, making it a beacon for nocturnal mariners. 'He does not guide his laden vessel by the light of Cynosura or the circling Bear, but by the divine light of the church itself. Yet not only does it guide the merchant at night, like the rays of the Pharos on the African shore: it also points the way to the living God.'

The provinces of Pamphylia and Cilicia in southern Asia Minor also produced two famous scholars of note during Justinian's reign, the jurist Tribonian and the philosopher Simplicius. Tribonian was born in Side, the ancient Pamphylian colony of Aeolian Cyme. He studied law in Constantinople, where he became the most renowned legal scholar of his day. He was a close friend of Justinian, who appointed him to head the commission that compiled the *Codex Justinianus*. Justinian also appointed Tribonian to high offices in the imperial administration, but at the beginning of the Nika Revolt he was forced to dismiss him on charges of corruption.

Simplicius was born in Cilicia and went on to study in Alexandria and Athens, where he studied with Damascius, the last director of the Platonic Academy before it was closed by Justinian in 529. After his exile in Persia, Simplicius returned to Athens, where he spent the rest of his days writing and doing research, but since he was a pagan he was no longer allowed to teach. He is renowned for his commentaries on Aristotle, which were very influential in the thirteenth-century European renaissance.

Justinian was succeeded by his nephew Justin II, whose wife Sophia was Theodora's niece. Justin's reign was a series of disasters, beginning in 565 when the Lombards overran northern Italy. This was followed by the loss of much of the Byzantine province in Spain to the Visigoths in 571–572, while Pannonia was invaded by the Avars, an Asian people who had migrated into south-eastern Europe. At the same time the Slavs began an invasion of Thrace, Macedonia and Greece, and ca. 590 they sacked Athens and left it in utter ruins.

Meanwhile Justin had provoked a war with Persia by refusing to pay the annual indemnity to Chosroes, who in 573 invaded Syria and captured the great Byzantine fortress at Dara. The fall of Dara unhinged Justin, and he had a nervous breakdown from which he never recovered. The empress Sophia persuaded Justin to turn over control of the government to his friend Tiberius, commander of the imperial guard, who was appointed Caesar. When Justin died in 578 Tiberius succeeded to the throne.

Tiberius ruled until his death in 582 and was succeeded by Maurice, a Cappodocian general who had commanded the army on the Persian frontier. Maurice brought the Persian War to a successful conclusion, signing a peace treaty with the new king, Chosroes II, in which much of eastern Armenia was ceded to the Byzantines. He also reorganised the remnants of Justinian's conquests in Italy and Africa to form the exarchates of Ravenna and Carthage, which became the outposts of Byzantine power in the West.

Early in the autumn of 602 the imperial army on the Danube revolted under a centurion named Phocas, who usurped the throne and beheaded Maurice and his five sons. During the next six years the Persians under Chosroes II conquered Mesopotamia, Syria and Palestine, after which they overran Asia Minor and penetrated all the way to the Bosphorus at Chalcedon, leaving death and destruction in their wake. By that time Constantinople was being torn apart by a series of riots and insurrections, all put down savagely by Phocas. At the same the Slavs and Avars overran the Balkans, while the Lombards forced the Byzantine exarch in Ravenna to cede them considerable territory in Italy, and it seemed as if the empire was on the verge of disintegrating.

When all seemed lost the empire was saved by Heraclius, the exarch of Carthage, who sent a fleet to Constantinople under his son, also named Heraclius. The fleet reached Constantinople on 3 October 610, whereupon an insurrection broke out in the city and overthrew Phocas, who was beheaded by Heraclius. Two days later Heraclius was crowned as emperor by the patriarch of Constantinople, beginning an illustrious reign that would last for thirty-one years.

Heraclius spent his long reign in almost continuous battle against the Persians and the Avars, both of whom at first continued their advances despite his efforts. The Persians captured Jerusalem in 613, slaughtering the Christian population, and two years later they overran Asia Minor, once again advancing as far as Chalcedon. By 620 the Persians occupied all of Cilicia, Mesopotamia, Syria, Palestine and Egypt, as well as most of Armenia. Meanwhile the Avars penetrated as far as the suburbs of Constantinople, but they were stopped by the great Theodosian walls and withdrew, carrying away more than a quarter of a million captives from Thrace.

The situation now seemed hopeless, and Heraclius thought of leaving Constantinople to establish his capital in Carthage. This caused panic among the people of Constantinople, and led the patriarch Sergius to have Heraclius swear that he would not abandon their city to the barbarians. Sergius then put much of the Church's wealth at the disposal of Heraclius, who used it to strengthen the imperial army in what was seen as a crusade to save the empire from being engulfed by the barbarians.

Heraclius agreed to a truce with the Avars so he could concentrate his efforts against the Persians, whom he defeated in Armenia in 622. He continued campaigning in eastern Anatolia, where in the next four years he won three more victories against the Persians. Nevertheless Chosroes II refused to come to terms, and in 626 he launched an invasion of Asia Minor that once again reached the shores of the Bosphorus at Chalcedon. At the same time Constantinople was attacked on its landward side by the Avars and their Slavic allies, who at one point almost broke through the Theodosian walls near the Golden Horn at Blachernae, where there was an ancient holy well dedicated to the Virgin. But the attackers were driven back by a miraculous appearance of the Virgin, or so said the Byzantine defenders. The siege continued through the summer, but then both the Avars and Persians ran out of supplies and withdrew under pressure from reinforcements sent by Heraclius. The populace then gave thanks to the Virgin at her holy well in Blachernae, singing a hymn composed by the patriarch Sergius – the *Akathistos* – which is still part of the Greek Orthodox liturgy, sung every year on the anniversary of the city's deliverance.

Heraclius then concentrated all of his forces on the Persian frontier, where on 12 December 626 he won a great victory over Chosroes II. Soon afterwards Chosroes was deposed and killed by his son Kavad II, who agreed to terms imposed by Heraclius, restoring the frontier between Byzantium and Persia as it had been in 602. The lost territory in Armenia, Mesopotamia, Syria, Palestine and Egypt was restored to the empire, and Heraclius was finally able to return to Constantinople in triumph.

Meanwhile a new and far more formidable power had emerged in Arabia, where the Islamic era began with the flight of the Prophet Muhammed from Mecca to Medina in 622. The armed might of Islam became evident in 636, when a Byzantine army under the emperor's brother Theodorus was virtually annihilated by the Arabs in the canyon of the river Yarmuk, south of Damascus. This opened all of Syria and Palestine to the Arabs, who captured Jerusalem in 638 and Alexandria in 641, at the beginning of their conquest of Egypt.

By this time Heraclius was a dying man, his spirit broken by the loss of all that he had fought so hard to regain. He finally passed away on 11 February 641 and was buried in the church of the Holy Apostles, along with his illustrious predecessors from Constantine to Justinian, whose empire in the East was now threatened with destruction.

11

Medieval Byzantium

Heraclius began a dynasty that lasted for more than a century, a period during which the empire stuggled to survive as invaders broke through both the eastern and western frontiers, destroying everything in their path. The long night of the Dark Ages had begun, leaving Constantinople as the last outpost of Graceo-Roman civilisation after the destruction of Rome and Athens.

The Arabs first invaded Anatolia in 641, at the beginning of the reign of Constans II, grandson of Heraclius, who was only eleven at the time. The young emperor's capable generals kept the Arabs at bay until he came of age. Then in 651 Constans himself led a successful campaign against the Arabs in Armenia and the Caucasus.

Meanwhile the Slavs had overrun the Balkans to the extent that Thrace became known as Sklavinia. The historian Theophanes notes in his chronicle for 656–657 that 'In this year the emperor made an expedition against Sklavinia, and many he captured and subjected.' Constans then resettled the Slavs in Asia Minor, where thenceforth their young men were taken into the Byzantine army.

The following year a civil war broke between the caliph Ali, son-in-law of the Prophet, and Muawija, the Arab governor of Syria. Constans took advantage of the situation to negotiate a favourable truce with Muawija, who emerged as caliph two years later after the assassination of Ali.

Constans took advantage of the truce to reorganise the army commands in Anatolia and the Aegean into districts known as *themata*,

118

or themes, a development that had begun during the reign of Heraclius and would dominate Byzantine military history for centuries to come. The Opsician Theme comprised Thrace and north-western Anatolia, including the old provinces of the Hellespont, Bithynia and Galatia. The Armeniac Theme comprised Paphlagonia, the Pontus and Armenia. The Anatolic Theme originally took in all of southern Anatolia, but in the following century its western half became the Thracesian Theme. The Anatolic Theme theme comprised western Cappadocia, Phrygia, Pisidia, Lycaonia and Cilicia Campestris (Clicia in the Plain), while the Thracesian Theme included Aeolis, Ionia, Lydia and Caria. The Carabisian Theme, which took its name from the Greek *karabis*, or ship, was a maritime district, with its capital on Samos, comprising Cilicia Tracheia (Rugged Cilicia), Pamphylia, Lycia, the Aegean isles and south-eastern Greece.

The soldiers in each of the four main themes in Anatolia received grants of land, where they supported themselves and stood in readiness to take up arms when summoned. Each of these districts was under the supreme command of a *strategos*, or general, who had his headquarters in the capital of the theme. The Opsician Theme had its capital at Ancyra, the Armeniac at Euchaita, the Anatolic at Amorium, and the Thracesian at Chonae, while the maritime Carabisian Theme a minor one, had its headquarters on Samos.

Constans was succeeded by his son Constantine IV, who was about nineteen when he came to the throne in Constantinople late in the summer of 668. Constantine spent much of his reign defending the empire against Arab invasions led by the caliph Muawija. The first of these reached the Sea of Marmara in the autumn of 670, when the Arabs established a base at Cyzicus. Two years later Muawija's forces occupied much of Cilicia and Rhodes before going on to capture Smyrna, after which the caliph began preparing for an assault against Constantinople. Constantine began building warships to reinforce his fleet, equipping them with a newly invented weapon called Greek Fire, an inflammable fluid that could be sprayed on enemy vessels.

The Arabs sailed into the Marmara with a huge fleet in the spring of 674, attacking Constantinople and ravaging the coasts around the city for six months before withdrawing to their base at Cyzicus. They renewed their assault the following spring and again in 676, when Muawija sent an army overland to Cyzicus under his son Yazid, but still they were unable to take Constantinople. Constantine had refrained from using Greek Fire because of the fear that it might destroy his own ships and men, But when the city was attacked again in 678 the Byzantines used their incendiary fluid for the first time with devastating effect, whereupon the Arab fleet and army broke off the siege and headed home.

Most of the surviving ships of the Arab fleet sank in a hurricane off the southern coast of Anatolia, while what was left of their army was virtually annihilated by a Byzantine force in Cilicia. This forced Muawija to begin negotiations for a truce, which was concluded in 679, the agreement calling on the Arabs to pay an annual tribute to the Byzantines. Two years later Muawija died and was succeeded by his son Yazid, who withdrew from Rhodes to avoid provoking the Byzantines, for he was faced with a war of succession by a descendant of Ali.

The Byzantine victory over the Arabs made a profound impression on the Slavs and Avars, both of whom sent envoys to Constantinople to pay homage to Constantine. Constantine then mounted an expedition against the Bulgars in 681, but his army was routed and he was forced to pay tribute to the Bulgar khan Asparukh.

Constantine died in July 685 and was succeeded by his son Justinian II, who was then sixteen. Two years later the young emperor led a successful campaign against the Slavs, whom he resettled in the region around Cyzicus, which had been depopulated by the Arab invasion. Justinian then broke his father's peace treaty and began a series of campaigns against the Arabs. This provoked the caliph 'Abd al-Malik, who in 694–695 made successful raids into both Cilicia and Armenia, indicating that the balance of power had shifted back to the Arabs.

Toward the end of 695 Justinian was deposed in a coup that placed the general Leontius on the throne. Leontius persuaded his supporters to spare Justinian, who had his tongue slit and his nose cut off, mutilations meant to disqualify him from ever ruling again, after which he was sent into exile in the Crimea. Justinian eventually made his way back to Constantinople in the spring of 705 and regained his throne. Justinian's second reign lasted until 711, when he was overthrown and killed by the Armenian general Philippicus Vardan, thus ending the Heracleian dynasty after 101 years.

Philippicus was the first of three ephemeral emperors who ruled in turn over the next six years, his successors being Anastasius II and Theodosius III, all three of them confined to monasteries after they were deposed.

Theodosius was deposed by the *strategos* of the Anatolic Theme, who on 25 March 717 was crowned in Haghia Sophia as Leo III, known as the Isaurian because of his supposed origin. Thus began the Isaurian dynasty, which would last until the beginning of the following century.

Meanwhile the Arabs invaded Anatolia under Maslamah, son of the late caliph 'Abd al-Malik, who appeared before Constantinople in mid-August 717 with a force said to number 120,000 men and 1,800 ships. During the particularly severe winter many of the Arabs perished from hunger and cold, leading Maslamah to lift his siege on 15 August 718, exactly a year after it began. The Arabs never again attacked Constantinople, which marked the high-water mark of their attempt to invade Europe from the East, just as Charles Martel's victory at Poitiers in 732 halted them on the West.

Leo's reign saw the beginning of the most serious religious controversy in the history of Byzantium, the Iconoclastic Crisis, which would trouble the empire for more than a century. The crisis began in 726 when Leo sent his imperial bodyguards to remove a large painting of Christ that hung over the entryway of the Great Palace, for he felt that religious images were perpetuating pagan idolatry. This provoked a riot by the iconodules, those who supported icon veneration, in which their leader and the commander of the imperial guard were killed.

Leo's iconoclastic policy led to revolts in both the army and navy, but he put them down easily. He formalised his iconoclastic policy in 730 with an edict banning religious images, which were then destroyed in all the churches and monasteries throughout the empire. At the same time he reorganised the administration of Anatolia, dividing the Anatolic Theme into two parts. He also published a revised version of the Justinianic code known as the Ecloga, which was published in Greek rather than Latin, which thenceforth became virtually a dead language in Asia Minor.

Leo died on 18 June 741 and was succeeded by his son Constantine V, who continued his father's iconoclastic policy. Constantine ruled until 775, when he died while on campaign against the Bulgars. He was succeeded by his son Leo IV, who continued his father's policy of iconoclasm. Leo's wife Eirene, an Athenian, was a devoted iconodule, but she kept this secret from her husband, who pursued his campaign against icons with a vengeance, confiscating the treasures of churches and monasteries and imprisoning monks and nuns who opposed him.

Leo died on 8 September 780 while on campaign against the Bulgars and was succeeded by his son Constantine VI. The new emperor was not yet ten, and so his mother Eirene was appointed regent. Eirene immediately set out to restore the veneration of sacred images, dismissing iconoclasts in the government and army and replacing them with iconodules. The climax of her efforts came when she convened the Seventh Ecumenical Council at Nicaea in the fall of 787, when the assembled bishops issued a decree restoring icons.

Eirene continued to act as regent until December 790, when the army in Anatolia revolted and forced her to give over power to her son, who then made her co-emperor. But Constantine's incompetence and cruelty antagonised the army, and when he repudiated his wife and remarried, the Church turned against him too.

Eirene then decided to take power into her own hands, and on 15 August 797 she had her bodyguards seize Constantine and imprison him in the Great Palace, where later that day she had him blinded so brutally that he died. Thus Eirene became sole emperor, the first woman to rule the empire in her own right.

Charlemagne, who had been crowned as emperor by Pope Leo III in 800, sent an embassy to Constantinople with a proposal of marriage to Eirene, 'and so unite the eastern and western parts' of the empire, according to Theophanes. But shortly after their arrival a palace coup overthrew Eirene, who on 31 October 802 was replaced by her former minister of finance, who took the throne as Nicephorus I. Eirene was then exiled to a convent on Lesbos, where she died soon afterwards.

Nicephorus spent most of his reign at war with the Arabs, the Slavs and the Bulgars. On his last campaign he and his son Stauricius took the field against Krum, the khan of the Bulgars, and early in the summer of 811 they captured Pliska, his capital. Then on 26 July of that same year the Byzantines fell into a trap near Adrianople and were slaughtered almost to a man, including Nicephorus, whose skull was fashioned into a silver-lined drinking mug by Krum. Stauricius was badly wounded, but he was rescued and brought back to Constantinople and acclaimed as emperor. He died of his wounds on 11 January 812, having abdicated three months before in favour of his brother-in law, Michael Rhangabe.

Michael ruled for only twenty months. On 21 June 813 he was defeated by Krum near Adrianople, after which he and his general Leo the

Armenian barely managed to make their way back to Constantinople. Michael then abdicated in favour of Leo and retired to a monastery on the Princes' Isles in the Marmara, where he died seven years later.

The new emperor was crowned as Leo V on 22 July 813. Five days before that Krum had put Constantinople under siege, but the Theodosian walls were too strong for him and he eventually withdrew, ravaging Thrace on his way home.

Leo was an iconoclast, and as soon as peace was restored he set out to renew the ban on images. He convened a synod in Haghia Sophia, and in April 815 the assembled clerics revoked the decrees of the Seventh Ecumenical Council and renewed the prohibition of icons.

On Christmas Day 820 Leo was attending services in the chapel of the Great Palace, when he was assassinated by supporters of Michael the Amorian, who was crowned that same day as Michael III. Thus began the Amorian dynasty, which was to last for nearly a century.

Michael died on 2 October 829 and was succeeded by Theophilus, who was sixteen at the time. Theophilus spent most of his reign in warfare against the Arabs, beginning with his expeditions against them in 829 and 830. After the latter campaign, which penetrated into the Arab domains in Cilicia, he strengthened the sea walls of Constantinople along the Golden Horn and the Marmara, where numerous inscriptions still bear his name.

Theophilus was an iconoclast, but like his father he was reasonably tolerant. His wife Theodora, on the other hand, was a devoted iconodule, though she had to keep her icons hidden from her husband. Theophilus died of dysentery on 20 January 842 and was succeeded by his son Michael III, who was only two at the time. The empress Theodora was appointed regent along with her brother, the Caesar Bardas, who was also an iconodule. Three years later regents convened a church synod that repealed the ban on icon veneration. A thanksgiving service was held in Haghia Sophia on 11 March 845, celebrating the return of sacred images to the churches and monasteries of Byzantium, a liturgy perpetuated in the Greek Orthodox Church as the Feast of Orthodoxy. Thus ended the Iconoclastic Period, which had riven Byzantium for more than a century.

Michael III is known as 'the Sot', for from his youth he spent his time carousing with his favourites while his mother and his uncle Bardas ran the empire. The regency ended on 11 March 856, when Michael reached the age of sixteen, whereupon he confined Theodora to a convent and appointed Bardas as prime minister and commander-in-chief of the army.

Bardas completely controlled the empire for the next decade, mounting several successful campaigns against the Arabs while he kept the Bulgars and Slavs at bay. He sparked a cultural renaissance in Byzantium by refounding the University of Constantinople, which had been closed for two and a half centuries, the Dark Ages of the Byzantine world. The leading figures in this renaissance were the theologian Photius, who became patriarch of Constantinople in 856; the mathematician Leo, whose ideas spread to the West and Islam; and the linguist Cyril, whose creation of the Slavonic script helped him and his fellow missionary Methodius convert the Slavs to Christianity.

Michael III was assassinated on 23 September 867 by Basil the Macedonian, a former groom in the royal stables who had become his favourite. The following day Basil was crowned as emperor, thus beginning the illustrious Macedonian dynasty, which was to rule Byzantium for nearly two centuries.

During the period of the Macedonian dynasty several outsiders ruled as co-emperor, either by usurping power or by becoming part of the royal family through marriage or adoption. The most notable of the usupers were two Armenian generals – Nicephorus II Phocas (r. 963–969) and then John I Tzimisces (r. 969–976) – who in turn were co-emperors with Basil II, both of them winning several notable victories over the Arabs. Basil II himself proved to be one of the great warrior emperors of Byzantium, ruling on his own in the years 976–1025, and after his crushing victories over the Bulgars he was called Bulgaroctonus, the Bulgar-Slayer, the name by which he is still known to Greeks today.

Basil was succeeded by his brother Constantine VIII, who was sixty-five when he came to the throne. Although he had been his brother's co-emperor for half a century he had played virtually no part in the governing of the empire, devoting his life exclusively to pleasure. After his death in 1028 he was succeeded in turn by three ephemeral emperors – Romanus III (r. 1028–1034), Michael IV (r. 1034–1041), and Michael V (r. 1041–1042) – who came to the throne in turn through their marriage to or adoption by his daughter Zoë. After the death of Michael V, Zoë ruled on her own for a few months before marrying Constantine IX Monomachus (r. 1042–1055).

Michael Psellus, the court chamberlain, describes the beginning of the new regime in his *Chronographia*. He writes of Constantine that 'Although he could scarcely be called an advanced student of literature, or, in any sense of the word, an orator, yet he admired men who were, and the finest speakers were invited to the imperial court from all parts of the empire, most of them very old men.'

Constantine's interests led to the re-establishment of the University of Constantinople in 1045, with faculties of philosophy and law. The faculty was presided over by Michael Psellus, who was given the title of 'consul of philosophers', while the school of legal studies was headed by John Xiphilinus, who was called 'the guardian of the law'. This was the culmination of a cultural renaissance that had been developing during the Macedonian dynasty, in which classical Greek philosophy was revived, principally by Michael Psellus, who describes his own education in this field:

> I met some of the experts in the art, and I was instructed by them how to pursue my studies in a methodical way. One passed me to another for tuition, the lesser light to the greater, and he recommended me to a third, and he to Aristotle and Plato. Doubtless my former teachers were well-satisfied to take second place to these two.

During the last year of Constantine's reign a serious dispute arose between Pope Leo I and the patriarch Michael Cerularius. The dispute reached its climax during an afternoon service in Haghia Sophia on 16 July 1054, when Cardinal Humbert, one of three papal legates, strode down the main aisle and placed a scroll on the high altar, a formal bull of excommunication against Cerularius and his supporters. Soon afterwards Cerularius convened a synod which excommunicated the three papal legates, causing a schism between the Greek Orthodox and Roman Catholic churches that continues to the present day.

Constantine outlived Zoë, who died in 1050, and when he himself died five years later he was succeeded by Zoë's sister Theodora. Theodora was about seventy-five when she began her reign. Despite her advanced years she showed few signs of age, taking full charge of the government. Nevertheless, there was full agreement among her councillors that she should appoint a man as her successor, but as long as she remained in good health she refused to do so. Toward the end of August 1056 Theodora was suddenly stricken with an abdominal illness that caused her severe pain, and it was apparent that her end was near. Her councillors then put forward their candidate for emperor, an aged civil servant named Michal Bringas, whom Theodora accepted as her successor. She died that same day, 31 August 1056, whereupon Bringas succeeded as Michael VI.

Theodora was the last of the Macedonian house, a dynasty that had ruled Byzantium for 189 years, beginning with her great-great-great grandfather Basil I. It was the end of an age in which Byzantium had been established as a great empire, its boundaries extending from Persia to Italy and from the Danube to the Aegean isles, the capital at Constantinople emerging from the darkness of the Middle Ages in a renaissance that made it a centre of classical culture in a world that had nearly descended to barbarism.

12

Seljuk Turks and Crusaders

The reign of the aged Michael VI lasted less than a year. During the spring of 1057 the general staff of the army, outraged by the criticism they had received from Michael, decided to overthrow him with one of their own number. The commander-in-chief Isaac Comnenus was the obvious choice, and the army in Anatolia proclaimed him as emperor on 8 June 1057. When news of this reached Constantinople the Senate forced Michael to abdicate, after which he fled to Haghia Sopha for sanctuary. He was then allowed to retire to a monastery, where he died soon afterwards.

Isaac Comnenus entered Constantinople at the head of his army on 1 September 1057 and received an enthusiastic welcome. Isaac immediately began a complete reform of the government, restoring the neglected armed forces of the empire. He successfully defended the empire's frontiers in both Asia and Europe, holding the Magyars at bay and leading a successful attack against the Patzinaks, a nomadic Turkic people from the south of Russia who crossed the Danube in 1059. But the expedition against the Patzinaks was to be his last campaign, for later that year he came down with pneumonia and never recovered.

During his last days Isaac considered the question of his succession, the likeliest candidate being his brother John. But the landowning military aristocracy persuaded him to pass over John and choose one of their own, Constantine Doucas. Doucas was thereupon crowned as Constantine X on 23 November 1059. Isaac then retired to a monastery, where he died the following year.

Constantine proved to be completely ineffective as an emperor. The emperor relied on the advice of his brother, the Caesar John Doucas, and his wife, the empress Eudocia Macrembolitissa, whom Psellus describes as 'a woman of great spirit and exceptional beauty'. Constantine neglected the armed forces, hiring unreliable foreign mercenaries, and he allowed the bureaucracy to become as bloated and corrupt as it had been before Isaac's reforms. Thus the government and the military were seriously weakened, and at a time when the empire was facing great danger from new and powerful enemies. The Normans under Robert Guiscard had overrun southern Italy, and the Seljuk Turks had conquered Persia and were beginning to raid deep into Anatolia.

When Constantine became seriously ill he designated his sixteen-year-old son Michael as his successor, appointing the empress Eudocia as regent. Constantine died in May 1067, whereupon his son succeeded as Michael VII, with his mother holding the title of autocrator, or senior emperor.

Eudocia ruled as regent and autocrator only until the end of the year, by which time she had arranged to marry the general Romanus Diogenes, who had been exiled by Constantine. After his return to Constantinople they were married on 1 January 1068, and that same day he was crowned as Romanus IV, junior co-emperor with Michael VII.

Romanus immediately reorganised the armed forces of the empire to take action against the Seljuks, leading expeditions against them in 1068 and 1069. Then in the summer of 1071 he set out against them with an even larger force, but on 26 August his army was virtually annihilated by the Seljuk sultan Alp Arslan at Manzikert in eastern Anatolia. Romanus was one of the few survivors and was released by Alp Arslan after promising to pay a huge ransom and a large annual tribute. But the ransom and tribute were never paid, for Romanus was deposed even before he returned to Constantinople. He was then exiled to a monastery on the Princes Isles, where he died on 4 August 1072.

Michael VII reigned only until the spring of 1078, when he was overthrown by the general Nicephorus Botaneiates. Botaneiates led his troops into Constantinople on 24 March 1078, and on that same day he was crowned in Haghia Sophia as Nicephorus III.

Botaneiates ruled for only three years before he was deposed by Alexius Comnenus, nephew of the late emperor Isaac I. Alexius was crowned as emperor in Haghia Sophia three days later, re-establishing the Comnenus dynasty. Alexius was about twenty-four when he came to the throne, while his wife Eirene, granddaughter of Caesar John Ducas, was not yet fifteen. Alexius and Eirene eventually had four sons and five daughters, their first born being Anna, who would later write the history of her father's reign in the *Alexiad*.

Alexius began his reign faced with menacing enemies on all sides. By then the Seljuks had overrun most of Anatolia, establishing a state known as the Sultanate of Rum, the latter being the Turkish for Rome, with its capital at Nicaea, Turkish Iznik. Besides the Sultanate of Rum, there were also several Türkmen *beyliks*, or emirates, contending for power in central and eastern Anatolia, the most powerful of which was the Danışmendid tribe, with branches in Sivas and Malatya.

At the same time the Normans under Robert Guiscard had invaded Greece, but Guiscard's dream of conquering Constantinople ended with his sudden death in 1085. No sooner had the Norman threat ended than new crises arose in the Balkans, and Alexius had to fight off invasions by the Patzinaks and another Turkic tribe called the Cumans. The Patzinaks besieged Constantinople in 1090, while at the same time the city was attacked from the sea by the fleet of Çaka, the Turkish emir of Smyrna. But the Byzantine navy destroyed the Turkish fleet in a blaze of Greek Fire, while Alexius defeated the Patzinak army. Alexius then entered into an alliance with the Seljuk sultan Kılıç Arslan, whom he persuaded to kill Çaka, removing a threat to both of them.

Early in 1095 Alexius sent envoys to Pope Urban II, appealing for help against the Turks who had overrun the Byzantine domains in Anatolia. That autumn, during a church council at Clermont in France, Urban called for a great expedition to free the eastern Christians from the Muslims and recapture Jerusalem.

This expedition, which came to be called the First Crusade, got underway the following year, the first contingent being a throng of peasants who arrived at Constantinople under the leadership of Peter the Hermit. Seeing that there were no professional soldiers among them, Alexius advised Peter to have his people wait in the vicinity of Nicomedia until the main crusading army arrived. But the Christian rabble went on a rampage when they arrived in Nicomedia, and they were soon slaughtered by the Turks. Those who survived were brought back across the Bosphorus by Alexius, who gave them refuge outside Constantinople.

The first of the regular armies of the crusaders arrived at Constantinople in the autumn of 1096, a contingent led by Hugh of Vermandois, brother of King Philip I of France. Three other contingents arrived during the following winter and spring, including one led by Count Bohemund of Taranto, son of the late Robert Guiscard. Alexius, after heated arguments and some violence, persuaded all of the crusader leaders to swear an oath of loyalty to him in which they vowed to restore all of the Byzantine territory they recaptured from the Turks.

The first objective of the crusaders was Nicaea, capital of the Seljuk Sultanate of Rum, which they besieged along with a Byzantine force. At the time Sultan Kılıç Arslan was in eastern Anatolia, which he was trying to take from the Danışmendid Türkmen tribe. As soon as he heard that the crusaders were threatening his capital he made a truce with the Danışmendid and rushed back to Nicaea, where he had left his wife and children and much of his treasure. By the time he arrived Nicaea was already surrounded by the crusaders, who defeated Kılıç Arslan's army and forced him to withdraw. The Turkish garrison in Nicaea then surrendered to the Byzantine commander rather than the crusaders, who had been outwitted by Alexius.

The crusaders then resumed their march across Anatolia for the Holy Land. The first section of the crusaders, commanded by Bohemund of Taranto, set out from Nicaea on 25 June, accompanied by a detachment of Byzantine troops, while the second left the following day under Raymond of St Gilles. The first stage of their march took them to Dorylaeum, where on 1 July they were ambushed by Kılıç Arslan and his Türkmen allies. The Turks surrounded Bohemund's troops and rained arrows upon them, putting the crusaders in a perilous position. But then at midday the second section of the crusader army under Raymond arrived to relieve Bohemund's beleagured troops, forcing Kılıç Arslan to withdraw his forces.

Kılıç Arslan by now realised that the Turks were no match for the more numerous and better armed crusaders, and he gave up active resistance, other than ordering that the Christians be harried and that their route across Anatolia be stripped of supplies.

The crusaders went on to capture Antioch, Edessa and Jerusalem, all three of which became capitals of Latin principalities. Godfrey of Bouillon was elected king of Jerusalem, and when he died on 18 July 1100 he was succeeded by his brother Baldwin. Raymond of Toulouse established himself as count of Edessa, and Bohemund of Taranto became count of Antioch. Meanwhile Kılıç Arslan established his headquarters at Iconium, Turkish Konya, where he was in a better position to contend for power in central and eastern Anatolia.

Pope Urban II died on 29 July 1099 and was succeeded by Paschal II, who continued the crusading policy of his predecessor. As a result of his appeals a new wave of crusaders began arriving in Constantinople early in 1101. The first to reach the capital were 20,000 Lombards. They were followed by two successive contingents of French knights, the second commanded by Count William of Nevers. The last was an enormous Franco-German force headed by William, Duke of Aquitaine, and Welf, Duke of Bavaria. All three contingents were ambushed and cut to pieces by the Seljuks and their Danışmendid allies as they marched across Anatolia, and thus the crusade of 1101 ended in disaster for the Christian cause.

Alexius spent the last two years of his reign campaigning against the Turks in Anatolia. His last campaign was a victorious expedition in western Anatolia against the Seljuk sultan Ruknuddin Mesut I in 1115. After Alexius returned to Constantinople following this campaign his health steadily declined, and he finally passed away on 15 August 1118, after thirty-seven years of rule, one of the longest and most illustrious reigns in the history of the Byzantine Empire.

Alexius was succeeded by his eldest son John II, who was nearly thirty-one at the time of his accession. John's first campaign was in 1119, when he cleared the Turks from Ionia, Lydia and Pamphylia. Then in the years 1121–1122 he defeated the Patzinaks, who thenceforth supplied troops to the imperial army.

John fought a war against Venice in the years 1122–1125, and in 1129 he defeated King Stephen II of Hungary. He then turned his attention eastward once again, leading campaigns against the Turks almost annually in the years 1130–1141, in which he reconquered the entire Black Sea coast of Anatolia from the Seljuks and Danışmendid. He set off in the spring of 1142 on a campaign to recapture Antioch from the Latin crusaders, spending the winter in Cilicia, where he reduced a number of Danışmendid fortresses. He was preparing to resume his march again the following spring when he was accidentally wounded by an arrow while hunting. The wound became badly infected and John passed away on 8

April 1143. The chronicler Nicetas Choniates writes that 'he was the crowning glory...of the Komnenian dynasty to sit on the Roman throne, and...that he equaled some of the best emperors of the past and surpassed the others.'

John was succeeded by his son Manuel, who was crowned in Haghia Sophia on 28 November 1143. Manuel's first campaign was against the Latins of Antioch, whom he defeated in 1144, forcing them to return several fortresses in Cilicia that they had taken when his father died. The Latins were now so weak that Edessa fell to the Seljuks, who put all the Christian men to the sword and enslaved the women and children. The fall of Edessa made a profound impression on western Europe, leading Pope Eugenius III to proclaim the Second Crusade in 1146.

One contingent of crusaders set out from Germany under King Conrad III, while a second left France led by King Louis VII, both of them planning to pass through Constantinople en route to the Holy Land. Conrad's army, the first to arrive, was decimated by the Seljuks at Dorylaeum, though he himself escaped and made his way back to Nicaea. King Louis led his army across Anatolia to Attaleia, where the Byzantine governor provided ships to take them to the port of Antioch. Louis decided to attack Damascus before going on to liberate Edessa. They reached Damascus on 24 July 1148, but after four days of heavy fighting they were forced to retreat, harried along the way by Türkmen cavalry. The failure of the expedition against Damascus was a great humiliation for the western knights, demoralising them to the extent that they abandoned the expedition. Thus the Second Crusade ended in a total fiasco, leaving the Seljuks in possession of Edessa.

Meanwhile Manuel was fighting against the Seljuks in Anatolia as well as leading campaigns in Europe against the Serbs, Hungarians, Normans and Venetians.

The conflict with Venice began on 12 March 1171, when Manuel evicted the Venetian merchants from Constantinople, where for nearly a century they had occupied a quarter on the shore of the Golden Horn adjacent to those of the Genoese and Pisans. The Venetians retaliated by sending their fleet to attack Byzantine ports in the Aegean, and in addition they formed alliances with the Germans and Normans against the Byzantines. An armed truce followed, but for the remainder of Manuel's reign all diplomatic relations between Byzantium and Venice were broken off. The alienation between Greek East and Latin West grew apace, with all of Roman Catholic Europe allied against the schismatic Byzantines, who on their part were contemptuous of the only recently civilised westerners and their upstart rulers. According to Nicetas Choniates: 'The accursed Latins...lust after our possessions and would like to destroy our race...between them and us there is a wide gulf of hatred, our outlooks are completely different, and our paths grow in opposite directions.'

Manuel's last diplomatic effort in the West was to arrange the betrothal of his son Alexius to Princess Agnes of France, daughter of Louis VII. The little princess, who was barely eight years old when she left France, took the name of Anna when she was married to the twelve-year-old Alexius in Haghia Sophia on 2 March 1180.

Manuel was at the time suffering through his last illness and had retired to the monastery of the Pantocrator, where he died on 24 September 1180. Manuel was succeeded by his son Alexius II, whose mother Maria of Antioch was appointed regent. Maria gave all the highest positions in her court to Latins, which made her extremely unpopular among the people of Constantinople, commoners and aristocracy alike, who referred to her contemptuously as Xena, 'the Foreigner'. This led them to give their support to Andronicus Comnenus, a nephew of John II who had been exiled by Manuel.

At the time of Manuel's death Andronicus was about sixty-five, living in retirement on his estate in Paphlagonia. Andronicus mustered his supporters and marched on Constantinople in the early spring of 1182, pausing when he reached the Bosphorus. He sent his troops across the strait into Constantinople, where they were joined by the townspeople in a general massacre of the Latins, after which he himself entered the city and took control. The empress Maria was convicted of treason and confined to a convent, where soon afterwards she was secretly drowned.

Andronicus declared himself regent for Alexius II, and in September 1182 he was crowned as co-emperor. Shortly afterwards Andronicus had Alexius strangled, leaving the empress Anna a widow at the age of eleven. Toward the end of the year Andronicus married Anna, though they differed in age by more than half a century, scandalising both Byzantium and western Europe.

Andronicus soon began a reign of terror, executing anyone he thought might be a threat to the throne. At the same time the empire came under attack by the Seljuks, the Hungarians and the Normans, who invaded Greece. The Normans took Thessalonica in the summer of 1185 and then advanced on Constantinople. The populace panicked at the approach of the Latins and castigated Andronicus for not making adequate preparations for defending the city.

The emperor responded by arresting all of his opponents and condemning them to death. Among them was a distant relative of the Comneni named Isaac Angelus, who escaped from his captors and took refuge in Haghia Sophia, where he called on the populace for support. They responded enthusiastically to his call, and on 12 September 1185 he was raised to the throne as Isaac II.

Andronicus fled, but he was captured and imprisoned in a tower of the Blachernae Palace. Soon afterwards he was dragged from his prison and paraded through the streets of the city riding backwards on a camel, which brought him to the Hippodrome. There he was mutilated and then hacked to death, his body left to rot for days afterwards, until his remains were finally flung into the sea. Thus ended the dynasty of the Comneni, who had ruled brilliantly over Byzantium for more than a century.

When Isaac II Angelus came to the throne the Normans were marching on Constantinople. But within a year he defeated the invaders and drove them back to Italy, where they had established a kingdom in the southern end of the peninsula, as well as in Sicily. Isaac was thirty years old when he became emperor, a widower with two daughters and a son, the future Alexius IV. His daughter Eirene was married in 1192 to King Roger of Sicily, who died eighteen months after their wedding. Then in 1197 Eirene was married to Philip of Swabia, brother of the German emperor Henry VI.

Ten years after Isaac came to the throne he had to deal with the onset of the Third Crusade. The Germans under Frederick I Barbarossa passed through Constantinople without incident, while the other crusaders travelled by sea to the southern shore of Anatolia and thence to the Holy Land. Barbarossa never reached the Holy Land, for on 10 June 1190 he drowned while fording the Calycadnus river above Seleucia on the Mediterranean coast.

Meanwhile Isaac had to deal with the Seljuks in Anatolia, keeping them at bay while in the Balkans he fought against the Bulgars, Serbs, Cumans and Vlachs, a Latin-speaking people from Dacia. The Vlachs and Bulgars defeated imperial armies in 1190 and again in 1194, after which

Isaac himself took the field against them. But while he was on campaign during the summer of 1195 his older brother Alexius staged a coup in the camp and took him prisoner, after which he was blinded. When they returned to Constantinople, Isaac was imprisoned in a tower of the Blachernae Palace, along with his son Alexius, while his brother had himself crowned as Alexius III.

During the first five years of his reign Alexius personally led several campaigns, fighting against the Seljuks in Anatolia and the Vlachs in the Balkans. While on campaign against the Vlachs in 1201 the emperor was accompanied by his young nephew Alexius, whom he had released from prison. Alexius took the opportunity to escape from his uncle and took refuge with his sister Eirene and her husband, Philip of Swabia, after which he began making appeals in the West to have his father Isaac II restored to the throne of Byzantium.

Pope Innocent III succeeded to the papal throne in January 1198, and in August he issued an encyclical calling for a Fourth Crusade. The nucleus of an expeditionary force came into being in November 1199, when a number of French nobles took the Cross, most notably Count Baldwin of Flanders. Envoys of the French counts went to Venice to arrange with Doge Enrico Dandolo and his council for ships to transport the crusaders overseas. The Venetians set a price for the transports they would supply, also contributing fifty of their own warships fully manned, on the condition that Venice would share fully with the crusader in any conquests made on the campaign. After the return of the envoys a council was held at Soissons, where the marquis Boniface of Montferrat was chosen to lead the crusade.

When the crusaders finally mustered their forces in Italy they had only some 11,000 fighting men, about a third of the number that they had expected. They were thus unable to pay the Venetians the sum that they had agreed upon, and at first it looked as if the expedition would be aborted. But Doge Dandolo struck a deal with them, in which Venice would defer payment of the remaining passage money if the crusaders helped them recapture the Dalmatian city of Zara, which had defected to the Hungarians. The knights agreed, whereupon they embarked at Venice on 8 September 1202, bound for Zara.

The fleet reached Zara on 10 November and attacked the city, which surrendered after a two-week siege. The garrison and populace were unharmed, but the crusaders stripped the city of all of its movable possessions. It was then too late in the season to sail on to the Aegean, so the expedition wintered in Zara.

Boniface joined the crusaders at Zara in mid-December. Two weeks later envoys arrived with a message from Alexius Angelus, who promised that if the expedition restored his father Isaac to the throne he would agree to a union of the Greek and Roman churches under the papacy. Moreover he would give a huge sum of money to the crusaders, as well as paying their expenses for an additional year. The crusader leaders accepted the offer, and Doge Dandolo agreed to divert the expedition to Constantinople.

The Latin fleet finally reached the Bosphorus on 24 June 1203, forcing their way into the Golden Horn and landing in Galata. Then on 17 July they broke through the sea walls along the Golden Horn and occupied Constantinople, burning down the whole neighbourhood on the slopes of the Fifth Hill in their attack. As soon as night fell Alexius III escaped from the city, taking with him 10,000 gold pieces and the crown jewels. That same night the blind Isaac II was released from his prison tower and restored to the throne. Isaac pledged to honour all promises that had been made to the Latins by his son, who was raised to the throne as Alexius IV and crowned as co-emperor in Haghia Sophia on 1 August 1203. The Latins then withdrew their troops from the city, encamping outside the land walls by the Blachernae Palace.

Alexius soon became very unpopular in Constantinople, for he spent all of his time carousing with the Latins who had placed him on the throne. The Latins were losing patience with him too, for he was unable to make good on the extravagant promises he had made to them, so they began seizing gold and silver objects from the churches of the city. This led to a riot on 19 August, when a mob stormed the Latin quarter on the Golden Horn, starting a fire that spread as far as the summit of the First Hill and damaged the porch of Haghia Sophia.

An opposition movement developed under the leadership of Alexius Doucas, known as Murtzuphlus, a great-great-grandson of Alexius I Comnenus. The supporters of Murtzuphlus raised him to the throne as Alexius V on 2 February 1204, having imprisoned Alexius IV, who was soon afterwards strangled, his father Isaac II having in the meantime passed away.

As soon as Murtzuphlus was in full control of the city he ordered the crusaders to clear out of his territory within a week, after which he began making preparations to defend the city against a renewed Latin assault.

The Latins began their attack on 9 April 1204 by trying to break through the land walls outside the Blachernae Palace above the Golden Horn, where they were unable to breach the defences. Three days later the Latin fleet attacked the sea walls along the Golden Horn, where the knights established a beachhead at the foot of the Fifth Hill, setting a fire that destroyed most of the buildings along the shore. Murtzuphlus fled from the city under cover of darkness on 13 April, whereupon his troops surrendered and opened the gates of the city to the Latins.

The Latins then proceeded to sack Constantinople for three days, in an orgy of killing, rape and plunder that left some 2,000 Greeks dead and much of the city in ruins, Haghia Sophia and all of its other churches stripped of their treasures and profaned by the crusaders. Nicetas Choniates describes the hellish scenes that he witnessed as he fled from the ruined city with his family and other refugees, in what seemed to be the final destruction of Byzantium:

> There were lamentations and cries of woe and weeping in the narrow ways, wailing at the crossroads, moaning in the temples, outcries of men, and the dragging about, tearing in pieces, and raping of bodies... Thus it was in the temples, thus in hiding places; for there was no place that could offer asylum to those who came streaming in... Thus it was that Constantine's fair city, the common delight and boast of all nations, was laid waste by fire and blackened by soot, taken and emptied of all wealth, public and private, as that which was consecrated to God by the scattered nations of the West.

Constantinople had fallen to Christian crusaders, who then abandoned their crusade to occupy the God-guarded city they had just sacked and ruined.

13

The Latin Occupation

After their conquest of Constantinople, the Latin leaders met on 9 May 1204 to elect a ruler for their realm, which they called Romania, the 'Empire of the Romans'. Twelve electors were chosen, six of them crusaders, the others Venetians. The first vote was nine votes for Baldwin of Flanders and three for Boniface of Montferrat. Boniface's supporters thereupon gave their support to Baldwin, who was thus unanimously elected on the second ballot. A week later Baldwin was crowned as emperor in Haghia Sophia. Boniface was then given Thessalonica, which became the capital of his kingdom.

The share of Venice included Haghia Sophia, and so Doge Dandolo appointed the Venetian noble Thomas Morosini to be the Latin patriarch of Constantinople, a choice that was eventually confirmed by Pope Innocent III.

Most of the Greek clergy either refused to recognise Morosini or fled to Nicaea, where a fragment of the Byzantine Empire was now developing in exile. This was one of two Byzantine states that emerged in Anatolia after the fall of Constantinople in 1204, the other being the Empire of Trebizond. The Empire of Nicaea was founded by Theodore Lascaris, son-in-law of Alexius III Angelus, who was crowned emperor in 1205. The Empire of Trebizond was established by two grandsons of Andronicus Comnenus, the brothers Alexius and David Comnenus, aided by their aunt, the Georgian queen Thamar. Alexius declared himself emperor in 1204, while David was given the title of Duke and took command of the army, ruling the western part of the empire.

Meanwhile, two deposed Byzantine emperors had managed to create small states in Thrace. Alexius III Angelus was at Mosynopolis on the Aegean coast, from where he controlled Western Thrace. Alexius V Doucas Murtzuphlus was at Tzurulum (Çorlu), between Constantinople and Adrianople, giving him a precarious foothold in Eastern Thrace. Soon after his election the emperor Baldwin launched an expedition against Murtzuphlus. Murtzuphlus fled to Mosynopolis and formed an alliance with Alexius III, who gave him his daughter Eudocia in marriage. But Alexius soon blinded his ally to eliminate him as a rival. Baldwin then captured Murtzuphlus, who was sent back to Constantinople and executed. Meanwhile King Boniface of Thessalonica captured Alexius III, who later ransomed him to Michael I Doucas of Epirus, the deposed emperor's cousin.

Late in 1204 the emperor Baldwin mounted an expedition into north-western Anatolia under the command of his brother, Henry of Hainault. Theodore Lascaris quickly mustered a force to oppose Henry, but his army suffered two successive defeats at the hands of the Latins, first at Poemanenum in December 1204, and then near Adramyttium (Edremit) in March 1205.

The Latins then prepared to attack Nicaea, but the Bulgar tsar Kaloyan invaded Thrace and Baldwin had to move his army across to Europe to meet the threat.

The Bulgars decisively defeated the Latins near Adrianople on 14 April 1206, capturing Baldwin, who died in prison soon afterward. As a result, the Latins had to abandon all the territory they had taken in north-western Anatolia, which reverted to the Byzantine Empire in Nicaea. Baldwin's brother Henry served as regent until 20 August 1206, when he was crowned emperor of Romania in Haghia Sophia by the Latin patriarch Thomas Morosini.

Henry then allied himself with David Comnenus against Theodore Lascaris. When Theodore was marching against David's headquarters in Heracleia Pontica, Henry attacked him from the rear, forcing him to turn back and fight against the Latins. During the winter of 1206–1207 Henry invaded Theodore's territory again, capturing Nicomedia and Cyzicus. Theodore retaliated by persuading Tsar Kaloyan to attack Adrianople.

This forced Henry to sign a truce with Theodore and give up Nicomedia and Cyzicus.

Theodore signed a non-aggression pact in 1206 with the Seljuk sultan Keyhüsrev, although neither party was committed to a long-term peace. A series of multiple conflicts then broke out in Anatolia, the first of them involving the empires of Nicaea and Trebizond contending with one another for territory along the Black Sea coast. At the same time Manuel Mavrozomes, the Greek father-in-law of Sultan Keyhüsrev, was trying to establish his own kingdom with Turkish help.

Theodore Lascaris won the first phase of this three-sided conflict, prevailing in turn over the forces of Manuel Mavrozomes and David Comnenus, who was aided by Latin troops from Constantinople. Theodore then forced David to come to terms, limiting his westward expansion to Heracleia Pontica, which thereafter marked the boundary on the Black Sea coast between the Byzantine empires of Trebizond and Nicaea.

Meanwhile Keyhüsrev attacked the Mediterranean port town of Attaleia, known to the Turks as Antalya, which he finally captured in March 1207. This gave the Seljuks a port on the Mediterranean, which they would soon exploit to make the Turks a sea power.

Two years later the deposed Alexius III Angelus suddenly reappeared on the political scene. After being ransomed by his cousin Michael I Doucas, Alexius made his way to Konya in the hope that Sultan Keyhüsrev could help him regain his throne. Keyhüsrev welcomed Alexius, whom he thought would be of great advantage to him in his struggle with Theodore Lascaris, the deposed emperor's son-in-law.

That same year Henry of Hainault entered into an alliance with Sultan Keyhüsrev, in which they agreed to take joint action against their common enemy, Theodore Lascaris. As part of the agreement, a detachment of Latin troops was sent to Konya, where they joined the sultan's forces in preparation for the coming campaign.

Keyhüsrev invaded Nicaean territory in 1211, ostensibly to overthrow Theodore Lascaris and replace him with Alexius, who accompanied the sultan on the campaign. Theodore defeated and killed Keyhüsrev in a battle near Philadelphia, after which the Seljuk army fled from the field. Alexius was left behind by the Turks and captured by Theodore, who brought his father-in-law back to Nicaea and had him confined to a monastery for the rest of his days.

Keyhüsrev left three sons: Izzeddin Keykavus, Alaeddin Keykubad and Keyferidun Ibrahim, all of whom contested the throne. The struggle was eventually won by the eldest, Keykavus, who imprisoned his brothers in remote fortresses when he succeeded to the throne.

As soon as Keykavus was established in Konya as sole ruler of the Sultanate of Rum, he agreed to a truce with Theodore Lascaris. Keykavus then signed a commercial treaty with Hugh I, the Lusignan king of Cyprus, which allowed the Seljuks to develop Antalya as a port for Mediterranean commerce, linking it up with the caravan trade in Asia.

Meanwhile the Latin emperor Henry invaded Nicaean territory and defeated Theodore's forces, occupying the north-western corner of Anatolia. A peace treaty was signed in 1212, leaving the Latins in control of the coast from Edremit on the Aegean to Izmit on the Sea of Marmara and Daphnusia on the Black Sea, extending as far inland as Achyracus (Balıkesir), with the Empire of Nicaea holding the territory south and east of that to the borders of the Sultanate of Rum.

After recovering from his defeat by the Latins, Theodore went to war with David Comnenus. The war ended when Theodore captured Heracleia Pontica, David's headquarters, forcing him to flee to Sinop.

Keykavus then attacked Sinop, defeating and killing David in a battle outside the city. Alexius Comnenus hastened from Trebizond to relieve the defenders in Sinop, but he was captured by the local Türkmen. Alexius, to regain his liberty, had to surrender Sinop to Keykavus and agree to become the sultan's vassal. This deflated the claim of Alexius to be the true Byzantine emperor, and thenceforth the Empire of Trebizond had little more than local significance.

The capture of Sinop now gave the Seljuks a port on the Black Sea. Keykavus invited merchants from elsewhere in Anatolia to resettle in Sinop, rebuilding its defence walls and harbour installations. Sinop then became the main base of the Seljuk fleet on the Black Sea, as well as the principal port for Turkish trade with the Crimea. This, together with the new Seljuk port at Antalya, opened up the Sultanate of Rum to trade from both the north and the south, greatly increasing its economic potential.

Keykavus died in 1220 and was succeeded by his brother Alaeddin Keykubad, who was released from his place of confinement and returned to Konya. (Keyferidun Ibrahim, the third son of Keyhüsrev, had died in the meantime.)

Theodore Lascaris died in the autumn of 1221, and since he had no son he was succeeded by his son-in-law John III Doucas Vatatzes. The following year Alexius Comnenus of Trebizond died, to be succeeded by his son-in-law, Andronicus Gidus Comnenus. Thus within two years there was a complete change of characters in the endless drama of Anatolian history, which was soon to enter a new phase.

John Vatatzes began his reign by moving his headquarters from Nicaea to Nymphaeum, south-east of Smyrna, hoping thus to keep out of the way of the Latins in Constantinople. John then turned his attention to his eastern frontier, where the Seljuks under Sultan Alaeddin Keykubad were raiding in the upper Maeander valley.

During the first year of his reign Keykubad captured Kalonoros, the enormous rocky promontory on the Mediterranean coast of Pamphylia, which had previously been held by the Armenians and before them by the Byzantines. The town was then renamed Alaiye (Alanya), after Alaeddin Keykubad, who soon afterwards erected the magnificent fortress that still crowns the heights of the promontory. Keykubad built the harbour works that can still be seen in Alanya, most notably the *tershane*, or naval arsenal, and the adjoining *tophane*, or armoury. Thus the Seljuks of Rum became a major naval power, their warships guarding their maritime commerce and extending Turkish influence around the shores of the eastern Mediterranean as well as the Black Sea. As a result, Keykubad now called himself 'Sultan of the Two Seas'.

Keykubad died at the end of May 1237 and was succeeded by his son Giyaseddin Keyhüsrev II. Keyhüsrev came to the throne just as the Mongols swarmed out of Central Asia, riding westward in an invasion that took them through Russia and into Poland, Bohemia, Moravia, Croatia, Bulgaria and the lands north of the Black Sea. The destruction and slaughter were so widespread that an anonymous chronicler of the time wrote that 'No eye remained open to weep for the dead.'

The Mongols then moved down into the great grazing lands of Azerbaijan, from where they could threaten the Caucasus, Anatolia, Mesopotamia and Syria. In 1239 the Mongol commander Chormaghan invaded and sacked Kars and Ani, the ancient Armenian capital, slaughtering the entire population of both cities. Then in the winter of

1242–1243 one Mongol army invaded Upper Mesopotamia, while another under the commander Bayju captured Erzurum, opening the way into eastern Anatolia.

When news of the fall of Erzurum reached Keyhüsrev he marshalled his forces at Sivas, summoning all his vassals, Christian and Muslim, to send him troops, including the emperor John Vatatzes of Nicaea. Keyhüsrev managed to muster about 80,000 troops, including about 3,000 Greeks and Latins, giving the overall command to the Georgian prince Shervashidze. The sultan then marched his army to the mountain pass of Kösedağ, some sixty miles north of Erzincan.

The Mongol army under Bayju, reinforced by Georgian and Armenian mercenaries, was somewhat smaller than the Seljuk force, but it made up for its fewer numbers by its greater discipline and experience and its far better leadership. The two armies collided on the morning of 26 June 1243 at Kösedağ, where the Mongols defeated the vanguard of the Seljuk army, killing Prince Shervashidze. Keyhüsrev fled in panic with the rest of the Seljuk army, leaving their camp with the tents of the sultan and other notables to be plundered by the Mongols.

After Bayju's victory he marched the Mongol army to Sivas, which surrendered without a struggle. The Mongols looted the city, but they did not destroy it or massacre its inhabitants. Tokat and Kayseri, on the other hand, tried to resist, and as a result they were brutally sacked and their inhabitants put to the sword.

Meanwhile Keyhüsrev had collected his treasure in Tokat and escaped to Ankara, sending his mother to take refuge with King Hethoum of Cilicia, who promptly handed her over to the Mongols. Keyhüsrev then finally made his way back to Konya, his sultanate a shambles, as the Türkmen tribes ran rampant through central and eastern Anatolia. Soon afterwards the sultan's vezir Muhadhdhab al-Din, on his own initiative, concluded a peace agreement with the Mongol chieftain Jurmaghan on condition that the Seljuks become vassals of the Mongols and pay an annual tribute in gold and silver.

The Mongol invasion relieved the pressure on the Nicaean emperor John Vatatzes, for the Seljuks were now reduced to vassalage and could no longer attack his eastern frontier. Vatatzes then secured his western frontier in 1244 by renewing a yearly truce with the Latins and that same year he married the princess Constance, daughter of the German emperor

Frederick II. The bride, who was only eleven or twelve, changed her name to Anna when the wedding was held in Nicaea. At the wedding party the court poet Nicolaus Irenikos recited a long *epithalamium*, or nuptial poem, a fragment of which may be roughly translated thus:

> Around the lovely cypress, the ivy gently windeth;
> The Empress is the cypress-tree, my Emperor is the ivy.
> Here in the world's wide garden-ground, he reaches from the centre,
> His tendrils softly encompassing the plenteous trees and herbage,
> And holds them flourishing and fair, and crowns them with his glory.
> The trees he grasps are cities great and lands and people many.
> Around the lovely cypress-tree, the ivy gently windeth,
> The Empress is the cypress-tree, my Emperor is the ivy.

Keyhüsrev died early in 1246. He left behind three young sons, who were raised to the throne as a triumvirate. These were Izzeddin Keykavus II, aged eleven, son of the daughter of a Greek priest; Ruknuddin Kılıç Arslan IV, aged nine, son of a Turkish woman of Konya; and Alaeddin Keykubad II, aged seven, whose mother was a daughter of the Georgian queen Russudan.

A three-sided struggle then took place as the advisors of the three young co-sultans strove for supremacy. The struggle was finally won by the emir Celaleddin Karatay, the *naib* or chief advisor of Izzeddin Keykavus, who in June 1249 reorganised the Sultanate of Rum as a triumvirate of the three co-sultans, with Izzeddin ruling at the capital in Konya, he himself holding the real power behind the throne with the title of *atabeg*.

John III Vatatzes died on 30 October 1254 in his palace at Nymphaeum, where he was buried on 4 November. Known in his time as 'John the Merciful', he was canonised as a saint in the Greek Orthodox Church. His memory was revered each year on 4 November by the clergy and people in the region around Nymphaeum, a custom that continued up until 1923, when the Greeks were expelled from Anatolia.

John was succeeded by his son Theodore II Lascaris, who was about thirty-three when he came to the throne. Theodore was a highly cultivated man and had studied with Nicephorus Blemmydes and George Acropolites, two of the most renowned scholars of the Nicaean Empire, which flowered in a cultural renaissance under the Lascarid dynasty.

Soon after he came to the throne Theodore came into conflict with Michael Palaeologus, a general and high government official whom he suspected of having designs on the throne. Michael was put on trial for treason, which led him to flee to Konya, where in the summer of 1256 he was given refuge by Izzeddin Keykavus. The sultan appointed Michael to a military command, his troops being exclusively Anatolian Greeks and other Christians.

Soon afterwards news came that Bayju had begun another Mongol incursion into Anatolia. Izzeddin Keykavus mustered an army under the command of a Seljuk vezir, reinforced by Michael Palaeologus and his contingent of Christian troops.

Bayju penetrated quickly into eastern Anatolia, where all the cities submitted to him without a struggle. He came up against the Seljuk forces south of Aksaray and defeated them decisively with little effort, for many of them were so terrified of the Mongols that they fled from the field. The Seljuk vezir was killed and Michael Palaeologus fled for his life, finding refuge with a Türkmen ally in Kastamonu before eventually making his way back to Nicaea.

Their defeat at the hands of Bayju sealed the fate of the Seljuks, and although the sultanate continued nominally for another half century it had little more than symbolic importance. The Turkish chronicler Karim al-Din Mahmud, reflecting on the demise of the Seljuk Sultanate of Rum, remarked that 'thorns replaced the rose in the gardens of excellence and prosperity, and the period of justice and security in the kingdom came to an end'.

Meanwhile there had been a change of regime in the Empire of Nicaea, where Theodore II Lascaris died on 16 August 1258, to be succeeded by his son John, who was only seven and a half years old. Just before he died Theodore appointed George Muzalon, his prime minister, to act as regent for his son. But nine days later the nobles of Nicaea assassinated Muzalon and replaced him as regent with Michael Palaeologus, their acknowledged leader. Three months later Michael was given the royal title of despot, and then in December he was proclaimed co-emperor. Early the following year the patriarch Arsenius performed the double coronation of Michael VIII Palaeologus and John IV Lascaris. Michael was crowned first, for there was no doubt in anyone's mind that he was the senior emperor, and the young John soon disappeared from sight as a virtual prisoner of his co-ruler.

The following year Michael's brother John won a decisive victory against a coalition of Latin forces at Pelagonia in northern Greece. Soon afterwards Michael's general Alexius Strategopoulus overran most of Epirus, forcing the despot John Doucas to flee to Cephalonia. Michael himself tried to take Constantinople in the spring of 1260, but after an unsuccessful attack on Galata he made a year's truce with the emperor Baldwin.

Michael then sought the aid of the Genoese in recapturing Constantinople, and on 31 March 1261 he signed a treaty with them at Nymphaeum, the second capital of the Nicaean Empire. The treaty gave the Genoese extensive commercial privileges in return for their support, particularly against Venice, whose powerful fleet was protecting the Latins in Constantinople. The privileges included Genoese control of Smyrna, the most important port by far on the Aegean coast of Anatolia.

Michael was on campaign in Greece in the summer of 1261, when he sent a small force under Alexius Strategopoulus to reconnoitre the environs of Constantinople. When Strategopoulus reached Selembria (Silivri) he was told that Constantinople was virtually undefended, since the Venetian fleet had left with most of the Latin garrison on a raid in the Black Sea.

Strategopoulus approached the city under the cover of night, and some of his men made their way through a secret passageway under the walls by the Gate of the Pege. They surprised the guards inside the gate, which they forced open to allow their comrades in before the alarm was raised. Early the following day, 25 July 1262, Strategeopoulus gained control of the city after some street fighting with the remnants of the Latin garrison. The noise awakened the emperor Baldwin II, who had been sleeping in the Blachernae Palace by the land walls near the Golden Horn, whereupon he quickly boarded a Venetian ship in the port and ordered it to sail away at once.

Strategopoulus, encouraged by the Greek populace, set fire to the buildings in the Latin quarter on the Golden Horn. When the Venetian fleet returned from the Black Sea the mariners found their families milling about on the shore of the Golden Horn 'like smoked out bees', according to an anonymous chronicler. All that the Venetians could do was load their families aboard their fleet and sail away, ending the Latin occupation of Constantinople.

The emperor Michael Palaeologus was in Greece when the great news arrived, whereupon he immediately struck camp and headed for Constantinople. He arrived at the walls of the city on 14 August and made his triumphal entry into Constantinople the next day, the Feast of the Assumption of the Virgin. The procession ended at Haghia Sophia, where Michael escorted the patriarch Arsenius to the patriarchal throne, a scene described by George Acropolites.

> The emperor entered the holy building, the temple of Divine Wisdom, in order that he might hand over the cathedra to the prelate. And finally there assembled with the emperor all the notables of the archons and the entire multitude. Then the emperor, taking the arm of the patriarch, said, 'Take your throne now, O lord, and enjoy it, that of which you were so long deprived.'

A service of thanksgiving was then held to mark the restoration of Byzantium to its ancient capital on the Bosphorus, after an exile that had lasted for fifty-seven years.

14

The Sons of Osman

After his triumphal return to Constantinople, Michael VIII Palaeologus was crowned once again in Haghia Sophia, with his wife Theodora enthroned as empress. At the same time their two-year-old son Andronicus was crowned as co-emperor and proclaimed as heir presumptive to the throne.

The legitimate emperor, the eleven-year-old John IV Lascaris, was not present at the ceremony, for Michael had left him behind in Nicaea. A few months later Michael had John blinded and confined to the fortress of Dakibyze on the Gulf of Nicomedia, where he seems to have remained for the rest of his days, unmentioned by any contemporary chroniclers.

Michael's first task after retaking Constantinople was the rebuilding and repeopling of the city, which had been left in ruins by the Latins and abandoned by many of its former residents.

The restored Byzantine Empire was only a small fraction of what it had been in the days of Justinian, and the enormous effort of restoring Constantinople brought the state to near bankruptcy. This eventually led Michael to reduce the Byzantine armed forces and merchant navy as an economy measure, relying on the Genoese to carry the empire's maritime commerce. The Genoese were allotted land across the Golden Horn from Constantinople in Galata, where they established an automous city-state governed by a podesta sent out each year by Genoa. The Genoese were forbidden to fortify their city, but they did so anyway, building defence walls that radiated down to the Golden

Horn and the Bosphorus from a huge hilltop bastion known as the Galata Tower.

Michael died on 11 December 1282 while on campaign in Thrace. He was succeeded by his son Andronicus II, who was twenty-three at the time, having been co-emperor for twenty-one years. Andronicus had been married at the age of thirteen to the Princess Anna of Hungary, who bore him two sons, Michael and Constantine. Andronicus had his eldest son crowned on 21 May 1294 as Michael IX, who ruled as co-emperor with his father until his death in 1320. The year after he became co-emperor Michael married the Princess Rita of Armenia, who then changed her name to Maria. Maria bore Michael two sons and two daughters, the oldest boy being the future Andronicus III, who succeeded as sole emperor on the death of his grandfather Andronicus II in 1328.

Giyassedin Mesut II, eldest son of Izzeddin Keykavus II was murdered in Kayseri in 1305. He was apparently the last Seljuk sultan, for by then the Sultanate of Rum had ceased to exist even as a puppet state of the Mongols.

The Mongol occupation was for the most part confined to eastern and central Anatolia, and thus it had much less of an effect on the western part of Asia Minor, where the Byzantine Empire was bordered by a number of Türkmen *beliks*, or emirates. The smallest and least significant of these *beliks* was that of the Osmanlı, the 'Sons of Osman', the Turkish name for the followers of Osman Gazi, whose last name means 'warrior for the Islamic faith'. Osman was known in English as Othman, and his dynasty came to be called the Ottomans. He was the son of Ertuğrul, leader of a tribe of Oğuz Turks who at the end of the thirteenth century settled as vassals of the Seljuk sultan around Söğüt, a small town in the hills of Bithynia, just east of the Byzantine cities of Nicomedia, Nicaea and Prusa.

The only contemporary Byzantine reference to Osman Gazi is by the Greek chronicler George Pachymeres, writing during the reign of Andronicus II Palaeologus (r. 1282–1328), who says he was living in a time when 'troubles confused the Emperor on all sides'. Pachymeres first mentions Osman in connection with an offensive mounted by Andronicus against the Turks in the spring of 1302. One detachment of the Byzantine army, about 2,000 men under a commander named Muzalon was driven back by a force of 5,000 Turkish warriors under a gazi, or 'warrior for the faith', whom Pachymeres calls Atman, actually Osman. According to

Pachymeres, this success attracted other Turkish warriors to join Osman Gazi from 'the region of the Maeander' and from Paphlagonia.

With these reinforcements Osman defeated Muzalon in 1302 in a pitched battle at Baphaeus, near Nicomedia. Soon afterwards Osman captured the Byzantine town of Belakoma, Turkish Bilecik, as well as other fortresses which he used to store the loot he had accumulated.

According to Pachymeres, after his victory at Baphaeus, Osman's forces subjected the countryside around Nicomedia 'to uncoordinated attacks from different quarters, mostly people finding easy foraging in the area, through grave lack of anyone to stop them... Some of the inhabitants were taken prisoners, others butchered, while some even deserted.'

Only the fortified Byzantine cities of Bithynia could withstand the Turkish attacks. Pachymeres writes of how Osman attacked Nicaea 'uprooting vineyards, destroying crops and finally attacking... the citadel'. But the walls of Nicaea proved too strong for the Turks, as did those of Prusa and Pegaia, a town on the Asian shore of the Marmara. Pachymeres describes the ordeal endured by the people of Pegaia during the Ottoman siege, when 'the surrounding population were confined within the city. Those who had escaped the sword suffered famine, and these bad conditions caused an epidemic of the plague.'

By now the Turks had made their way across the Dardanelles into Europe. One band of them hired themselves out as mercenaries to King Stephen Milutin of Serbia. Another, headed by a chieftain named Halil, pillaged the countryside throughout Thrace, making land communication impossible between Constantinople and Thessalonica. Andronicus, after calling on the Serbs and Genose for help, finally managed to trap Halil and his men in 1312 on the Gallipoli peninsula, where they were annihilated, fighting to the last man.

Osman Gazi died in 1324 and was succeeded by his son Orhan Gazi, the first Ottoman ruler to use the title of sultan, as he is referred to in an inscription. Two years after his succession Orhan captured Prusa, Turkish Bursa, which became the first Ottoman capital. He then renewed the siege of Nicaea, which had been begun by his father Osman Gazi.

Andronicus III Palaeologus, who had succeeded to the throne in May 1328, mounted an expedition to relieve Nicaea in the spring of the following year. The emperor, accompanied by his prime minister John Cantacuzenus, mustered a force of 4,000 to 5,000 veterans and ferried them across the Bosphorus to Chrysopolis (Üsküdar), from where they began to march along the shore of the Gulf of Nicomedia. But they were defeated by Orhan's troops in a battle at Pelekanon in which Andronicus himself was wounded in the leg. Andronicus was brought safely back to Constantinople, leaving Cantacuzenus to lead the defeated Byzantine army on its homeward march, beating off attacks by the Turks.

Thus no relief came to Nicaea, which finally fell to Orhan's forces on 1 March 1331. After the fall of Nicaea, which the Turks called Iznik, Orhan laid siege to Nicomedia. Andronicus agreed to a truce with Orhan by paying him a large sum not to make further attacks in Bithynia. But Orhan eventually broke the truce and renewed the siege of Nicomedia, known to the Turks as Izmit. The fall of the city is recorded by Nicephorus Gregoras in his account of events in the year 1337: 'When the emperor was occupied with other things, Nicomedia, the chief city of Bithynia, was captured, reduced by great famine brought on by the obstinate siege of the enemy.'

This virtually completed the Ottoman conquest of Bithynia, by which time Orhan had also absorbed the neighbouring Karası *beylik* to the south, so that he now controlled all of westernmost Anatolia east of the Bosphorus, the Sea of Marmara and the Dardanelles.

Andronicus III died on 15 June 1341 and was succeeded by his nine-year-old son John V Palaeologus. John Cantacuzenus was appointed regent, and later that year his supporters proclaimed him emperor. This began a civil war that lasted until 8 February 1347, when Cantacuzenus was crowned as John VI, ruling as senior co-emperor with John V.

Cantacuzenus had hardly begun his reign when Constantinople was struck by the Black Plague, which first appeared in the city in Genoese ships from the Crimea. By the time the worst of the plague was over, in the following year, a third of the population of Constantinople had died.

Meanwhile Orhan had signed a peace treaty in 1346 with John Cantacuzenus. Cantacuzenus sealed the treaty by giving his daughter Theodora in marriage to Orhan, who wed the princess in a festive ceremony at Selymbria, in Thrace on the European shore of the Marmara forty miles west of Constantinople. Cantacuzenus ruled as co-emperor until 10 December 1354, when he was deposed by the supporters of John V, after which he retired as a monk and wrote his chronicle, the *Historia*, one of the most important sources for the history of the Byzantine Empire during the rise of the Ottoman Turks.

Throughout his reign Cantacuzenus honoured the alliance he had made with Orhan. During that time Orhan thrice sent his son Süleyman with Turkish troops to aid Cantacuzenus on campaigns in Thrace. On the third of these campaigns, in 1352, Süleyman occupied a fortress on the Dardanelles called Tzympe, which he refused to return until Cantacuzenus promised to pay him 1,000 gold pieces. The emperor paid the money and Süleyman prepared to return the fortress to him, but then, on 2 March 1354, the situation changed when an earthquake destroyed the walls of Gallipoli and other towns on the European shore of the Dardanelles, which were abandoned by their Greek inhabitants. Süleyman took advantage of the disaster to occupy the towns with his troops, restoring the walls of Gallipoli in the process.

A Florentine account of the earthquake and its aftermath says that the Turks then 'received a great army of their people and laid siege to Constantinople', but after they were unable to capture it 'they attacked the towns and pillaged the countryside'. Cantacuzenus demanded that Gallipoli and the other towns be returned, but Süleyman insisted that he had not conquered them by force but simply occupied their abandoned ruins. Thus the Ottomans established their first permanent foothold in Europe, which Orhan was able to use as a base to make further conquests in Thrace.

Orhan also extended his territory eastward in Anatolia, as evidenced by a note in the *Historia* of Cantacuzenus, saying that in the summer of 1354 Süleyman captured Ancyra (Ankara), which had belonged to the Eretnid *beylik*, thus adding to the Ottoman realm a city destined to be the capital of the modern Republic of Turkey. A Turkish source says that Süleyman captured the Thracian towns of Malkara, Ipsala and Vize. This would have been prior to the summer of 1357, when Süleyman was killed when he was thrown from his horse while hunting.

Orhan Gazi died in 1362 and was succeeded by his son Murat, who had been campaigning in Thrace. At some time in the 1360s Murat captured the Byzantine city of Adrianople, which as Edirne soon became the Ottoman capital, replacing Bursa. Murat used Edirne as a base to campaign ever deeper into the Balkans, and during the next two decades his raids took him into Greece, Bulgaria, Macedonia, Albania, Serbia,

Bosnia and Wallachia. At the same time his forces expanded the Ottoman domains eastward and southward into Anatolia, conquering the Germiyan, Hamidid and Teke *beyliks*, the latter conquest including the Mediterranean port of Antalya.

Meanwhile John had gone to Italy to seek help from the pope. He left Constantinople in charge of his eldest son, who had been crowned co-emperor as Andronicus IV, while his second son Manuel, was appointed governor of Thessalonica. John met with Pope Urban V in Rome on 21 October 1367, agreeing to a union of the Greek and Roman churches under the papacy. Urban then sent an encyclical to the princes of western Europe saying that John was now a Roman Catholic and fully deserving of assistance.

After being detained in Venice for his inability to pay a large debt he owed the Venetians, John finally returned to Constantinople in October 1371. A year after his return he signed a treaty with Murat acknowledging his suzerainty to the sultan. Early in 1373 John was in Murat's camp in Anatolia fighting in a campaign as the sultan's vassal. This led the pope to remark that the emperor, though now a Catholic, had been reduced to making 'an impious alliance' with the infidel.

When John was off on campaign he once again left Andronicus to rule in Constantinople as his regent. Andronicus took the opportunity to revolt against his father in May 1374, but John quickly quelled the rebellion when he returned. This was the first in a series of civil wars that lasted until the death of John V on 16 February 1391, by which time Andronicus had also died. John VII, son and successor of Andronicus IV, held Constantinople for six months before he was forced out by Manuel II, son and heir of John V, who became sole emperor late in 1391.

Meanwhile Murat's army occupied Thessalonica in 1387 after a four-year siege, by which time the Ottomans controlled all of southern Macedonia. Murat's capture of Niş in 1385 brought him into conflict with Prince Lazar of Serbia, who organised a Serbian-Kosovar-Bosnian alliance against the Turks. Four years later Murat again invaded Serbia, opposed by Lazar and his allies, who included King Trvtko of Bosnia.

The two armies clashed on 15 June 1389 near Pristina at Kosovo Polje, the 'Field of Blackbirds', where in a four-hour battle the Turks were victorious over the Christian allies. At the climax of the battle Murat was killed by a Serbian nobleman who had feigned surrender. Lazar was captured and beheaded by Murat's son Beyazit, who then slaughtered all of the other Christian captives, including most of the noblemen of Serbia. Serbia never recovered from the catastrophe, and thenceforth it became a vassal of the Ottomans, who were now firmly established in the Balkans.

Soon afterwards Beyazit murdered his own brother Yakup to succeed to the throne, the first instance of fratricide in Ottoman history. Beyazit came to be known as Yıldırım, or Lightning, from the speed with which he moved his army, campaigning both in Europe and Asia, where he extended his domains deep into Anatolia.

Beyazit's army included an elite infantry corps called *yeniçeri*, meaning 'new force', which in the West came to be known as the Janissaries. This corps had first been formed by Sultan Murat from prisoners of war taken in his Balkan campaigns. Beyazit institutionalised the Janissary Corps by a periodic levy of Christian youths called the *devşirme*, first in the Balkans and later in Anatolia as well. Those taken in the *devşirme* were forced to convert to Islam and then trained for service in the military, the most talented rising to the highest ranks in the army and the Ottoman administration, including that of grand vezir, the sultan's first minister. They were trained to be loyal only to the sultan, and since they were not allowed to marry they had no private lives outside the Janissary Corps. Thus they developed an intense *esprit de corps*, and were by far the most effective unit in the Ottoman armed forces.

Beyazit mounted a campaign into Anatolia late in 1389 against the emirates of Saruhan and Aydın, both of which he subjugated. The most important result of this campaign was Beyazit's capture of Smyrna, which gave the Ottomans a port on the Aegean, although they were not yet in a position to exploit its commercial and military potential.

The Genoese, who had been given control of Smyrna by Michael VIII Palaeologus, were besieged there in 1328 by Umur Bey, son of the emir Mehmet, ruler of the Türkmen emirate of Aydın. Umur captured the Castle of St Peter, which protected the harbour of Smyrna, but he was unable to take the acropolis on Mount Pagos, where the Genoese garrison and the Greek townspeople continued to hold out. Then in 1344 Pope Clement VI launched a crusade to free Smyrna from Umur Bey who had in the meanwhile succeeded his father as emir of Aydın. The Crusader fleet, commanded by Martino Zaccharia, the former Genoese lord of Chios, recaptured the Castle of St Peter, and when Umur Bey tried to retake it four years later he was killed. The Genoese then had sole control of Smyrna until 1374, when Pope Gregory XI transferred custody of the Castle of St Peter to the Knights Hospitallers of St John on Rhodes. The knights retained the castle until 1389, when Beyazit took Smyrna.

Beyazit laid siege to Constantinople in May 1394, erecting a fortress at Anadolu Hisarı on the Asian shore of the Bosphorus at its narrowest stretch, to cut off the city from the Black Sea. While the siege continued Beyazit led his army into Wallachia, capturing the fortress of Nicopolis on the Danube in 1395.

King Sigismond of Hungary appealed for a crusade against the Turks, and in July 1396 an army of nearly 100,000 assembled in Buda under his leadership.

The Christian army comprised contingents from Hungary, Wallachia, Germany, Poland, Italy, France, Spain and England, while its fleet had ships contributed by Genoa, Venice and the Knights of St John on Rhodes. Sigismund led his force down the Danube to Nicopolis, where he put the Turkish-occupied fortress under siege. Two days later Beyazit arrived with an army of 200,000, and on 25 September 1396 he defeated the crusaders at Nicopolis and executed most of the Christian captives, though Sigismund managed to escape.

Beyazit then renewed his siege of Constantinople, where the Greeks had been reinforced by 1,200 troops sent by Charles VI of France under Marshall Boucicaut, a survivor of the battle of Nicopolis. The marshal realised that his force was far too small, and so he persuaded the emperor Manuel to go with him to France so that he could present his case to King Charles. Manuel went on to England, where on 21 December 1400 he was escorted into London by King Henry IV, who welcomed him as 'a great Christian prince from the East'. But although help was promised it never materialised, and Manuel returned to Constantinople empty-handed early in 1403.

By then the situation had completely changed, for the previous spring Beyazit had lifted his siege of the city and rushed his forces back to Anatolia, which had been invaded by a Mongol horde led by Tamerlane. The two armies collided on 28 July 1402 near Ankara, where Mongols routed the Turks, many of whom deserted at the outset of the battle. Beyazit himself was taken prisoner and soon afterwards he died in captivity, tradition holding that he had been penned up in a cage by Tamerlane.

Five of Beyazit's sons – Süleyman, Mustafa, Musa, Isa and Mehmet – also fought in the battle. Mustafa and Musa were eventually freed by Tamerlane, though while the former was still captive a pretender known as Düzme Mustafa appeared to claim the throne.

Meanwhile Tamerlane went on to capture and sack Bursa, Konya, Tire, Ephesus, Smyrna and Phocaea, slaughtering the inhabitants. An anonymous Greek source says that after the massacre at Smyrna Tamerlane 'had the heads collected and built two towers from them, from which great fear affected all who saw them'. Tamerlane then departed from Anatolia in the summer of 1403, never to return, exciting tribute from the places he had subjugated. The Aragonese diplomat Ruy Gonzales de Clavijo, who passed through Anatolia in 1404 on his way to Samarkand, reports that everywhere he saw piles of human skulls erected by Tamerlane to create terror wherever he rode.

The Ottoman state was almost destroyed by the catastrophe at Ankara. After his victory Tamerlane reinstated the emirs of the Anatolian *beyliks* that had fallen to the Ottomans, turning over Smyrna to Cüneyt Bey, Umur Bey's grandson, while in the Balkans the Christian rulers who had been Beyazit's vassals regained their independence.

The next eleven years were a period of chaos, as Beyazit's surviving sons fought one another in a war of succession, at the same time doing battle with their Turkish and Christian opponents. The struggle was finally won by Beyazit's youngest son, Mehmet, who on 5 July 1413 defeated and killed his brother Musa at a battle in Bulgaria, their brothers Süleyman and Isa having died earlier in the war of succession.

Mehmet ruled for eight years, virtually all of which he spent in war, striving to re-establish Ottoman rule in Anatolia and the Balkans. The year after he became sole ruler of the Ottoman Empire he recaptured Smyrna from Cüneyt Bey, the Aydınıd emir. Mehmet's last campaign was a raid across the Danube into Wallachia in 1421, shortly after which he died following a fall from his horse. He was succeeded by his son Murat II, who although only seventeen was already a seasoned warrior, having fought in at least two battles during his father's war of succession.

At the outset of Murat's reign he had to fight two successive wars of succession of his own, first against the pretender Düzme Mustafa and then against his own younger brother, also named Mustafa, both of whom he defeated and killed. Both of the pretenders had been supported by the emperor Manuel II, and so after Murat eliminated them he sought to take his revenge on the emperor, putting Constantinople under siege on 20 June 1422. But the Byzantine capital was too strongly fortified for him to break through, and at the end of the summer he decided to abandon the siege and withdraw.

Manuel suffered a critical stroke during the siege, whereupon his son John was made regent. Manuel died on 21 July 1425, whereupon his son succeeded as John VIII. The chronicler George Sphrantzes writes of Manuel's funeral that it was attended 'with such mournings and such assemblages as there had never been for any of the other emperors'.

Murat's two wars of succession had cost him territory in both Anatolia and Europe, and now he set out to recover his losses. In 1423 he launched a campaign against the Isfendiyarid emir of Sinop on the Black Sea, forcing him to return the territory he had taken and to resume his status as an Ottoman vassal. Immediately afterwards Murat returned to Europe and marched against the ruler of Wallachia, Vlad II Drakul, the historical prototype of Dracula, and he too was forced into vassalage and had to give up the land he had seized.

Murat then set out to regain Thessalonica, which his uncle Süleyman had ceded in 1403 to the Byzantines, who two decades later gave the city over to the Venetians since they were unable to defend it themselves. When Murat besieged Thessalonica the Venetians made an alliance with the Aydınid emir Cüneyt, supporting him in his effort to regain the territory his *beylik* had lost to the Ottomans, most notably Smyrna which he recaptured in 1422. Murat sent his commander Hamza against Cüneyt, who in April 1425 was defeated and killed, restoring Smyrna to the Ottoman Empire and bringing the Aydınid *beylik* to an end. Hamza went on to invade the Menteşe *beylik*, and that same year it too was conquered and terminated. During the next five years Murat further enlarged his territory in Anatolia, taking the Canik region along the Black Sea coast and annexing the Germiyan *beylik*, as well as putting down a number of rebellious Türkmen tribes.

Murat then turned his attention back to Thessalonica, leading his forces in a final attack that brought about the city's surrender on 29 March 1430, after which 7,000 of its inhabitants were carried off into slavery. This led John VIII to seek help from the West, and he proposed to Pope Martin V that a council be called to reconcile the Greek and Latin churches, which had been estranged for four centuries.

This gave rise to the Council of Ferrara-Florence, in which the Byzantine delegation was headed by John VIII and the patriarch of Constantinople Joseph II. The union of the churches was finally agreed upon on 5 July 1439, uniting the Greek and Latin churches under the aegis of the pope, Eugenius IV, who then called for a crusade to save Constantinople from the Turks. But the union was very unpopular among the people and clergy of Constantinople, and so the Byzantine Empire was deeply divided as it faced a showdown with its mortal enemy.

During the summer of 1439 Murat's army captured Ioannina in north-western Greece before invading Albania, while his navy raided the Ionian islands. During the next three years Murat conquered much of Albania, and in the following two years he mounted campaigns in Serbia and Bosnia as a prelude to an invasion of Hungary, which he began in 1438. He put Belgrade under siege in April 1440, according to the Turkish chronicler Aşıkpaşazade, who notes that the sultan 'knew that Belgrade was the gateway to Hungary and aimed to open that gate'. But, as Aşıkpaşazade adds, 'many men and lords from the Muslim army were killed', and Murat was forced to lift the siege in October of that year.

The following year Murat mounted an expedition into Transylvania under the commander Mezid Bey. But the invasion was stopped by an army led by John Hunyadi, the voyvoda, or princely governor, of Transylvania, who killed Mezid and routed his forces. Murat sought vengeance and sent another army against Hunyadi, who defeated the Turkish force in Wallachia in September 1442.

Hunyadi's victories encouraged the Christian rulers of Europe to form an anti-Ottoman alliance. On 1 January 1443 Pope Eugenius IV called for a crusade against the Turks, in which the rulers of Burgundy, Poland, Hungary, Wallachia and Venice agreed to join forces with the papacy against Murat, who that winter put down a revolt in central Anatolia by the Karamanid emir Ibrahim Bey.

Between campaigns Murat usually returned to his capital at Edirne, though he also spent time in the old capital of Bursa, where in the years 1424–1426 he erected an imperial mosque complex called the Muradiye. A decade later he built a mosque of the same name in his new capital as well as a palace called Edirne Sarayı, where he housed his Harem. The palace comprised a number of pavilions on an island in the Tunca, one of two rivers that nearly encircle the city.

During the summer of 1443 Murat learned that a Christian army had crossed the Danube and was headed south-eastward through Ottoman territory, led by John Hunyadi and Ladislas, King of Poland and Hungary. Murat mobilised his army and in December 1443 he set out to do battle with the crusaders, leaving his son Mehmet behind with the grand vezir Halil Çandarlı, who was to await the arrival of troops from Anatolia. The crusaders defeated the Ottomans twice in the winter of 1443–1444 between Sofia and Niş, with both sides suffering heavy losses, after which Hunyadi and Ladislas led their troops back to Buda and Murat returned to Edirne.

Murat, faced with a new revolt by the Karamanid emir Ibrahim Bey, decided to negotiate a peace with Ladislas, and on 12 June 1444 a ten-year truce was signed at Edirne by the sultan and envoys of the king, who himself signed the treaty at Szeged in Hungary around 1 August of that same year. That left Murat free to deal with the revolt in Anatolia, and he appointed his twelve-year-old son Mehmet to serve as regent in his absence under the guidance of the grand vezir Çandarlı Halil Pasha. Murat then led his Janissaries into Anatolia to deal with Ibrahim Bey, who immediately surrendered and agreed to resume his status as the sultan's vassal.

After Ibrahim's surrender Murat did not return directly to Edirne, but instead he rode to Bursa, visiting the royal tomb at the Muradiye where his son Alaettin Ali was buried. Soon afterwards, around 1 September 1444, Murat stunned his court by announcing that he was abdicating in favour of Prince Mehmet, saying 'I have given my all – my crown, my throne – to my son, whom you should recognize as sultan.'

Murat's vezirs tried to dissuade him, particularly Halil Pasha, who had seen how immature Mehmet was when the young prince served as his father's regent. But Murat was adamant, and, accompanied by Ishak Pasa and Hamza Bey, he retired to Manisa to spend his time in study and contemplation, leaving Mehmet to govern under the direction of Halil Pasha. But Mehmet's immaturity and inexperience led Murat to resume his reign in September 1446, whereupon Mehmet was made provincial governor in Manisa.

Meanwhile John Hunyadi had mustered an army and tried to join forces with the Albanian rebel leader Skanderbeg to fight against the Turks.

Murat caught up with Hunyadi's army at Kosova, where the Serbs had gone down fighting against the Turks in 1389. The outcome of the second battle of Kosova, fought from 17 to 20 October 1448, was the same as the first, with the Turks completely routing the Christians.

John VIII died on 31 October 1448. He was survived by three of his brothers – Constantine, Demetrius and Thomas – as well as by his mother Helena Dragas. Constantine, the oldest, used the surname Dragases, the Greek form of his mother's name. At the time of John's death Constantine and Thomas were in Mistra, capital of the Despotate of the Morea (the Peloponnesos), while Demetrius was in Selymbria, a day's ride from Constantinople.

As soon as he received news of John's death Demetrius rushed back to Constantinople to make a claim for the throne. But Helena was determined that Constantine should succeed, and so she stopped Demetrius from taking control and asserted her right to serve as regent in the interim. She then despatched a courier to Mistra to inform Constantine that he had succeeded his brother John. When the news arrived at Mistra, Constantine was acclaimed as emperor. It was decided that the coronation should be performed there rather than in Constantinople, and so on 6 January 1449 he was crowned as Constantine XI in the church of St Demetrius in Mistra.

Constantine was forty-four when he became emperor. He had been married twice, but both wives had died without bearing a child, and so after coming to the throne efforts were made to arrange a dynastic marriage, but without success.

After his coronation Constantine divided the Despotate of the Morea between his brothers, with Demetrius to rule in Mistra and Thomas in Achaia, in the western Peloponnesos. He then left Mistra for Constantinople, where he arrived on 12 March 1440. Shortly afterwards he sent a courier to Murat, conveying his greetings and asking for a peace agreement.

Constantine began his reign in a divided city, for most of the clergy and people were totally opposed to the decree of Union of the Greek and Roman churches which had been signed by John VIII. Constantine was determined to uphold the Union, for he believed that it offered the only hope of obtaining aid from the West. The principal opponent of this policy was the monk George Scholarios, who in

1450 left the emperor's service and retired to the monastery of the Pantocrator as a monk.

Murat II died at Edirne on 3 February 1451. His death was kept secret by the grand vezir Halil Çandarlı so that Prince Mehmet could make his way to take control in Edirne, He arrived on 17 February 1451, and on the following day he was acclaimed by the army as Sultan Mehmet II, one month before his nineteenth birthday. But despite his youth he now seemed ready for the task, at least according to Kritoboulos of Imbros, Mehmet's contemporary Greek biographer, who writes of the young sultan's soaring imperial ambition:

> When he became heir to a great realm and master of many soldiers and enlisted men, and had under his power already the largest and best parts of both Asia and Europe, he did not believe that these were enough for him nor was he content with what he had: instead he immediately overran the whole world in his calculations and resolved to rule it in emulation of the Alexanders and Pompeys and Caesars and kings and generals of their sort.

Mehmet exchanged emissaries with a number of rulers, both Christian and Muslim, including John IV Comnenus, the Byzantine emperor of Trebizond. The Greek chronicler George Sphrantzes, who was serving as ambassador from Constantine XI to Trebizond, tells of how he warned John IV about Mehmet. 'This man, who just became sultan, is young and an enemy of the Christians since childhood, he threatens with proud spirit that he will put into operations certain plans against the Christians. If God should grant that the young sultan be overcome by his youth and evil nature and march against our City, I know not what will happen.'

15

The Fall of Byzantium

Immediately after Mehmet became sultan he appointed Halil as grand vezir, although he loathed his father's old advisor. Mehmet felt that Halil had undermined his first attempt to rule as sultan, and he suspected that the grand vezir had been taking bribes from the Byzantines. Nevertheless he allowed Halil to continue as grand vezir for the time being, while he waited for the right moment to eliminate him.

At the beginning of the second year of his reign Mehmet took the first step in the plan that he had made to attack and conquer Constantinople. According to Kritoboulos, Mehmet decided 'to build a strong fortress on the Bosphorus on the European side, opposite to the Asiatic fortress on the other side, at the point where it is narrowest and swiftest, and so to control the strait'. The fortress, known as Rumeli Hisarı was completed in three months in the summer of 1452, directly opposite Anadolu Hisarı, the fortress built earlier by Beyazit I.

The two fortresses enabled Mehmet to cut off the Byzantines from their grain supplies on the Black Sea in preparation for his siege of Constantinople. The siege began an hour before sunrise on 5 April 1453, when, according to the Venetian physician Nicolo Barbaro, Mehmet 'moved with a great part of his forces to within about a quarter of a mile from the city walls, and they spread in a line along the whole length of the city walls from the Sea of Marmara to the Golden Horn'.

Modern estimates put the number of Mehmet's troops at about 80,000, while the defenders in Constantinople were probably no more than 7,000, including Constantine's Venetian and Genoese allies, the latter commanded by Giovanni Giustiniani-Longo. Constantine and his men fought valiantly for more than seven weeks, as Mehmet launched one infantry attack after another against the great Theodosian walls, which had protected Constantinople from its enemies for 1,000 years. The Ottoman artillery, which included a gigantic cannon made by the Hungarian engineer Urban, kept up an almost continuous bombardment that reduced much of the fortifications to rubble, while the defenders and the townspeople strove to repair the damage.

At dawn on 28 May, Mehmet ordered his troops to take their assigned positions for the assault the following day, and some 2,000 ladders were brought up before the walls. Meanwhile the clergy and townspeople formed a procession, holding aloft the icon of the Virgin Hodegitria and holy relics from all of their churches, singing hymns as they walked through the city and out to the Theodosian walls. Doukas writes of the repeated cries of supplication that were heard throughout the city, as the townspeople implored Christ and the Virgin to save them from the Turks: 'Spare us, O Lord, from Thy just wrath and deliver us from the hands of the enemy!'

That evening everyone who was not on duty along the walls began congregating in Haghia Sophia, praying for the city's salvation. The chronicler Melissourgos describes how Constantine prayed in Haghia Sophia and then stopped at the Palace of Blachernae, where he 'asked to be forgiven by all. Who can describe the wailing and tears that arose in the palace at that hour? No man, even if he were made of wood and stone, could have held back his tears.'

The Turkish engineering battalions had been working throughout the night filling in the foss in front of the Theodosian walls along the Mesoteichion, the middle arc of the defence walls, where the main attack would be made. About two o'clock in the morning of Tuesday 29 May, Mehmet gave orders to begin the attack. The first assault was made by the irregular light infantry known as the *başıbozuks*, who charged with wild battle cries to the din of drums and the skirl of bagpipes. The watchmen on the towers of the Theodosian walls heard the noise and sounded the alarm, and soon all the church bells within the city were rung to alert the populace. Meanwhile the *başıbozuks* had made their way across the foss and set up scaling ladders against the outer walls, some of them ascending to the battlements before they were cut down by the defenders. After two hours of intense fighting the *başıbozuks* were withdrawn, having worn down the defenders with their unrelenting attack.

Mehmet then launched the second wave, the regular Anatolian infantry under the command of Ishak Pasha and Mahmut Pasha, their charge accompanied by heavy bombardment from the Turkish artillery. An hour before dawn a huge cannon ball fired by Urban made a direct hit on the outer wall of the Mesoteichion, creating a breach through which some of the Turkish infantry tried to make their way into the city. But they were quickly surrounded and slaughtered by the defenders, led by the emperor himself. This broke the brunt of the assault, forcing Ishak Pasha to withdraw his infantry.

Mehmet then brought on the Janissaries, leading them himself as far as the foss. The defenders fought with desperation, holding back the Janissaries for an hour. But then at daybreak about 300 Janissaries forced their way through the breach that Urban had made in the outer wall near the Gate of St Romanus, where both Constantine and Giustiniani had their command posts.

The Janissaries had still not penetrated the inner wall, but then the tide of battle turned when Giustiniani suffered a severe wound and, despite Constantine's pleas that he remain at his post, he allowed himself to be carried to a Genoese ship in the harbour. Constantine tried to stem the tide as the Janissaries now penetrated the inner wall, and when last seen he was at his command post, fighting valiantly alongside his faithful comrade John Dalmata and his kinsmen Theophilus Palaeologus and Don Francisco of Toledo.

The Turkish star and crescent was soon waving from the towers of the Theodosian walls and the Palace of Blachernae, as the Turkish troops now made their way through the inner wall, killing or capturing the defenders on the Theodosian walls and then fanning out through the city. The last pockets of resistance were mopped up before the morning was over, with many of the surviving Italians escaping aboard Venetian ships, leaving the Greeks to face their fate.

Mehmet then turned loose his troops to sack the city for three days, as he had promised them. The Greek and Italian chroniclers write of how the Turkish soldiers killed those they did not enslave, and stripped Haghia Sophia and the other churches of their sacred relics and treasures, plundering the imperial palace and the houses of the rich. Kritoboulos says that nearly 4,000 Greeks were slain in the siege and its aftermath, and that more than 50,000 were enslaved, virtually the entire population of the city, which was stripped bare of everything that could be carried away by the looters.

Mehmet had given his soldiers permission to sack the city on condition that they did not destroy its public buildings, which now belonged to him. But from contemporary accounts it would appear that the Turkish forces did considerable damage to the city during their orgy of looting, enslavement, rape and massacre. Kritoboulos writes of Mehmet's reaction to the death and destruction he saw when he first entered the city he had conquered.

> After this the Sultan entered the City and looked about to see its great size, its situation, its grandeur and beauty, its teeming population, its loveliness, and the costliness of its churches and public buildings. When he saw what a large number had been killed, and the wreckage of the buildings, and the wholesale ruin and desolation of the City, he was filled with compassion and repented not a little at the destruction and plundering. Tears fell from his eyes as he groaned deeply and passionately: 'What a city have we given over to plunder and destruction.'

Sultan Mehmet II made his triumphal entry into the city late in the afternoon of the day he captured it, Tuesday 29 May 1453, passing through the Adrianople Gate, now known as Edirne Kapı. As he passed through the gate he was acclaimed by his troops as Fatih, or the Conqueror, the name by which he would thenceforth be known to the Turks. The city that he had conquered had been known to the Turks as Kostantiniye, but after the Conquest its name in common Turkish usage became Istanbul, a corruption of the Greek '*eis tin polin*', meaning 'in the city' or 'to the city'.

Mehmet rode into the city along the Roman thoroughfare known as the Mese, or Middle Way, which took him from the Sixth Hill to the First Hill, the ancient acropolis of Byzantium. This brought him to Haghia Sophia, the Great Church of the Divine Wisdom. Before Mehmet entered the building he dismounted and fell to his knees, pouring a handful of earth over his turban in a gesture of humility, since Haghia Sophia was as revered in Islam as it was in Christianity. He then surveyed the church and ordered that it be immediately converted to Islamic worship under the name of Aya Sofya Camii Kabir, the Great Mosque of Haghia Sophia, where he attended the first noon prayer in the mosque that Friday, 1 June 1453.

After Mehmet's first visit to Haghia Sophia he also inspected the remains of the Great Palace of Byzantium on the Marmara slope of the First Hill. Mehmet was deeply saddened by the noble ruins, and those who were with him heard him recite a melancholy distich by the Persian poet Saadi: 'The spider is the curtain-holder in the Palace of the Caesars./ The owl hoots its night-call on the Towers of Afrasiab.'

Some of the younger males of the Byzantine aristocracy survived the siege and were taken by Mehmet into his household. Kritoboulos writes that Mehmet 'appointed some of the youths of high family, whom he had chosen according to their merits, to be in his bodyguard and to be constantly near him, and others to other service as his pages'. These captives included two sons of Thomas Palaeologus, brother of the late emperor Constantine XI, who came to be known as Hass Murat Pasha and Mesih Pasha. Hass Murat was a particular favourite of Mehmet, probably his lover, and eventually was appointed *beylerbey* of Rumelia. Mesih also rose to high rank in Mehmet's service, and during the reign of the Conqueror's son and successor Beyazit II he thrice served as grand vezir. Other Christian converts who rose to high rank in Mehmet's service include four who served him as grand vezir: Zaganos Pasha, Mahmut Pasha, Rum Mehmet Pasha and Gedik Ahmet Pasha.

News of the fall of Constantinople reached Venice on 29 June on a ship from Corfu, and on the following day the Senate wrote to inform Pope Nicholas V 'of the horrible and most deplorable fall of the cities of Constantinople and Pera'. The pope, who received the news on 8 July, referred to the fall of Constantinople as the 'shame of Christendom'.

Three weeks after the Conquest, Mehmet left Istanbul for Edirne. According to Tursun Beg, before leaving for Edirne, Mehmet announced 'to his vezirs and his commanders and his officers that henceforth his capital was to be Istanbul'. At the same time Mehmet appointed Karıştıran Süleyman Bey as prefect of Istanbul.

Kritoboulos describes Süleyman Bey as 'a most intelligent and useful man, possessed of the finest manners', and he writes that Mehmet 'put him in charge of everything, but in particular over the repopulating of the City, and instructed him to be very zealous about this matter'.

Mehmet then spent the summer in Edirne Sarayı, which he had expanded and embellished the year before the Conquest. One of Mehmet's first orders of business at Edirne Sarayı was to order the execution of the grand vezir Çandarlı Halil Pasha, who had been undermining him since he first came to the throne, and whom he had suspected of being in the pay of the Byzantines. Mehmet then appointed Zaganos Pasha as grand vezir, ending the virtual monopoly that the powerful Çandarlı family had held on that office.

When Mehmet returned from Edirne to Istanbul, his first concern was to repopulate the city. According to Kritoboulos,

> He sent an order in the form of an imperial command to every part of his realm, that as many inhabitants as possible be transferred to the City, not only Christians but also his own people and many of the Hebrews… He gathered them there from all parts of Asia and Europe, and he transferred them with all possible care and speed, people of all nations, but more especially Christians.

The non-Muslims among the townspeople and new settlers were grouped into *millets*, or 'nations', according to their religion. Thus the Greek *millet* was headed by the Orthodox patriarch, the Armenian by the Gregorian patriarch, and the Jewish by the chief rabbi. The authority granted to the head of each *millet* extended not only to religious matters but also to most legal questions other than criminal cases, which were always tried before the sultan's judges. The *millet* system instituted by Mehmet was continued by his successors right down to the end of the Ottoman Empire, forming the core of its multi-ethnic character.

There was no Greek Orthodox patriarch of Constantinople at the time of the Conquest, for the last to hold that position before the siege, Gregory III Mammas, abandoned the city in August 1451 and fled to Rome, never to return.

Thus it was that Mehmet decided to choose a new patriarch to head the Greek *millet*, as Melissourgos writes: 'He issued orders for the election of a patriarch, according to custom and protocol… The high clerics who happened to be present, and the very few members of the church and the lay population designated the scholar George Scholarios, and elected him patriarch under the name Gennadios.'

Gennadios took office on 6 January 1454, when he was consecrated by the metropolitan of Heracleia on the Black Sea. Before the ceremony

Mehmet received Gennadios and invited him to share his meal, after which he presented him with a silver sceptre and a palfrey from the royal stables. Mehmet then personally escorted Gennadios in the first stage of his procession to the church of the Holy Apostles on the Fourth Hill, which had been assigned to the new patriarch as his headquarters. The sultan later issued a *firman* which guaranteed to Gennadios 'that no one should vex or disturb him; that unmolested, untaxed, and unoppressed by an adversary, he should, with all the bishops under him, be exempted from taxes for all time'.

Mehmet began the reconstruction of his new capital in the summer of 1453, when he issued orders for the repair of the Theodosian walls and the other fortifications damaged in the siege. Since both the Great Palace of Byzantium and the Blachernae Palace were in ruins, Mehmet began construction of a new imperial residence on the Third Hill, on a site described by Kritoboulos as 'the finest and best location in the centre of the City'. This came to be known as Eski Saray, the Old Palace, because a few years later Mehmet decided to build a new palace on the First Hill, the famous Topkapı Sarayı.

Kritoboulos, in writing of Eski Saray, also notes that Mehmet at the same time 'ordered the construction of a strong fortress near the Golden Gate' in the south-western corner of the city, a monument that came to be called Yedikule, the Castle of the Seven Towers. Then, at the beginning of his chronicle for the year 1456, Kritoboulos reports the sultan's satisfaction at the completion of Eski Saray and Yedikule, as well as his initiation of new construction projects, most notably the great marketplace known as Kapalı Çarşı, or the Covered Bazaar.

Six years after the Conquest, according to Kritoboulos, Sultan Mehmet issued a 'command…to all able persons to build splendid and costly buildings inside the City'. Kritoboulos goes on to say that Mehmet 'also commanded them to build baths and inns and marketplaces, and very many and beautiful workshops, to erect places of worship, and to adorn and embellish the City with many other such buildings, sparing no expense, as each man had the means and ability'.

Mehmet himself led the way by selecting a site on the Fourth Hill, where a decade after the Conquest he began building an enormous complex known as Fatih Camii, the Mosque of the Conqueror. The ancient church of the Holy Apostles occupied a large part of the site, and so Mehmet had it demolished to make way for his new mosque complex. Kritoboulos also notes Mehmet's orders to build a new palace on the First Hill, the pleasure dome that would come to be known as Topkapı Sarayı.

A number of Mehmet's vezirs also erected mosque complexes in Istanbul. The earliest of these is Mahmut Pasha Camii. This mosque complex was built on the Second Hill in 1462 by Mahmut Pasha, who succeeded Zaganos Pasha as grand vezir three years after the Conquest. Mahmut Pasha, who by all accounts was the greatest of all of the Conqueror's grand vezirs and one of the best who ever held that post in the Ottoman Empire, was eventually executed by Mehmet.

The mosques and other structures built by Mehmet and his vezirs marked the first phase of the transition in which Greek Constantinople, capital of the Byzantine Empire, became Turkish Istanbul, capital of the Ottoman Empire. One can see this transition in the famous Buondelmonti maps, the earliest of which is dated 1420 and the latest 1470. The city looks essentially the same in these two maps, but in the later one we can see the castles of Rumeli Hisarı and Yedikule, the mosques of the Conqueror and Mahmut Pasha, the palaces of Eski Saray and Topkapı Sarayı, the Covered Bazaar, and even the minaret on what was now the Great Mosque of Haghia Sophia, which in itself symbolises the transition from Byzantine Constantinople to Ottoman Istanbul.

After establishing his capital in Istanbul, Mehmet launched the first of a series of campaigns into Serbia in the spring of 1454, in which he captured the town of Novo Brdo, noted for its gold and silver mines. But in 1456 he failed in his attempt to take Belgrade, the only major defeat in his otherwise victorious career.

Meanwhile his forces captured the Genoese colonies of Nea Phocaea and Palaeo Phocaea on the Aegean coast of Asia Minor north of Izmir. This gave Mehmet control of the lucrative alum mines that the Genoese had developed there.

Despite their humiliating defeat at Belgrade, Mehmet's forces continued their march of conquest, and in the summer of 1456 an Ottoman army under Ömer Bey besieged Athens, which since 1385 had been held by the Florentine dynasty of the Acciajuoli. Ömer Bey's forces occupied the lower city while the defenders retreated to the acropolis, where they held out until they finally surrendered in June 1458.

Mehmet himself led a major expedition into the Peloponnesos in the spring of 1458, his pretext being that the two surviving brothers of the deceased emperor Constantine, Demetrius and Thomas Palaeologus, the despots of the Morea, were three years in arrears with the tribute that had been levied upon them. Corinth surrendered to Mehmet on 2 August. Shortly afterwards he concluded a treaty with Thomas Palaeologus, who surrendered to him Patras and other places in the northern Peloponnesos, which were put under the governorship of Ömer Bey.

On his homeward march Mehmet took the opportunity to see Athens, whose defenders had finally surrendered to Ömer Bey just two months before. Kritoboulos describes Mehmet's enthusiasm on seeing the famous city he had read about in his Greek studies.

> He saw it and was amazed, and he praised it, and especially the Acropolis as he went up into it. And from the ruins and the remains, he reconstructed mentally the ancient buildings, being a wise man and a Philhellene and as a great king, and he conjectured how they must have been originally. He noted with pleasure the respect of the city for their ancestors, and he rewarded them in many ways. They received from him whatever they asked for.

Mehmet lead a campaign into Serbia in the spring of 1459, his objective being the capture of Smederova, which surrendered to him without a struggle on 20 June. The fall of Smederova led all the smaller fortresses of northern Serbia to surrender as well. By the end of 1459 all of Serbia was under Mehmet's control, with some 200,000 Serbs enslaved, beginning an Ottoman occupation that would last for more than four centuries.

At the beginning of January 1459 civil war erupted in the Peloponnesos between Thomas and Demetrius Palaeologus, a struggle in which the Turkish forces, papal troops and Albanian marauders also became involved. Mehmet at first left the war to his local commanders, but then in May 1460 he mustered his forces in Edirne and led them into the Peloponnesos. According to Sphrantzes, Mehmet 'marched straight into Mistra, where the despot Lord Demetrius was…Demetrius had no alternative but to surrender to the sultan, who took possession of Mistra and imprisoned Demetrius.'

Mehmet then went on to conquer the rest of the Peloponnesos, apart from Monemvasia and the Venetian fortresses at Koroni, Methoni and Nauplion.

When he captured the Byzantine stronghold at Gardiki, according to Sphrantzes, Mehmet slaughtered all 6,000 inhabitants, including women and children, a savage example that led Greeks in other places to surrender to him without a struggle.

The despot Thomas Palaeologus fled to Corfu, which was held by the Venetians. Thomas then made his way to Rome, carrying with him the head of St Andrew, which had been preserved in the metropolitan cathedral of Patras. On 12 April 1462 he presented the Apostle's head to Pope Pius, who had it enshrined in the basilica of St Peter. Thomas then spent the rest of his days as a guest of the pope in Rome, where he died on 12 May 1465, his wife having passed away three years before. One of their two sons, Andreas, died a pauper in Rome in 1502, while the other, Manuel, moved to Istanbul, where he may have converted to Islam.

After his conquest of the Peloponnesos Mehmet took Demetrius Palaeologus and his wife and daughter back with him to Edirne. Mehmet then gave Demetrius an endowed estate at Aenos, where he and his family lived comfortably for the next decade. Demetrius then retired to a monastery in Edirne, where he died in 1470, his wife and daughter passing away in the same year.

Meanwhile Mehmet sent his grand vezir Mahmut Pasha on an expedition against the port town of Amasra, Genoa's principal commercial colony on the Black Sea coast of Anatolia. The Genoese surrendered without a struggle in the autumn of 1459, after which two-thirds of the populace were carried off to Istanbul as slaves.

Then in the spring of 1461 Mehmet launched an expedition against the Byzantine Empire of Trebizond, sending a fleet of 300 vessels along the Black Sea coast of Anatolia under Kasım Pasha, while he and Mahmut Pasha led an army overland, a force estimated as 80,000 infantry and 60,000 cavalry in addition to the artillery and supply train. By the time that Mehmet's army reached Trebizond the fleet under Kasım Pasha had begun to besiege the city, which was held by the emperor David Comnenus, the last Byzantine ruler still holding out against Mehmet.

David agreed to surrender and Mehmet took possession of Trebizond on 15 August 1461, exactly two hundred years to the day after Michael VIII Palaeologus had recaptured Constantinople from the Latins. David Comnenus was allowed to move with his family and all of his portable possessions to Edirne, where Mehmet gave him an estate in Thrace. David lived comfortably there for nearly two years, but then on 26 March 1463 Mehmet had him and the male members of his family arrested and brought to the Castle of the Seven Towers in Istanbul. There, on 1 November 1463, David was executed along with six of his seven sons and a nephew. Mehmet spared David's wife Helena, their youngest son George and their daughter Anna. The empress Helena buried her six sons and died soon afterwards. George, who was only three, was given to a Turkish family and raised as a Muslim; when he came of age he fled to Georgia and reverted to Christianity, after which he disappeared from history, the male imperial line of the Comneni vanishing with him.

Thus Mehmet, who had now added nearly the whole Black Sea coast of Anatolia to his realm, extinguished the last embers of Byzantium in Trebizond, having previously dispossessed the branch of the imperial line that had ruled in the Peloponnesos. Byzantium had passed away and its former dominions in Europe and Asia from the Mediterranean to the Black Sea were now ruled by Mehmet the Conqueror, who could thus style himself 'Sultan of the two Continents and Emperor of the two Seas'.

16

The Tide of Conquest Turns

After his conquest of Trebizond, Mehmet's next campaign began in the spring of 1462, when he put down a revolt in Wallachia by Vlad II Drakul, the historical prototype of Dracula, who was forced to flee and take refuge with King Matthias Corvinus of Hungary. That same summer Mehmet accompanied Mahmut Pasha on a campaign against Niccolo Gattilusio of Lesbos, who surrendered his fortress at Mytilene after a siege of fifteen days.

At the beginning of the Mytilene campaign Mehmet had visited the site of ancient Troy. Kritoboulos says the Mehmet 'inquired about the tombs of the heroes – Achilles and Ajax and the rest. And he praised and congratulated them, their memory and their deeds, and on having a person like the poet Homer to extol them.' He said proudly that he had settled the score with the ancient Greeks for their victory over the 'Asiatics' at Troy, where he was referring to the Mysian people who inhabited the Troad in antiquity.

The following year Mehmet led a campaign into Bosnia together with Mahmut Pasha. After the Ottomans captured the Bosnian capital at Jajce King Stephen VII of Bosnia fled to Ključ, where Mehmet had him beheaded after Mahmut Pasha captured the city. Stephen's death marked the end of the kingdom of Bosnia, which remained under Ottoman rule for the next four centuries. Mahmut Pasha then went on to conquer most of Hercegovina, whose ruler, Duke Stephen Vukčić, fled to Hungary.

Ömer Bey, the Ottoman commander in Athens, launched an attack in November 1462 on the Venetian fortress at Naupactos, on the northern shore of the Gulf of Corinth, and nearly captured it. Then the following spring Isa Bey, the Turkish commander in the Peloponnesos, besieged the Venetian fortress at Argos, which he captured on 3 April 1463. This led the Venetian senate to make a formal declaration of war against the Ottoman government on 28 July 1463.

On 12 September 1463 Venice entered into an anti-Turkish alliance with King Matthias Corvinus of Hungary. At the end of September Corvinus led an army of 4,000 troops into Bosnia and attacked Jajce, which surrendered after a siege of three months. By the end of the year more than sixty places in Bosnia surrendered to the Hungarians without a struggle. Duke Stephen Vukčić regained possession of Hercegovina when the Ottoman forces withdrew.

Thus began a war between the Ottoman Empire and Venice that would last for sixteen years, with Hungary and other Christian powers of Europe involved as well. During that time Mehmet mounted campaigns in both the Balkans and Anatolia, leading most of them himself, aided by Mahmut Pasha and his other commanders.

Mehmet mounted a campaign in 1464 under Mahmut Pasha that recovered most of Bosnia from the Hungarians, who continued to hold Jajce and a few other strongholds in the north. Then when Stephen Vukčić died in 1466 Mehmet annexed Hercegovina.

Two years later Mehmet launched a campaign against the fortress of Kruje in Albania, held by the Albanian leader Skanderbeg with the aid of Venetian reinforcements. But the garrison held out against repeated attacks over the course of twelve years, and the fortress did not surrender until 15 June 1478, a decade after Skanderbeg passed away. Kruje, known to the Turks as Akhisar, then remained in Turkish hands until 1913, the year after Albania won its freedom from the Ottoman Empire.

Mehmet's biggest victory against the Venetians came on 12 July 1471, when he captured their fortress at Negroponte, commanding the strait between the island of Euboea and the mainland of eastern Greece. The Venetians reacted with shock and consternation when news of the fall of Negroponte, the 'glory and splendor of Venice', reached the lagoon on 27 July, as the Milanese ambassador reported to his duke: 'All Venice is in the grip of horror; the inhabitants, half dead with fear, are saying that to give up all their possessions on the mainland would have been a lesser evil.'

Pope Sixtus IV called for a crusade against the Turks, and in response to his summons a Christian fleet was launched and sailed to Rhodes, where the various contingents assembled in June 1472. The fleet comprised fifteen transports and eighty-five galleys, the latter including thirty-six from Venice, twelve from the Venetian-controlled cities on the Dalmatian coast, eighteen from the papacy, seventeen from Naples, and two from the Knights of St John on Rhodes.

The Venetian contingent attacked and took Silifke and two other fortresses to its east, which he handed over to the Karamanid emir Kasım Bey. The entire Crusader fleet then sailed to Antalya in August 1472, breaking through the chain that blocked the entrance to the fortified port and landing troops who laid waste the environs of the city. But the Crusaders were unable to break through the powerful Roman walls of the fortified city, and so after a brief siege the fleet sailed back to Rhodes.

At that point the Neapolitan leaders, who had been in continual disagreement with the Venetian commanders, withdrew their contingent from the armada and sailed back to Naples. The rest of the Crusader fleet attacked Izmir on 13 September 1472, and after a bloody battle with the Ottoman defenders the city was sacked and burned to the ground.

Mehmet's principal campaign in Anatolia took place in the years 1472–1473, when he fought Uzun Hasan, chieftain of the Akkoyunlu Türkmen tribe, who controlled a vast empire that extended from eastern Anatolia through Persia, Mesopotamia and Syria. Mehmet finally destroyed the Akkoyunlu forces on 11 August 1473 in the mountains of north-eastern Anatolia, forcing Uzun Hasan to flee for his life, only to be killed soon afterwards. This victory permanently established Ottoman power throughout all of Anatolia except Cilicia and Upper Mesopotamia, which remained marchlands with the Muslim powers to the south and east.

Later that year the Karamanid emirs recaptured some of their former possession within and to the south of the Taurus Mountains. The following year Mehmet sent an army to Karaman under Gedik Ahmet Pasha, who took the towns of Ermenek and Minyan within the Taurus, as well as Silifke and other fortresses south of the mountains and along the Mediterranean coast. This was the end of the Karamanid as an independent *beylik*, for although they continued to exist as a tribe after 1474 their territory was controlled by the Ottomans, becoming a province of the empire the following year. By that time all of the other independent *beyliks* in Anatolia had come to an end too.

A dynastic dispute among the Tartars gave Mehmet the excuse to intervene in the affairs of the Genoese colony of Kaffa in the Crimea affairs. He launched an expedition under Gedik Ahmet Pasha, who conquered Kaffa on 6 June 1474. All of the Genoese in Kaffa were then resettled in Istanbul, where the census of 1477 recorded that they occupied 277 houses and had two churches.

The Ottoman fleet then went on to capture all of the other Genoese possessions in the Crimea, as well as the Venetian colony of Tana (now Azov) in the Sea of Azov. This ended the long Latin presence in the Crimea and its vicinity, which for the next four centuries remained under the control of the Ottomans, extending their dominions around most of the Black Sea.

Meanwhile a large force of Turkish *akincis*, or raiders, penetrated into Friuli beyond the Tagliomento river, which took them to within forty miles of Venice. The Venetian commander in Friuli, Geronimo Novello, gave battle to the *akincis* at the Tagliomento, but he and most of his men were killed.

The Venetian Senate decided to send 2,000 infantry and 6,000 cavalry to Friuli, as well as arming an additional force of 20,000 troops to defend Venetian territory against Turkish raids. But the Turkish attacks continued nonetheless, one *akinci* force penetrating as far as Pordenone, pillaging and destroying everything in its path, the smoke of burning villages clearly visible to observers atop the campanile of the basilica of San Marco in Venice. According to the chronicler Domenico Malipiero, the Venetian nobleman Celso Maffei cried out in despair to Doge Andrea Vendramin, 'The enemy is at our gate! The axe is at the root. Unless divine help comes, the doom of the Christian name is sealed.'

The Turkish raids in Friuli, coming after sixteen years of warfare, finally convinced the Signoria to come to terms with Mehmet. The secretary of the Senate, Giovanni Dario, a Venetian who had been born on Crete, was sent to Istanbul late in 1478, empowered to make an agreement without receiving further instructions. The result was a peace treaty signed in Istanbul on 28 January 1479 ending sixteen years of war between the Venetian Republic and the Ottoman Empire. The Venetians promised to pay within two years a reparation of 100,000 gold ducats, agreeing also to an annual payment of 10,000 ducats for the right of free trade in the Ottoman Empire without import and export duties.

Mehmet's health was now failing, but despite this he launched two major campaigns in 1479. The first of these was an attempt to take Rhodes, where the Knights of St John withstood a five-month siege before the Ottoman commander Mesih Pasha finally sailed his fleet back to Istanbul. That same year Gedik Ahmet Pasha captured Otranto on the heel of Italy, which the Ottomans held for only a few months before withdrawing.

Mehmet began making preparation for yet another campaign, possibly to invade Egypt. No one ever learned the sultan's plans, for at the end of the first day's march into Anatolia, 3 May 1481, his illness finally laid him low and he died the following day 'at the twenty-second hour,' according to the Italian chronicler Gianmaria Angiolello.

Mehmet was forty-nine when he died, having reigned for more than thirty years, most of which he had spent at war. As Tursun Beg wrote in his biography of the Conqueror: 'Beside the gracious gift of the Conquest of Constantinople, Fatih [Mehmet] wrested twenty or more independent lands from the enemies of his High Estate.'

News of Mehmet's death reached Venice on 29 May 1481, twenty-eight years to the day after the conquest of Constantinople. The doge sent a courier to Rome with news that the Grande Turco was dead, and the pope had cannons fired from Castel Sant' Angelo, ordering that all the church bells in the city be rung to alert the populace. The pope then led a procession to the church of Santa Maria del Popolo, where a ceremony of thanksgiving was held, and as night fell Rome was illuminated by bonfires and a tremendous fireworks display. As news spread that the Grand Turk had passed from the world the scene was repeated throughout western Europe.

After the death of Mehmet the Conqueror there was a brief war of succession between his two sons, Beyazit and Jem. Beyazit won and Jem fled to Cairo, where he gathered support for a second attempt to take the throne. But he failed in that attempt too and was forced to flee to Rhodes where he was given refuge by Pierre d'Aubusson, grand master of the Knights of St John.

Jem spent the rest of his life in exile as a prisoner in turn of the Knights of St John in Rhodes and France, of popes Innocent VIII and Alexander VI in Rome, and then of King Charles VIII of France, all of whom used him as a pawn in their negotiations with Beyazit until his death in Naples on 25 February 1495.

Now that Beyazit no longer had to be concerned about Jem, he was free to resume the campaigns of conquest that had been interrupted by the death of his father fourteen years before. Beyazit mounted a campaign against Lepanto, the Venetian fortress-town at the north-west end of the Gulf of Corinth, which surrendered after a fifteen-day siege on 29 August 1499, a severe blow to Venetian prestige.

Venice tried to make peace with Beyazit, but to no avail, and the Ottoman attacks on the Venetian fortresses in Greece continued relentlessly. The Turkish forces took Methoni in August 1500 after a six-week siege led by Beyazit himself, the first time that he had commanded his troops in battle as sultan. The fall of Methoni soon led the garrisons at Koroni and Navarino to surrender as well, defeats from which Venetian power in the Morea never recovered. The Venetians were forced to sue for peace, on terms dictated by Beyazit in mid-December 1502, a date long remembered in Venice as the beginning of the decline of the Serenissima's maritime empire.

The fall of Lepanto and the Venetian fortresses in the Morea led Pope Alexander VI to make a desperate plea for a renewed crusade against the Turks. But the internal conflicts in Christian Europe once again made this impossible, and the sudden death of Alexander on 12 August 1503, effectively ended the crusade before it began.

The Turks were less of a threat to Europe during the years 1500–1511, when the Ottoman Empire was involved in a war with Persia. While the war with Persia was still raging Beyazit became seriously ill in 1508, and for the next three years he was bed-ridden. By that time a three-sided war of succession had developed between his three surviving sons, Ahmet, Selim and Korkut, all of whom were serving as provincial governors in Anatolia. Selim knew that Beyazit planned to abdicate and leave the throne to Ahmet, the eldest, and to forestall that he took his army across to Europe in the summer of 1511 and camped near Edirne, raising the pay of his soldiers so that he drew recruits from his father's forces.

The following spring Beyazit was forced to submit to Selim, who entered Istanbul with his army on 23 April 1512 and took control of the city. The same day Selim met with his father, whom he had not seen in twenty-six years, and he forced Beyazit to abdicate. The next day Selim was girded with the sword of Osman and became the ninth sultan in the Osmanlı dynasty, the third to rule in Istanbul.

Selim allowed Beyazit to retire to Demotika in Thrace, his birthplace. But the deposed sultan died halfway there, passing away in great agony on 26 May 1512. A number of those in his entourage believed that Beyazit had been poisoned by his Jewish physician Hamon on the orders of Sultan Selim.

Selim was forty-two when he became sultan, having served for eighteen years as provincial governor in Trazon, the Greek Trebizond. His fierce mein and cruel manner led the Turks to call him Yavuz, or the Grim. Shortly after his accession Selim set out to deal with his rivals to the throne. During the next year he defeated and killed his brothers Ahmet and Korkut, after which he executed six of his nephews. His campaign to eliminate all possible rivals to the throne did not stop there, and on 20 December 1512 he executed three of his own sons, whom he suspected of plotting against him. This left Selim with only a single male heir to the throne, his son Süleyman, whom he was grooming as his successor.

The Christian powers of Europe enjoyed a respite from Ottoman aggression during Selim's reign, which was distinguished by two victorious campaigns in Asia. In the first of these campaigns Selim defeated Shah Ismail of Iran at the battle of Çaldıran on 23 August 1514, adding all of eastern Anatolia and western Persia to the Ottoman domains. In the second campaign Selim conquered the Mamluks of Egypt, capturing Cairo on 20 January 1517, thus extending the boundaries of the Ottoman Empire around the eastern Mediterranean. Tradition has it that at this time the caliph al-Mutawakkil transferred the rights of the caliphate to Selim, whose successors added this to their title of sultan right down to the end of the Ottoman Empire.

Selim prepared for a campaign into Europe in the summer of 1520, probably intending to invade Hungary, though he had not divulged his plans to his pashas. The sultan led his army out from Istanbul in early August, but a day's journey short of Edirne he became so seriously ill that the march had to be halted. Selim never recovered, and after suffering for six weeks he finally passed away on 22 September 1520. The cause of his death is suggested by the remark of an anonymous European chronicler, who noted that 'Selim the Grim died of an infected boil and thereby Hungary was spared.'

Ferhat Pasha, the commanding Ottoman general, kept Selim's death a secret so that Süleyman, the deceased sultan's only surviving son, who was serving as provincial governor in Manisa, could rush to Istanbul to take control of the government and ensure his succession to the throne.

Süleyman was nearly twenty-six when he came to the throne. Foreign observers found him to be more pleasant than his grim father, and they were hopeful that his reign would bring better relations between the Ottomans and Christians. As the Venetian Bartolomeo Contarini wrote just before Süleyman's accession: 'He is said to be a wise lord, and all men hope for good from his reign.'

Soon after his accession Süleyman and his grand vezir Piri Pasha began making preparations for a campaign into Europe. Süleyman's objective was Belgrade, the gateway to all of the lands along the middle Danube, which he captured on 29 August 1521.

The following year Süleyman launched an expedition against Rhodes, which his great-grandfather Mehmet had failed to take in 1480. Süleyman began the siege of Rhodes on 28 June 1522, when his fleet of 700 ships crossed the strait from Marmaris carrying a force of some 100,000 troops, vastly outnumbering the knights and their allies. The defenders fought on valiantly for nearly six months, but then on 22 December the grand master, Philip Villiers de L'Isle Adam, finally agreed to surrender, on condition that he and his men would be allowed to leave the island unharmed, along with all of the Rhodians who chose to accompany them.

Süleyman honoured the terms of the surrender, and on 1 January the grand master and his 180 surviving knights sailed away from Rhodes, along with 4,000 Rhodians. The Knights of St John had held Rhodes for 223 years, blocking Turkish expansion in the eastern Mediterranean, which was now open to Süleyman. The knights first retired to Crete, and then in 1530 they moved to Malta, where they constructed a mighty fortress that became a bulwark against Turkish expansion into the western Mediterranean.

Meanwhile the balance of power had shifted with the rise of the Hapsburgs. Charles V, grandson of Maximilian I, had through his inheritances become the most powerful ruler in western Europe, his possessions in Spain, the Netherlands and Germany hemming in France.

The French king, Francis I, believed that his territories were threatened and that Charles wanted 'to be master everywhere'. Francis was captured after his army was defeated by the forces of Charles V at Pavia in 1525. While in captivity Francis wrote secretly to Süleyman, suggesting that the sultan attack Hungary.

Süleyman agreed to the proposal and invaded Hungary the following year, with the Ottoman army under the command of the grand vezir Ibrahim Pasha. The campaign climaxed on 29 August 1526 at the battle of Mohacs, when the Ottomans utterly defeated the Hungarians in a battle that lasted less than two hours. King Lewis II and most of the Hungarian soldiers died in the battle, and the few who survived were executed immediately afterwards by Süleyman, who had ordered that no prisoners be taken.

After his victory at Mohacs, Süleyman led his army back to Istanbul, where he remained for six months before starting off on his next campaign into Europe, with Ibrahim Pasha once again in command. The goal of the expedition was Vienna, which the Ottoman forces besieged unsuccessfully. After suffering heavy losses Süleyman was forced to raise the siege on 15 October 1529, so as to march his army back to Istanbul before the winter began. Early in 1532 Süleyman mounted another expedition against Vienna under Ibrahim Pasha, but his army penetrated only as far as the Austrian frontier.

Süleyman's failure to capture Vienna was the only major setback he suffered in more than four decades of campaigning in Europe, while at the same time his buccaneering fleets were the terror of the Mediterranean, capturing most of the Venetian-held islands in the Aegean. Süleyman mounted a powerful expedition against Malta in 1565, but the Knights of St John defended the island with their usual valour, and the Ottoman forces were compelled to withdraw, having lost some 35,000 men, including their commander Dragut Pasha. The defeat at Malta marked the limit of Ottoman expansion in the Mediterranean, just as their failure at Vienna was the high-water mark of their penetration into Europe.

Süleyman died a year after the failure of his forces to capture Malta, passing away on the night of 5/6 September 1566 while leading his army in another invasion of Hungary. The Ottoman Empire had reached its peak during his reign, the longest and most illustrious in the history of the Ottomans.

Süleyman was succeeded by his son Selim II, nicknamed 'the Sot', the first in a succession of weak and inactive sultans, some of them insane, who ruled during the long decline of the Ottoman Empire that began in the late sixteenth century. During Selim's reign the sultan left the direction of the government largely to his capable grand vezir, Sokollu Mehmet Pasha, who had been the last to hold that post under Süleyman. After the Ottomans were defeated by a Christian fleet at the battle of Lepanto in October 1571, Sokollu Mehmet rebuilt the Turkish navy during the following winter and used it to conquer Cyprus in 1573 and to take Tunis from the Spaniards the following year.

Selim died on 15 December 1574, having collapsed in a drunken stupor while bathing in the Harem. He was succeeded by his son Murat III, who on the day of his accession had his five younger brothers murdered so that they would not contest the throne. Sokollu Mehmet continued as grand vezir under Murat III until 12 December 1579, when he was assassinated by a mad Bosnian soldier.

After the death of Sokollu Mehmet the power behind the throne was Nurubanu, the *valide sultan*, or queen mother. This began a period in Ottoman history known as the 'Sultanate of Women', when a succession of *valide sultans* exerted considerable influence on their sons, one of the causes of the decline of the Ottoman Empire after the death of Süleyman. The most powerful of these women was Kösem, a Greek girl from the Aegean island of Tinos who became the favourite wife of Sultan Ahmet I (r. 1603–1617). Kösem was *valide sultan* during the successive reigns of her sons Murat IV (r. 1623–1640) and Ibrahim the Mad (1640–1648). She continued to be the power behind the throne during the early years of the reign of her grandson Mehmet IV, who was only five when he came to the throne. Kösem finally met her end on 2 June 1651, when she was murdered in the Harem on orders of Mehmet's mother Turhan Hadice, who then took her rightful place as *valide sultan*. When Mehmet came of age his favourite wife was Rabia Gülnus, a Greek girl from Crete, who became *valide sultan* during the successive reigns of her sons Mustafa II (r. 1695–1703) and Ahmet III (r. 1703–1730).

Despite the evident decline in the empire the Ottoman forces still won occasional victories, most notably Murat IV's capture of Erivan in 1635 and Baghdad in 1638, as well as the final conquest of Crete in 1669, during the reign of Mehmet IV (r. 1648–1687). Mehmet IV mounted an expedition against Vienna in the spring of 1682 under the grand vezir Kara Mustafa Pasha, who had persuaded the sultan that when he took the city 'all the Christians would obey the Ottomans'. But after besieging the city for two months the Ottoman army was routed by a Christian force and fled in disorder. The defeat cost Mustafa Pasha his head and Sultan Mehmet his throne, for he was deposed in 1687 in favour of his brother Süleyman II (r. 1687–1691).

The Ottoman defeat at Vienna encouraged the Christian powers of Europe to form a Holy League for another crusade against the Turks. Emissaries from Austria, Poland and Venice met in March 1684, with the support of Pope Innocent XI, and the following year they invaded the Ottoman dominions on several fronts, beginning a war that would last for thirty years.

The crusade mounted by the Holy League was the first in a series of wars between the European powers and the Turks that would continue to the end of the Ottoman Empire, which lost successive chunks of territory in the peace treaties that followed each of these conflicts. The Treaty of Karlowitz, signed on 26 January 1699, ended the war with the Holy League, in which the Christian powers were victorious on both land and sea against the Ottomans, who ceded Hungary to the Austrians and Athens and the Morea to the Venetians. The Ottomans recovered their lost territory in Greece within fifteen years, but most of Hungary was lost to the empire forever.

The Treaty of Passarowitz, which ended another war with the Christian powers on 21 July 1718, cost the Ottomans all of their remaining territory in Hungary, along with much of Serbia, Bosnia and Wallachia. The Treaty of Küçük Kaynarca, signed on 21 July 1774, ended a war in which Russia conquered Moldavia, Wallachia and the Crimea. By that time the decay of the Ottoman Empire was such that the western powers began to refer to Turkey as the 'Sick Man of Europe', as they prepared to divide up its remaining territory. In the Treaty of London, signed in 1827, Britain, France and Russia agreed to intervene in the Greek War of Independence from the Ottoman Empire, leading to the foundation of the modern Greek kingdom six years later.

Meanwhile Mehmet Ali, the Turkish viceroy of Egypt, set out to establish his independence from Sultan Mahmut II, sending an army under his son Ibrahim Pasha to invade Ottoman territory in the summer of 1831.

Within a year Ibrahim conquered Palestine, Lebanon and Syria, taking Damascus on 18 June 1832. Ibrahim then led his troops across the Anatolian plateau, defeating two Ottoman armies, and on 12 February 1833 he took Kütahya, only 150 miles from Istanbul. Sultan Mahmut was so frightened by this that he called on the Russians for help. Tsar Nicholas sent a fleet to Istanbul, and on 20 February they landed troops on the Asian shore of the upper Bosphorus at Hünkâr Iskelesi. This led Ibrahim to come to terms with Sultan Mahmut, and he signed a peace treaty in Kütahya which gave Mehmet Ali control of Egypt, Syria, Arabia and Crete. Ibrahim thereupon evacuated his troops from Anatolia.

Representatives of Tsar Nicholas and Sultan Mahmut signed a treaty at Hünkâr Iskelesi on 8 July 1833, in which Russia and the Ottoman Empire concluded an eight-year non-aggression pact, in which the sultan agreed to close the Bosphorus and the Dardanelles to the ships of any countries who were in conflict with either of the two nations. This agreement alarmed the British and French who saw the prospect of the Tsar taking control of the straits, and thenceforth they were determined to protect the Ottoman Empire and defend it against Russian encroachment.

A crisis arose in 1840 when the Ottoman admiral Ahmet Fevzi Pasha sailed the Ottoman fleet to Alexandria and surrendered it to Mehmet Ali, for fear that the grand vezir Mehmet Husrev Pasha would turn it over to the Russians. The foreign minister Mustafa Reşit Pasha negotiated with the European powers – Britain, France, Russia, Austria and Prussia – to intervene, promising that Sultan Abdül Mecit would institute far-reaching reforms in the Ottoman Empire. The five powers intervened and forced Mehmet Ali to allow the Ottoman fleet to be returned to Istanbul, on the promise that Abdül Mecit would make him the governor of an autonomous Egypt.

Mustafa Reşit then worked with Abdül Mecit on the reforms he had promised the western powers. These were embodied in a *Hatti Şerif,* or imperial decree, proclaimed by Abdül Mecit at a pavilion in the lower gardens of Topkapı Sarayı known as Gülhane, the Rose Chamber. The Gülhane decree announced that Abdül Mecit thenceforth would rule as an enlightened monarch, protecting the lives and property of all his subjects – Muslims, Christians and Jews alike – and that he would create a government in which there would be equitable taxation, regular legislative councils, and a fair system of conscription to obtain manpower for a modern army and navy. This was the beginning of the *Tanzimat*, or Reform Movement, which would continue under Abdül Mecit's immediate successors.

Another crisis arose in October 1853, when Russia refused to evacuate Moldavia and Wallachia, the trans-Danubian principalities that had been taken from the Turks in 1774. This gave rise to the Crimean War, which began on 28 March 1854, when the British and French joined the Turks in fighting against the Russians on the Crimean peninsula. The Crimean War ended with the Treaty of Paris, signed on 30 March 1856. The terms of the treaty left the map much as it had been before the war. Turkey was admitted to the Concert of Europe, the harmonious family of civilised European nations, and the other signatories undertook 'to respect the independence and the territorial integrity of the Ottoman Empire'.

Abdül Hamit II succeeded as sultan on 7 September 1876, and three months later, under pressure from the Great Powers and the Turkish reform movement, he agreed to the adoption of a constitution. The constitution provided for the creation of an Ottoman parliament, which met for the first time on 19 March 1877.

Russia declared war on the Ottoman Empire on 16 April 1877, invading Turkish territory in both eastern Anatolia and the Balkans, capturing Edirne and penetrating to the suburbs of Istanbul before they were stopped by pressure from the great powers of Europe. The war was officially ended by the Treaty of Berlin, signed on 13 July 1878, in which part of Bulgaria became independent of the Ottoman Empire along with all of Montenegro, Serbia and Rumania, while a large part of north-eastern Anatolia was ceded to Russia, to which Sultan Abdül Hamit II agreed to pay a huge indemnity. Aside from the financial losses, the Treaty of Berlin cost the Ottoman Empire forty per cent of its territory and twenty per cent of its population, of whom almost half were Muslims. Another casualty of the war was the Ottoman parliament, which Abdül Hamit dissolved on 14 February 1878, suspending the constitution as well.

That same year the Ottoman Empire entered into a defensive alliance with Great Britain. As part of the agreement Britain took over the administration of Cyprus as a British protectorate, seeking to safeguard its sea-lanes to Egypt.

The movement of reform in the Ottoman Empire was led by a group known as the Young Turks, who formed a number of loosely knit coalitions, among which the Committee of Union and Progress (CUP) eventually came to the fore. On 23 July 1908 the leaders of the CUP gave an ultimatum to Abdül Hamit, warning him that unless the constitution was restored within twenty-four hours the army in Macedonia would march on Istanbul. The sultan was terrified, and on the following day he restored the constitution and declared that the parliament would be reconvened. After elections, the Second Turkish Parliament opened on 17 December 1908, with Abdül Hamit now reduced to the status of a constitutional monarch.

Meanwhile the neighbours of the Ottoman Empire had taken advantage of its weakness to grab whatever Turkish territory they could. On 6 October 1908 Austria annexed Bosnia and Hercegovina from the Ottoman Empire. On that same day all of Bulgaria declared its independence, including the part that had remained Ottoman territory in 1878. Then on the following day Greece announced its annexation of Crete, which had been under the control of the great powers after the Ottomans were forced to remove their troops from the island in 1898.

Abdül Hamit was deposed by an army coup on 23 April 1909 and replaced as sultan by his brother Mehmet V Reşat, who was merely a puppet of the Young Turks, a group of officers led by Talat, Cemal and Enver, who controlled the Ottoman government for the next decade.

Italy's designs on North Africa led it to declare war on the Ottoman Empire on 29 September 1911, putting Tripoli under blockade. The Italians opened another front by occupying the Ottoman-held island of Rhodes and bombarding the forts at the entrance to the Dardanelles.

The Balkan states now sought to take advantage of the Tripolitan War by forming alliances against the Ottomans in the summer and early autumn of 1912, their coalition comprising Greece, Bulgaria, Serbia and Montenegro. The First Balkan War began when Montenegro invaded Ottoman territory in northern Albania on 8 October 1912, with the other allies beginning offensives against the Turks shortly afterwards. The war continued until an armistice was arranged on 30 May 1913, by which time the Bulgars were at Çatalca, less than twenty-five miles from Istanbul, having captured Edirne, while the rest of the Ottoman possessions in Europe were occupied by the other Balkan allies. Ten days later the Treaty of London was signed, establishing the boundaries of the Ottoman Empire in Europe as close as sixty miles from Istanbul.

The Second Balkan War began on 29 June 1913 when the Bulgars launched surprise attacks on the Greeks and Serbs, who were soon aided by Romania and Montenegro. The four allies proved too much for the Bulgars and soon forced them to surrender. Enver Pasha seized the opportunity and led an army to recapture Edirne on 21 July. The war was officially ended by the Treaty of Bucharest, signed on 10 August 1913, in which Greece took most of Epirus and Western Thrace from the Ottoman Empire.

Enver Pasha had been busy behind the scenes preparing the way for a pact with Germany, for he knew that Russia was now entering an alliance with Britain and France known as the Triple Entente. A treaty of alliance between the Ottoman Empire and Germany was signed secretly on 2 August 1914, just as the Triple Entente and the Central Powers were declaring war on one another. Three months later the Ottoman Empire entered the First World War as an ally of Germany. Then on 2 October 1914 Britain annexed Cyprus, declaring it a crown colony of the British Empire.

The Allies thought that they could take Turkey out of the war quickly by sending a fleet through the Dardanelles to attack Istanbul, but on their first attempt, on 15 March 1915, several British and French battleships and cruisers were sunk by mines and by German and Turkish gun crews. The Allies then decided to land British and Commonwealth troops on the European shore of the Gallipoli peninsula, while at the same time the French landed a diversionary force of Senagalese troops on the Asian shore.

The Senegalese troops landed near the mouth of the Dardanelles, about where Agamemnon would have beached his ships as the Achaeans began their siege of Troy. The Senegalese made their way as far as the mound at Hisarlık, the site of ancient Troy, before they were driven back by the Turkish troops, who killed many of them before they could be picked up by the French fleet. The Turks then buried the fallen Senegalese on the Trojan plain, on the same ground as the Achaeans who had died in the siege of Troy, near the mound that marked the Tomb of Achilles.

The Turkish forces under Mustafa Cemal Pasha fought the Allies to a standstill and kept them confined to the western end of the Gallipoli peninsula. The Allies finally abandoned the Gallipoli campaign after eight months of fighting, which cost the lives of some 100,000 men on both sides, ending another chapter in the endless history of the struggle between East and West.

During the First World War the Ottoman forces were engaged on several other fronts: fighting against the Russians in the Caucasus and eastern Anatolia; and against the British and French in the Persian Gulf, Iraq, Syria, Palestine and Thrace, where in 1917 the Allies were joined by the Greeks.

The Young Turks were in complete control of the government throughout most of the war, with Talat Pasha appointed grand vezir on 3 February 1917, forming a triumvirate with Cemal and Enver. Mehmet V Reşat died on 2 July 1918 and was succeeded the following day by his brother Mehmet VI Vahidettin, fated to be the last sultan of the Ottoman Empire.

Meanwhile the Ottoman forces had suffered a series of defeats in both Iraq and Syria, where Mustafa Cemal Pasha commanded the Seventh Army. Damascus fell to the British on 1 October 1918 and the French took Beirut the following day, as the Ottoman army retreated to make a last stand in Anatolia. As they did so Mustafa Cemal sent a cable to the sultan urging him to form a new government and sue for peace.

Talat Pasha resigned as grand vezir on 8 October, and soon afterwards he and Enver and Cemal fled from Turkey on a German warship. Six days later the sultan appointed Ahmet Izzet Pasha as grand vezir, and he immediately began making overtures to the British for peace. An armistice was signed at Mudros to come into effect on 31 October 1918, eleven days before fighting between Germany and the Allies stopped on the western front. The Mudros Armistice called for total and unconditional surrender of the Ottoman army, with all strategic positions in Turkey to be occupied by Allied forces. A large Allied fleet sailed through the straits and reached Istanbul on 13 November, landing troops to begin the occupation of the city.

The Ottoman Empire was in ruins, helpless before the western powers, who now set out to divide up its remains.

17

Tourkokrateia and the *Rhomaioi*

The period of Turkish rule is known in Greek as *Tourkokrateia*, which for the Greeks in Anatolia lasted for some six centuries. The subject Greeks of the Ottoman Empire were part of the Rum *millet*, headed by the Greek Orthodox patriarch of Constantinople, who was also head of the Orthodox Christians in the Balkans, until they formed their own autocephalic churches in the nineteenth century. The Greeks of Constantinople and Anatolia in particular were known to the Turks as *Rum*, while they called themselves *Rhomaioi*, literally 'Romans' of the former Byzantine Empire, whose culture, at once Hellenic and Christian, they preserved after the fall of Byzantium to the Turks.

But the prospects for the survival of the *Rhomaioi* in Anatolia looked bleak after the Turkish conquest. Gennadios, the first patriarch of Constantinople under Ottoman rule, wrote that the Orthodox Church was in the same situation it had been prior to the reign of Constantine the Great, for 'we are now bereft of an empire, a free church, and outspokenness, as we were before'.

Gennadios resigned as patriarch in 1456 and retired to a monastery. There he wrote a work entitled *Lament*, in which he deplored what had happened to the Church and Hellenism under Turkish rule, his only hope being that the clergy would resume their role of enlightening the faithful. 'For if our nation is ever to see the sun shine again, it will only be because the clergy and the monks will have resumed intellectual leadership and, by exercising great power and solicitude, thereby create the great hope that, through charity, our entire nation shall recover completely.'

The preservation of Hellenic Christian culture was extremely difficult without schools, which the more remote communities of *Rhomaioi* had little access to before the mid-nineteenth century, when philanthropists in the modern Greek kingdom began subsidising educational institutions in Anatolia. The Bishop of Caesarea wrote in 1873 to Leon Melas, president of the Educational Society in Athens, thanking him for sending books to the Greek community in the Cappadocian town of Nevşehir. According to the Bishop, the community was Turcophone but 'Greek in spirit', having made efforts 'to regain their mother tongue and culture, and they do this to the extent that it is possible…' He refers to them as 'Greek brothers who had been in disapora for a long time among other nations…and who had experienced moral and social tribulations and who were almost severed from their race.' The Bishop also speaks of his hope that through proper schooling the Greek community of Nevşehir will be imbued 'by a pure and unadulterated Hellenism in religion, education and language'.

Only a fragment of the Anatolian Greek population survived in the fifteenth century, their numbers having been diminished by the Turkish conquest and by the conversion of many subject Christians to Islam. By the late fifteenth century, of a total of seventy-two metropolitanates subordinate to the patriarch of Constantinople only seventeen survived in Anatolia, and there remained but three bishoprics.

The historian William Ramsay, writing in 1897, remarked on the ethnic and linguistic diversity of the Anatolian *Rhomaioi*, many of whom, particularly in the more remote areas in the central plateau, had by his time all but lost their Greek language, immersed as they were in a sea of Muslim Turks: 'They have not the tie of common blood, but are the direct descendants of the most diverse races, Cappadocians, Pisidians, Isaurians, Pamphylians, men of Pontus, and so on… They are divided by difference of language: some use Greek alone, some Turkish alone, many are bilingual…'

According to Ramsay, although their ethnic origins might be diverse, the common bond of the Anatolian *Rhomaioi* as Hellenes was their membership in the Orthodox Church:

Throughout Turkey the power of religion as a unifying force is especially conspicuous in the Orthodox Church. All members of the Orthodox

Church call themselves Hellenes, all feel themselves to be so. They differ in race and in language, and are widely separated from one another, like islands in the estranging sea of Islam. But small communities in Isauria and Pisidia, in Cappadocia and in Pontus, feel themselves one with the Hellenes of Greece, because they are united in the Orthodox Church.

Even among the Greeks who retained their faith those in isolated areas lost their mother tongue and became Turkish speakers. Some of these lost communities of Anatolian Orthodox Christians came to the attention of western scholars in late Ottoman times. Spyridon Lambros wrote in 1908 of 'pitiable remnants of the once flourishing and dense Christian population of the region around which the barbarian flood lapped but which it never wholly swamped, though it did obliterate every Christian monument and indeed the entire civilisation of middle Asia Minor'.

A century or so after the Conquest, Greeks from the Aegean islands and mainland Greece began migrating to Anatolia, which had become depopulated in the early Ottoman era. Pericles Triandaphyllidis describes what the new settlers found in central Anatolia:

> When the Greeks recovered and reinhabited the lands that they had formerly abandoned or had taken away from them they found nothing to indicate that those lands had once been Christian; not a single church, not a single Greek name remained. Only a few towns which had avoided the tempest and destruction and which on this account never became entirely bereft of human life retained their original names, though in Turkish version – Kemack (from Kamschos), Sivas (Sebastia), Changra (Gangra), and so on. But very rarely today does one encounter a village or indeed any place with a Greek or Christian name, and the very few of these have only recently been given.

According to official Turkish records examined by the Turkish scholar Ömer Lütfi Barkan, in the period 1520–1535 there were 78,783 Christian households in Anatolia, which would amount to about 400,000 people. This included not only Greeks but also Armenians and other Christians. Barkan estimated that the total population of Anatolia at the time was about 5,000,000, which means that Christians amounted to only about eight per cent. Within half a century the Christian population almost doubled in certain areas of western Anatolia through the influx of Greek settlers.

Most of the new Greek settlers in Anatolia came through Izmir, which once again became the principal port on the Aegean coast of Asia Minor after the Turkish capture of Chios in 1566. The Greek settlers moved inland from Izmir through the valleys of the Hermus (Gediz) and Maeander (Menderes) rivers, the same route followed by the Hellenes in the great migration at the beginning of the first millennium BC.

Some of the new arrivals moved northward along the Aegean coast and settled in Ionia, Aeolia and the Troad, reviving ancient Greek settlements that had been virtually uninhabited for centuries. Records indicate that in 1586 Greek workmen were brought into the Troad to build the Ottoman fortress of Kum Kale at the entrance to the Dardanelles. Some of the workmen settled in two villages named Yenişehir and Nichor on Cape Sigeum, the ridge on the Aegean shore that rises above the Trojan plain by the tumuli of Achilles and Patroclus. The Turks I met on my first visit to the Trojan plain in 1961 were from Yenişehir, and the oldest of them still remembered with affection his Greek neighbours there, all of whom left in the population exchange in 1923.

Prior to the arrival of the new settlers there were small communities of Greeks in what were once the most famous and populous Greek cities in Asia Minor. When the German traveller Dernschwam visited Nicaea in 1555 he found that the Greek community numbered only eleven, along with an illiterate priest. When Stephan Gerlach visited Nicaea in 1575 he was told that there were fifty Greek communities in the vicinity of Nicaea. But in Nicaea itself the Greek community remained very small, and in the following century it increased to only some fifty souls, as evidenced by an entry in the diary of the Rev. John Covel, the Anglican chaplain at Pera in Istanbul, recording a visit he made to Nicaea in February 1677:

> When we first came to the town I desired to lodge at a Greek house if possible; we were at last brought to ye church (the Dormition), where ye papas [the priest], hearing strangers enquiring for him, ran and hid himself... There are not above 10 Greek families here now left, and about 50 Armenians; ye rest are all Turks. None of the Greeks know how to speak their own tongue, the papas himself, who (after he was better informed and his fear was over) came to us and begged our excuse, could understand well enough what we spoke to him in Greek, but would by no means answer in the same language. They, continually practising only Turkish, have in a manner quite forgotten their own language. The priest

hath got by heart…several prayers…and with these he makes a shift to entertain his hearers, though neither he nor they understand not one word in twenty. He was the most miserably poor, and the saddest ignorant soul that ever I yet met…

During the seventeenth century the Greek populations of Antalya and Side in Pamphylia and Myra in Lycia were a mixture of new arrivals and the original local inhabitants, who were said to have survived the difficult years of Ottoman dominance 'living secretly'. The Greeks in Antalya apparently lost their native tongue because the more numerous immigrants were Turkish-speaking Greeks from Isparta, less than three days' journey across the Taurus Mountains. However, by the end of the seventeenth century many of the Turkophone Greeks in the area were receiving a Greek education in an elementary school and used Greek books imported from Venice.

Bursa, ancient Prusa, the first Ottoman capital, had a Greek community of some 300 families when the French traveller Joseph Tournefort visited it in 1702. This was just two per cent of the total population of Bursa, which before the Turkish Conquest had been entirely Greek.

The population of some of the Greek and other Christian communities in central Anatolia began to increase significantly half a century after the fall of Byzantium, largely due to immigration. Turkish records show that in the sixteenth century the number of Christian families in Ankara increased from 590 to 1,347, from 570 to 1,889 in Kastamonu, from 81 to 483 in Çankırı and from 27 to 1,993 in Kocaeli. Bolu, which previously was completely Muslim Turkish, counted 134 Christian families in the census of 1570–1580. The French geographer V. Cuinet concluded from oral tradition that the Greeks of Çankırı were descended partly from the ancient inhabitants of Paphlagonia and partly from Greek merchants of Kayseri and Ankara who arrived between 1650 and 1700.

The population of Smyrna had declined considerably during the Byzantine era, and the port and its hinterland were desolate when the Ottomans took control. A census taken in 1528/1529 records a population of only about 1,000 of which about 150 were Greeks and the rest Muslim Turks. By the mid-seventeenth century the population of Smyrna had increased to some 80,000, including about 50,000 Muslim Turks, 15,000 Greeks, 7,000 Armenians, 7,000 Jews and 1,000 others, mostly Levantine Europeans. The great increase in population resulted from the redevelopment of Izmir as a port beginning in the late sixteenth century, after the Ottoman conquests of Egypt in 1517 and Rhodes in 1520 opened up the eastern Mediterranean to Turkish trade. After the conquest of Chios by the Turks in 1566 more and more Chiot merchants settled in Smyrna. By the mid-seventeenth century Izmir had become Turkey's second most important port after Istanbul.

During the reign of Süleyman the Magnificent (r. 1520–1566) the Ottomans began granting commercial concessions to European powers in order to develop the trade of the empire. Murat III (r. 1574–1595) wrote to Queen Elizabeth I to promote this trade, assuring her that he had signed an imperial decree which safeguarded any of her representatives 'as shall resort hither by sea from the realm of England'. This led to the incorporation of a group of English merchant adventurers called the Levant Company, also called the Company of Turkish Merchants, who in September 1581 were given a seven-year charter by the sultan which enabled them to set up trading stations in Izmir and Istanbul.

The Dutch traveller Cornelis de Bruyn, writing in 1678, noted that 'for commerce, Smyrna is the premier city in all the Levant'. The French traveller Tournefort observed in 1702 that in Smyrna 'the taverns were open all hours of the day and night. Inside they played music, ate wholesome food, and danced à la Franga, à la Greca, à la Turca...' indicating that Izmir had once again risen from its ashes.

The English antiquarian Richard Pococke, who visited Izmir in 1739, estimated the population to include 84,000 Muslim Turks, 8,000 Greeks, 6,000 Jews and 2,000 Armenians. Besides these there were probably several hundred European merchants, known locally as 'factors', the most numerous being those of the English Levant Company.

The English traveller Richard Chandler, who first visited Izmir in 1764, writes that 'The factors, and other Europeans settled at Izmir, generally intermarry with the Greeks, or with natives of the same religion.' His description of the rich ethnic and religious mixture in the port city indicates why Turks referred to it as *Gavur Izmir*, or Infidel Izmir, for although the Turks were the majority, the non-Muslims lived as if they were in Europe.

> The conflux at Smyrna of various nations, differing in dress, in manners, in language, and in religion, is very considerable. The Turks occupy by far the greater part of the town. The other tribes live in separate quarters.

The protestants and Roman catholics have their chapels, the Jews a synagogue or two; the Armenians a large and handsome church, with a burying ground near it. The Greeks, before the fire, had two churches...

Chandler remarked on the beauty of the Greek girls of Izmir, particularly those who had come there from Tinos and the other Aegean isles: 'Girls of inferior rank from the islands, especially Tinos abound; and are many of them as beautiful in person, and picturesque in appearance. They excel in a glow of colour, which seems the effect of a warm sun, ripening the human body as if it were into an uncommon perfection.'

Chandler made an extensive tour of the Aegean coast of Asia Minor in 1764–1765, looking for the remains of the ancient Ionian cities, some of which he found to be still inhabited by small Greek communities. Chandler writes of his first view of the Trojan plain at dawn on 25 August 1764, when his ship entered the Dardanelles: 'We now saw a level and extensive plain, the scene, as we conceived, of the battles of the Iliad, with barrows of heroes, and the river Scamander, which had a bank or bar of sand at its mouth.'

Chandler reports that there were two Greek hamlets on Cape Sigaeum, on the Aegean coast of the Trojan plain, one of them being Yenişehir, the village that I had seen myself on my first visit to Troy in 1961, the home of the horsemen who had ridden down to the Tomb of Achilles to greet us. Chandler describes Yenişehir as 'a Greek village, so miserable, as scarcely to to furnish grapes, wine, eggs, and oil to fry them, sufficient for our breakfast'.

Ephesus, one of the most famous of all the ancient Ionian cities, was a virtually uninhabited ruin when Chandler visited the site in September 1764. He reports that 'The Ephesians are now but a few peasants, living in extreme wretchedness, dependence and insensibility; the representatives of an illustrious people, and inhabiting the wreck of their greatness...'

Chandler had gone to Ephesus in search of the famous temple of Artemis, though earlier travellers had been unable to find a trace of it, and at the end of his visit he reported that he too had failed to discover any of its remains. As he wrote at the end of his visit to Ephesus: 'We now seek in vain for the temple; the city is prostrate; and the goddess gone.'

Chandler then went on to visit Miletus, which at the time was the site of a Turkish village known as Balat, which he describes as 'a very mean place', making no mention of any Christian community there. North of

Miletus, Chandler visited the site of ancient Priene, where he came upon Greeks celebrating Easter in a small village near the ruins of the ancient city.

> A small bier, prettily decked with orange and citron buds, Jasmine, flowers, and boughs, was placed in the church, with a Christ crucified rudely painted on board, for the body. We saw it in the evening; and before daybreak were suddenly awakened by the blaze and crackling of a large bonfire, with singing and shouting in honour of the resurrection. They made us presents of coloured eggs, and cakes of Easter-bread.

Chandler later visited Philadelphia, one the Seven Churches of Apocalypse, the last Byzantine city in Anatolia to be conquered by the Ottomans. He found a Greek community of some 300 families there, but neither they nor their chief priest could really speak their native tongue, as he was told: 'We were assured that the clergy and laity in general knew as little of Greek as the proto-papas; and yet the liturgies and offices of the church were read as elsewhere, and have undergone no alteration on that account.'

The town of Ayvalık, on the Aegean coast of Asia Minor opposite Lesbos, was known to its Greek inhabitants as Kydonies. The history of Ayvalık is obscure up until the last quarter of the nineteenth century, when a stroke of good luck suddenly brought it into prominence.

The historic incident that changed the fortunes of Ayvalık occurred on 6/7 July 1770, when the Russian fleet virtually annihilated the Ottoman navy in the harbour of Çeşme, at the tip of the peninsula south of Izmir. The only Turkish captain who escaped was Cezayirli Hasan, who managed to sail his badly damaged ship as far as Ayvalık, where he ran it aground. The Greeks of Ayvalık rescued Hasan and his crew and escorted them to Çanakkale on the Dardanelles, from where a ship brought them safely back to Istanbul. Four years later Hasan was made Kaptan Pasha of the Ottoman fleet and then in 1789 he became grand vezir. Hasan Pasha never forgot the Greeks of Ayvalık for saving his life, and in 1783 he obtained from Sultan Selim III an imperial decree granting the town special privileges enjoyed by few other places in the Ottoman Empire.

According to the decree, all Muslims in Ayvalık were to be relocated in the surrounding villages; no Ottoman soldiers were allowed in the town; the townspeople were spared all taxes except for a specified annual amount which was significantly less than had been paid previously; and they were allowed to appoint their own Turkish governor, with the right to dismiss him if they felt it necessary.

This privileged status attracted Greeks from all over the Ottoman Empire to Ayvalık. It soon became the most prosperous and cultured town in Asia Minor, with an Hellenic academy in which 600 students received a classical education in the liberal arts, science and mathematics, using books published by their own press. A Viennese Greek periodical in 1820 described it as this 'New Miletus, metropolis of learning for the whole of Asia Minor'. The Rev. R. Walsh, British chaplain in Istanbul in the mid-nineteenth century, called Ayvalık 'a free republic of active and intelligent Greeks, equal to any that formerly existed among their Ionian ancestors, in opulence, spirit and a feeling of independence'. According to the American scholar Charles N. Eliot, 'Ayvalik was for half a century a sort of oriental Boston, famed for its fine streets, public gardens, University, libraries, and municipal buildings, for the wealth, culture and refinement of its inhabitants.' Arnold Toynbee described it as 'the first piece of free Greek soil in modern times'.

The beginning of the Greek War of Independence brought down savage reprisals on some of the Greeks in the Ottoman Empire. On Easter Sunday 1821 the patriarch Gregory VI was hanged from the main gate of the patriarchate in Istanbul, where his body remained suspended for three days before being thrown into the Golden Horn.

The following summer an Ottoman force under Kara Ali Pasha attacked Chios, killing about a quarter of the island's population and enslaving nearly half of the islanders. Among the captives were four Chiote boys who were sold in the slave market in Istanbul and purchased by the grand admiral Hüsrev Pasha, who later became grand vezir. One of the boys, who took the name Ibrahim Ethem when he converted, became the protégé of Hüsrev Pasha and rose through the highest ranks in the Ottoman service, becoming grand vezir in 1877 under Abdül Hamit I, who gave him one of his granddaughters in marriage.

Ayvalık was also destroyed in 1822, with many of the townspeople fleeing to Greece along with refugees from Chios. The town gradually recovered, and by the end of the nineteenth century it was once again a prosperous community, with a population of nearly 30,000, almost all of whom were Greek.

After the Greek War of Independence thousands of Greeks from the Aegean islands still under Ottoman control began migrating to Anatolia, many of them finding work on the farms of wealthy Turkish landowners. This was remarked upon half a century later by the British scholar Charles Wilson, who wrote that the migration of the Greeks

> has resulted in the almost entire displacement of the Moslem population by Greek colonists from the Turkish islands of the Archipelago. Every year the islands send out fresh immigrants; the coast districts from Assos to Scala Nuova [Kuşadası] are now almost entirely owned by Greeks and the rich lands in the valleys of the Maeander and the Hermus are gradually passing into the hands of the Christians.

Among the new arrivals were Greeks from Laconia in the Peloponnesos who early in the nineteenth century settled along the shores of the Dardanelles in the Troad. These immigrants spoke Tsakonian, a language deriving from ancient Doric Greek rather than the Ionian koine of Athens that became the standard tongue of most Hellenes. Two of these Tsakonian villages in the Troad survived up until 1923, speaking a language that would have been intelligible to the Achaeans of Agamemnon's army when they were besieging Troy, but then they too were uprooted in the population exchange.

The new Greek migration was dramatically evident in the Turkish–Greek ratio in the population of Izmir. The population of the city in 1830 was estimated to be about 80,000 Turks and 20,000 Greeks, along with other minorities. Three decades later the proportions had been reversed and there were now some 75,000 Greeks to 41,000 Turks.

Greek immigration into central Anatolia sharply increased after 1856, when British investors were given a concession to build a railway from Izmir to Aydın. This was the first of several lines that during the next half century would connect Izmir with the central Anatolian plateau and the coastal plains along the Marmara and in Cilicia. A handbook published by the British Foreign Office in 1918 reports that 'A number of factories have been erected and new industries created along its route, and there has been a notable increase of the Christian population owing to the peace and security prevailing in adjacent districts.' It also noted that the railway lines 'have greatly stimulated the production of fruits, especially raisins and olives, and in the last years before the war the population near the lines, which was largely Greek, enjoyed unprecedented prosperity'.

The demographics were quite different in Cappadocia, where, because of its relative remoteness, the Greek population diminished as people left for Istanbul and the coastal regions in search of work. Archives of the Greek Orthodox metropolitan of Caesarea, the ancient capital of Cappadocia, show that almost sixty per cent of the able-bodied Greek men of the city migrated to Istanbul or other places to work. This is reflected in the census figures for Kayseri, which had 3,000 Greeks in 1890 and less than 900 in 1923, while in that same period the number of Turks increased from 600 to 1,000.

The town of Sinasos in Cappadocia was distinguished by the high level of Orthodox Hellenic culture that it maintained, when other Greek communities around it were losing their native tongue. Sinasos founded a school for boys in 1840 and a girls' school in 1872, both of which were considered to be among the best in Anatolia, attracting students from the surrounding region, including Kayseri and Konya. The subjects taught were languages, both ancient and modern Greek as well as Turkish and French; mathematics, including both theoretical and applied arithmetic, geometry and cosmography; Greek, Roman and general history; along with religion, art and music.

The Turcophone Greeks came to be known as Karamanlides, since many of them were from Karamania, the region in southern Cappadocia that had been ruled by the Karamanid Türkmen. The ethnic origins of the Karamanlides has been a matter of some controversy, a question summarised by Richard Clogg:

> Greek scholars incline to the view that the Karamanlides were of Greek descent and adopted Turkish as their vernacular, either by force or as a result of their isolation from the Greek-speaking Christians of the coastal regions. Turkish scholars regard them as the descendants of Turks who had migrated to Byzantine territories before the conquest or had served as mercenaries in the Byzantine armies and had adopted the religion but not the language of their new rulers.

Speros Vryonis concluded from his own extensive research that 'It would seem more likely that the Karamanlides were in origin largely Greek-speaking Christians of Byzantine Anatolia, who under Seljuk and Ottoman rule were Turkified liguistically, abandoned the use of Greek, and adopted a number of Turkish customs and practices.'

Half a century after the establishment of the Greek kingdom efforts were made to rehellenise the Karamanlides and other Greeks of Anatolia. The most active of the organisations founded for this purpose was the 'Society of Anatolians, the East', founded in Athens in 1891. Its objective was to educate young Greeks from Anatolia, either at the University of Athens or theological schools in Greece, or in the Greek academies of Istanbul and Izmir. Those who graduated from these schools were meant to go back to teach their compatriots in Anatolia.

One of the members of the Society argued that it was the duty of Orthodox parents to imbue their children with 'the divine language of Plato and Aristotle'. Thus the Society's schools taught the *katharevousa* form of modern Greek favoured by intellectuals of the Greek kingdom, which, according to one advocate of the 'purified' speech was free 'of the foreign usages, mutilated words and barbarous phrases with which the language of the uneducated free Greeks is unfortunately replete'.

Izmir's prosperity and large Greek population put it far ahead of all other Anatolian cities in the number and level of its Hellenic educational institutions. The most prominent of these was the Evangelical School, which had been founded in 1728 and continued to function until 1922. By the last quarter of the nineteenth century the Evangelical School had under its direction two primary schools, a Greek school, a gymnasium, and several primary schools on the Lancastrian model, with a total of some 1,400 students. Besides this, the Greek community in Izmir had two primary schools, one of them for girls, as well as a commercial school and several private academies operated by Greeks, not to mention schools run by foreign missionaries.

But the new education programme had relatively little success in the more remote areas of Anatolia, and many travellers in the late nineteenth and early twentieth century report that Greek was losing ground to Turkish among Orthodox communities. Nevertheless, the divine liturgy was still recited in Greek, though often the congregation may have been Turcophone, as Clogg noted in an article on the Karamanlides:

> During the early years of the present [twentieth] century, an Orthodox priest in Nicaea told a British traveller that, although his flock knew no Greek, 'though having heard the liturgy all their lives they knew fairly well what the prayers meant'. When certain prayers used would have been

strange to his congregation the priest had himself translated the Greek text into Turkish.

Some of the Anatolian Greeks who converted to Islam, secretly retained their Christian faith. The earliest reference to these crypto-Christians is in a pastoral letter from Patriarch John IV Kalekas in 1338 addressed to the Greeks of Nicaea, which had recently been conquered by the Ottomans. The letter implies that many of the Nicaeans had been forced to convert to Islam, and it offers two possible choices to the apostates who wished to attain salvation, and these were either martyrdom or crypto-Christianity. Those who were not courageous enough to give up their lives were told that they would be received back into the fold if they practised Christianity in secret: 'As many as wish to live in secret practising and keeping in their heart the Christian way, because of the fear of punishment against them, these also shall attain salvation.'

Crypto-Christianity appears to have been most prevalent in the Pontus, where in remote mountain communities villagers remained Christian long after the fall of Trebizond in 1461. Trebizond was presumably 100 per cent Christian when Mehmet II conquered the city in 1461, but the Ottomans soon brought in Muslim settlers. The first Ottoman register of the city, ca. 1486, showed the population to be 19 per cent Muslim and 81 per cent Christian; ca. 1543 the ratio of Muslims to Christians was 48 per cent and by 1583 it was 54 per cent. By 1583, 43 per cent of the Muslims were identified as being first or second generation converts, though many or most continued to speak Greek. Many of these converts became crypto-Christians, whose existence is reported by travellers in the Pontus in late Ottoman times. William Hamilton, writing in 1842 of his observations in the mountains above Trebizond, said: 'I have seldom seen such a wild and savage-looking set of beings. For some time we could not make out who or what they were: by degrees, however, we learnt that they were Christians, although they seemed afraid of confessing their religion.'

When Sultan Abdül Mecit issued the imperial edict known as the *Hatt-i Hümayun* on 18 February 1856, affirming the principle of religious freedom in the Ottoman Empire, the crypto-Christians of the Pontus emerged from obscurity. On 15 July 1857 forty-four crypto-Christian leaders sent an appeal to the Ottoman government and the ambassadors of the European powers in Istanbul. This led the British embassy in Istanbul to ask its acting vice-consul in Trebizond, George Stevens, for further details. Stevens responded with detailed information about the crypto-Christians, whom he called Kooroomlees, after Kromni, one of the remote villages in the mountains above Trebizond where they predominated. Stevens reported, that there were about 17,260 crypto-Christians in the Pontus, the densest concentrations being in the villages of Matzouka (Maçka), Argyroplis (Gümüşhane) and Kromni.

The British scholar R. M. Dawkins was of the opinion that the crypto-Christians of the Pontus were the descendants of the Byzantines of the Empire of Trebizond, and that they were 'most earnestly Christians'. He wrote that 'These people felt that they represented a remnant of the high civilisation of their country and that only by concealment could they be kept together.'

During the forty years after the publication of the *Hatt-i Hümayun* approximately 1,000 new churches were built in the Pontus alone. The crypto-Christians of the Pontus found that the Ottoman reforms were a mixed blessing, for Christians were no longer exempt from military service and could escape service only by paying enormous bribes. Consequently many of them who were of military age fled from Turkey to Russia or Greece, as Dawkins found when he returned to the Pontus in 1914 after an absence of five years:

> Then, when I went to the Pontus in 1914, there were hardly any males left in the Christian villages between the ages of twenty and sixty, except a few priests and schoolmasters, who had paid the heavy bribes necessary. All the rest were away. The population had indeed only been kept going by the practice of contracting very early marriages; so that these exiles would often have left a baby or two behind them, and the women were doing all the work and looking after the herds and crops in the hopes of the better times which never came.

Such was the situation in the Pontus just before the outbreak of World War I, at the beginning of a decade in which the tides of history would once again surge across Anatolia, sweeping away the Greeks and other Christians and leaving their survivors scattered as exiles from a land where their ancestors had lived since time beyond memory.

18

Megali Idea and *Catastrophia*

When the Greek kingdom was created in 1833 it comprised only the southern provinces of modern-day Greece and the central Aegean isles, its northern frontier extending roughly from the Gulf of Lamia to the Gulf of Arta. The northern provinces of Epirus, Thessaly, Macedonia and Thrace were still under Turkish rule, as were Cyprus, Crete and the eastern Aegean isles, not to mention the Greeks in Constantinople and Anatolia.

There were roughly three times as many Greeks under Ottoman rule as there were in the Greek kingdom. Nationalists of the new kingdom were inspired by the dream of creating an enlarged Hellenic state that would include the 'captive' Greeks of the Ottoman Empire. This came to be known as the *Megali Idea*, or 'Great Idea', whose classic expression is that of Ioannis Kolettis, a hellenised Vlach, in a speech before the Constituent Assembly at Athens in 1844:

> The Kingdom of Greece is not Greece; it is merely a part, the smallest, poorest part of Greece. The Greek is not only he who inhabits the Kingdom, but also he who inhabits Ioannina or Salonika or Serres or Adrianoupolis or Constantinople or Trebizond or Crete or Samos or any other region associated with Greek history or the Greek race ... There are two main centres of Hellenism: Athens is the capital of the Kingdom. Constantinople is the great capital, the City, the dream and hope of all Greeks.

Classical Greece and Byzantium were the inspiration for those who advocated the *Megali Idea*. Adamantios Korais was the leader of those who looked back to the glories of the classical world, while the followers of Rhigas Pheraios felt that the common heritage of the Byzantine Empire was what united Greeks of the kingdom with those still under Turkish rule. The followers of both Korais and Pheraios were dedicated to the redemption of Hellenic Asia Minor, which the Greeks called *I kath'imas Anatoli*, 'Our East'.

The Orthodox Church had kept the Byzantine heritage alive during the *Tourkokrateia*, the period of Turkish rule, and those who advanced the *Megali Idea* were determined to regain the ancient capital of the empire and the great church of Haghia Sophia. The British economist Nassau Senior, writing in 1859, quotes a Greek intellectual in this regard:

> Do not think that we consider this corner of Greece as our country, or Athens as our capital, or the Parthenon as our national temple. The Parthenon belongs to an age and a religion with which we have no sympathy. Our country is the vast territory of which Greek is the language, and the faith of the Orthodox Greek church is the religion. Our capital is Constantinople; our national temple is Santa Sophia, for nine hundred years the glory of Christiandom. As long as that temple, that capital and that territory are profaned and oppressed by Mussulmans, Greece would be disgraced if she were tranquil.

The first enlargement of the Greek kingdom came on 29 March 1864, when Great Britain ceded the Ionian islands to Greece. The next expansion came on 24 May 1881, when the Ottoman government, under pressure from the Great Powers, ceded most of Thessaly and the district of Arta in southern Epirus, extending the northern frontier of Greece from the Vale of Tempe to the Gulf of Arta.

The French scholar A. Synvet, writing in 1878, estimated the number of Greeks in Asia Minor at 1,188,094, with an additional 230,000 in Istanbul. The Greek population of European Turkey amounted to a further million and a half. According to Richard Clogg: 'In the large commercial cities of the empire there was also a large population of Greek citizens of the Greek kingdom, including some 45,000 in Izmir, more than in Piraeus, the port of Athens.'

According to the official Turkish statistics for 1910, the population of the Ottoman Empire in Europe, including Istanbul, was 1,940,040, comprising 974,000 Turks, 676,500 Greeks, 113,500 Bulgarians and 176,040 'Others'. The total population in Anatolia was 10,823,095, including 8,192,589 Turks, 1,777,146 Greeks, 594,539 Armenians, 39,370 Jews and 219,451 'Others', with the greatest concentration of Greeks in Ionia, Bithynia and the Pontus.

Then in the Treaty of Bucharest, signed on 10 August 1913, ending the Second Balkan War, the Ottomans ceded to Greece southern Epirus and southern Macedonia, including Thessalonica and Kavala. This expanded the area of Greece by nearly seventy per cent, the frontier of the kingdom now stretching from the Corfu Strait to the Rhodope Mountains in Western Thrace. At the same time Greece also acquired Crete and the north-eastern Aegean islands, including Thasos, Samothrace, Limnos, Lesbos, Chios and Icaria, all together increasing the population of the kingdom from some 2,700,000 to 4,800,000.

According to the Ottoman Ministry of Refugees, during the Balkan Wars in 1912–1913, 177,352 Muslim refugees fled from Rumeli, or Eastern Thrace, before the advancing Bulgarian army; then, after the Turkish–Bulgarian Treaty of 1913, 120,566 more Muslims evacuated Macedonia, with many of them taking refuge in Istanbul. Arnold Toynbee, writing in 1922, estimated that the number of Muslims driven out of the Balkans during the Balkan Wars was 413,992.

This upheaval, the first ethnic cleansing of the twentieth century, inevitably led to Turkish reprisals against the Anatolian Greeks, whose dispersal made room for the resettlement of Muslim refugees from the Balkans. The attacks were made by armed bands known as *chettés*, the Turkish equivalent of the Bulgarian *comitadjis* who had driven the Muslims out of the Balkans. In fact, some of the *chettés* were Muslim refugees taking their revenge on Christians, as Toynbee pointed out: 'The terror attacked one district after another, and was carried on by "chetté" bands, enrolled from the Rumeli refugees as well as from the local population and nominally attached as reinforcements to the regular Ottoman gendarmerie.'

After Turkey entered the First World War on the side of Germany, many Greeks from the Aegean coast of Asia Minor were resettled in central Anatolia. This forced resettlement was apparently instigated by General Liman von Sanders, commander of the German forces at Gallipoli, who sent a report to the Ottoman government in which he wrote that 'he would be unable to take the responsibility for the security of the army until the Greeks had been moved away from the coast'. He went on to write that he wanted to begin the expulsion as soon as he arrived in Ayvalık, asking 'Couldn't we just throw these infidels into the sea?' As a result virtually all Greek males in Ayvalık were resettled in central Anatolia.

A report written in June 1918 by the British Intelligence Services states that 'The number of persons dispatched from Thrace and Anatolia exceeds 1.5 million; half of this number were either killed or died due to distressed conditions.' At the Paris Peace Conference in 1919 the Greek prime minister Eleftherios Venizelos announced that 300,000 Greeks had been killed in Thrace and Anatolia and 450,000 had fled to Greece. Celal Bayar, third president of the Turkish Republic, who redistributed confiscated Greek properties to Muslim Turks, wrote in 1966 that the number of Greeks deported from Turkey at the beginning of World War I was about 130,000.

The year 1918 ended with the Ottoman Empire defeated and on the brink of destruction, Istanbul occupied by the Allied powers, whose armies had also moved into Thrace and Anatolia.

At the Paris Peace Conference, which began in January 1919, the Allies considered various plans for dividing up what was left of the Ottoman Empire. Greece, which had come in on the Allied side in the summer of 1917, put in a claim for Izmir and its hinterland in western Asia Minor, an area that stretched in a great arc from the Gulf of Ayvalık to the delta of the Maeander river, with the Smyrnaic Gulf at its focal point. This would have been the realisation of the *Megali Idea*, which envisioned a revived Byzantine Empire that would include Greece itself and north-western Asia Minor. The area in Anatolia claimed by Greece had a population in 1912 that included about 2,250,000 Muslim Turks, 975,000 Greeks, 155,000 Armenians and 92,000 'Others'. Venizelos had proposed a Greek expansion into Asia Minor as early as 1915, when he first tried to bring Greece into the war on the side of the Allies; as he wrote, looking ahead to the fall of the Ottoman Empire and the realisation of the *Megali Idea*:

> It is true for a number of years, until we organize all our military forces on the basis of the new resources yielded by the mobilization of the greater Greece, we shall be forced in case of war in the Balkan peninsula to employ part of our forces in Asia Minor in order to avert a local uprising there – an uprising which is extremely unlikely, since with the complete dissolution of the Ottoman state, our Muslim subjects will be excellent

and law-abiding citizens. The force to be disposed for this purpose will anyway be provided within a very short time by the Greek population of Asia Minor.

The Greeks of the Pontus had been trying to establish an independent Greek Republic, but Venizelos refused to support their effort, for he felt that such a state would be too remote for Greece to protect and too weak to defend itself against the Turks. And so he proposed the the province of Trebizond be incorporated in the new state that the Armenians were trying to form in eastern Turkey and the southern Caucusus. The Greek Republic of Pontus never became a reality, and in the abortive struggle to create it the Pontic Greeks were displaced with enormous loss of life.

The Italians also had territorial ambitions in Asia Minor, and on 29 March 1919 they landed troops at Antalya and began moving north-westwards toward Izmir. Lloyd George was alarmed by this, and decided that the Greeks should be granted permission to send an expeditionary force to Izmir to forestall the Italians. The final decision was made on 6 May 1919 at a meeting of President Woodrow Wilson, Lloyd George and Georges Clemenceau, who called in the Greek prime minister Eleftherios Venizelos to advise him.

The Big Three – Lloyd George, Wilson and Clemenceau – then called in the Italian prime minister Vittorio Orlando and his foreign minister Baron Sonnino, and together they divided up western Anatolia into three mandates. The Greeks were to be given the zone from Ayvalık to the Maeander delta, extending in a great arc around Smyrna; the Italians were to have the Mediterranean coast of Pamphylia around Antalya; and the French were to take Cilicia and south-eastern Anatolia.

Venizelos received support from Lloyd George and Clemenceau to send an expeditionary force to Asia Minor, and on 14 May 1919 an armada of Greek, French and British ships reached Izmir and began to land detachments of troops, including units of the Greek 1st Division. The following day the rest of the 1st division landed and were blessed by the metropolitan of Smyrna Chrysostomos, some of the soldiers doing a little dance on the quay to the cheers of the Smyrniote Greeks who had gathered to welcome them. When the Greek troops marched through Konak Meydanı, the main square on the waterfront, a Turkish civilian in the crowd fired a shot that killed the standard-bearer of the 38th regiment of Evzones. The Greek soldiers opened fire on the government building and the military barracks in the square, and after half an hour of fighting the Turkish troops inside surrendered, after which some of them were killed by both the Greek soldiers and civilians. During the course of the day some 300 to 400 Turks and about 100 Greeks, including two soldiers, were killed in this and other incidents in Izmir and its surroundings.

Venizelos appointed Aristeidis Stergiadis as governor of Smyrna, his immediate goal being to restore law and order in the city. After court-martialling those responsible for killing and looting on May 15–16 he established an efficient administration, gendarmerie and judicial system in which the Turks and Greeks of Smyrna were treated impartially. He resettled some 100,000 Greek refugees, established an experimental farm to introduce them to more productive methods of agriculture, and founded a university to restore Smyrna as a cultural centre.

Meanwhile the Greek army, now numbering about 120,000, moved inland without opposition, and by mid-summer they had penetrated up the Maeander valley into the interior of Anatolia as well as northward up the Ionian coast as far as Ayvalık.

The Ottoman government of Sultan Mehmet VI Vahidettin continued to function under the aegis of the Allied High Commissioners. Meanwhile a national resistance movement was developing under the leadership of Mustafa Cemal Pasha. On 19 March 1920 Cemal announced that the Turkish nation was establishing its own parliament – the Grand National Assembly – in Ankara. The new parliament met for the first time on 23 April 1920, choosing Cemal as its first president.

During the summer of 1919 two separate boards of enquiry were established by the Allies to examine the Greek expedition in Asia Minor. One of them, headed by General George Milne, commander of the British forces in Turkey, arose from the disputes between the Greeks and the Italians over the limits of their zones of operations in the Maeander valley. Milne established the limits of the Greek zone of occupation, which extended from the Gulf of Edremit at Ayvalık to Aydın on the lower Maeander, its eastern boundary sixty miles inland from Izmir. He wrote in his report that any Greek advance beyond this boundary, which came to be called the Milne Line, would encounter determined resistance from the Turks.

The other investigation was conducted by the Interallied Commission of Enquiry, headed by generals from Britain, France and the US, with the

Greek colonel Mazarakis as a non-voting observer. The Commission, which issued its report in August, was highly critical of the Greek army, which they held responsible for the violence in Smyrna at the time of their landing, as well as for the bloodshed and destruction in their advance into the interior of Anatolia. The last of their conclusions was that 'the Turkish national sentiment, which has already manifested its resistance, will never accept this annexation. It will submit only to force, that is to say, before a military expedition which Greece alone could carry out without any chance of success.'

Venizelos disagreed with the commission's final conclusion, maintaining that the Greek army in Asia Minor, with its twelve divisions, had nothing to fear from the Turkish Nationalists under Cemal, who had only 70,000 men under arms.

The Greeks went into action again on 22 June 1920, beginning an offensive across the Milne Line in four directions, moving inland along the valleys of the Maeander, Cayster and Hermus, and heading northward along the railway line from Manisa to Bandirma on the Marmara. After Bandirma was taken a cavalry brigade rode eastward along the Marmara shore to take Bursa on 8 July. Then in August the Greeks ended the offensive by moving up onto the Anatolian plateau above the Maeander to take Uşak, some 120 miles inland from Izmir. Another Greek army invaded Eastern Thrace in July, and within a week it was within striking distance of Istanbul, from which it was held back only by Allied pressure.

The Allies agreed on the post-war boundaries of the Ottoman Empire at the Treaty of Sèvres, signed on 10 August 1920. The treaty greatly reduced the extent of the empire, putting the straits under international control, leaving Istanbul nominally under the sultan's rule. Thrace would be ceded to Greece, which would be sovereign in Izmir and its hinterland for five years, after which the League of Nations would decide whether western Asia Minor would become an integral part of the Greek kingdom.

The Greek army advanced deeper into Anatolia in October 1920 with the encouragement of Lloyd George, who wanted to put pressure on the Turks, both the sultan's government in Istanbul and the Nationalists under Cemal in Ankara, to sign the Treaty of Sèvres.

Venizelos fell from power in a general election on 14 November 1920, following the death of King Alexander from the bite of a pet monkey.

Alexander was succeeded by his father Constantine, who had been deposed in 1917. A new government was formed under Dimitrios Gounaris, whereupon Venizelos and several of his ministers went into exile. About 150 Venizelist officers in the army resigned, including four generals, and the new government replaced them with its own supporters, many of whom had been forced to retire when Venizelos came to power in 1915. Consequently, by the spring of 1921 only two of the nine corps and divisional commanders of the Greek army in Anatolia remained, most of the Venizelist regimental commanders also having been replaced, mostly by inexperienced Royalist officers.

By December 1920 the Greek army had advanced as far as Eskişehir, where fierce resistance from the Nationalists forced them to return to their original positions. Another Greek offensive was repelled by the Nationalists under Ismet Pasha on 11 January 1921 at the Inönü river just north of Kütahya, the first major victory for the Turks. This led to proposals by the Allies to amend the Treaty of Sèvres at a conference in London, which was attended by representatives of both the Istanbul and Ankara governments.

At the first full meeting of the conference, on 21 February, the Greek representatives presented a strong case for the continuation of Allied support of their operations in Asia Minor. The Greek position was supported by Lloyd George and their army renewed its offensive in Anatolia on 23 March 1921. The offensive was two-pronged, the southern one heading from Uşak toward Afyon and the northern from Bursa toward Eskişehir. The Greeks took Afyon on 27 March, but their northern group was defeated by Ismet Pasha at the second battle of Inönü, a four-day struggle that ended 30 March, after which they were forced to retreat to Bursa.

The Greeks regrouped and prepared for a summer offensive. On 11 June 1921 King Constantine, who had declared himself Supreme Commander of the Greek army in Asia Minor, departed for Izmir with the Chief of the General Staff, Victor Dousmanis. The King and Dousmanis established their headquarters in Izmir, while General Anastasios Papoulas, the commanding general of the army in Asia Minor, left with his staff to direct the offensive, which began on 10 July.

The offensive was a three-pronged attack whose objective was to take the railway line that ran from Afyon through Kütahya to Eskişehir. The Greeks captured Kütahya on 17 July and moved on toward Eskişehir, hoping to encircle the Turkish forces commanded by Ismet Pasha. Cemal Pasha came from Ankara and, after assessing the situation, ordered a general retreat, whereupon the Greeks occupied Eskişehir on 19 July. The Turkish Nationalist Assembly voted to make Cemal commander-in-chief of the army, with full powers to direct preparations to halt the expected Greek attack on Ankara.

King Constantine met with his generals and political leaders to consider their next move, and it was decided to pursue the enemy. The Greek army began marching eastward from Eskişehir on 14 August, following the railway line along the Porsuk river to its confluence with the Sakarya, where the latter makes a great U-bend some forty miles west of Ankara.

The Greeks reached the Sakarya on 23 August, and by 2 September they had taken the Turkish position on the heights of Çal Dağ east of the Sakarya, some twenty-five miles from Ankara, as the battle raged in the Phrygian highlands, within sight of the tumuli that marked the tombs of the kings of ancient Lydia. After a week-long lull the Turks counterattacked on 8 September. The Greek line held for two days, but then on 11 September General Papoulas ordered a general retreat back to Eskişehir, having suffered over 20,000 casualties.

The Turks were unable to follow up on their victory, and the Greeks moved back to the lines that they had held before their offensive. A long stalemate followed, during which various proposals were put forward for a settlement of the conflict. But the Turkish Nationalists refused an armistice without a simultaneous Greek evacuation of Asia Minor. There was also a movement, known as the *Mikrasiatiki Amyna*, which proposed to set up an independent Greek state in western Asia Minor with Smyrna as its capital, to be defended by a volunteer army. But in the end nothing came of the movement, and as the months dragged on the morale of the Greek troops in Asia Minor declined inexorably.

Meanwhile Cemal had been building up the strength of the Nationalist army, and during the early summer of 1922 he began concentrating his troops along the Greek lines in north-western Anatolia. Then on 26 August the Turkish army under Cemal began what came to be known as the *Büyük Taarruz*, the Great Offensive, moving forward on a line stretching from Izmit to Afyon. Izmit fell on the first day of the offensive, and four days later the Turks utterly defeated the Greeks at Dumlupınar, thirty miles west of Afyon. Half of the Greek army involved in the battle was either killed or captured, including General Trikoupis, who only after his surrender learned that he had been appointed commander-in-chief of the Greek forces in Asia Minor.

The Turks captured Eskişehir on 2 September, and the government in Athens asked Britain to arrange a truce in which the Greeks could at least keep Smyrna and its environs, but Cemal rejected the proposal. Balıkesir fell on 6 September, and on the following day the Turks took Aydın and Manisa, which was burned to the ground by the Greeks when they evacuated the town. Turkish cavalry entered Izmir on 9 September, and two days later Gemlik and Mudanya surrendered.

Meanwhile units of the retreating Greek army had bypassed Izmir to the south and marched out to the end of the peninsula at Çeşme, where ships took them across to Chios. Some units retreated to Mudania and Bandirma, where they were shipped across the Sea of Marmara to Thrace, while one regiment made its way down to Dikili and was taken to Lesbos. Thus by 19 September all of the Greek troops had been evacuated, leaving much of western Asia Minor in ruins after atrocities on both sides. Greek civilian refugees crowded the roads leading toward the sea, and by 5 September they were arriving in Izmir at the rate of 30,000 a day, according to American observers, all hoping to get aboard one of the ships in the harbour.

Cemal entered Izmir on 10 September, escorted by a division of cavalry to the Konak, the government building on the waterfront square, which had been the scene of the first fighting when Greek troops had landed in the city more than three years before.

Looting and violence had already started in Izmir on the evening of 9 September, and within the next four days many Greek and Armenian civilians were killed, including the metropolitan of Smyrna, Chrysostomos, who was savagely mutilated by a mob. Late in the afternoon of 13 September fire broke out in the Armenian quarter, evidently arson. The fire spread rapidly and almost totally destroyed the Armenian, Greek and European quarters, leaving the Turkish and Jewish quarters untouched. The inhabitants of the burning neighbourhoods fled down to the waterfront, where many drowned while trying to escape from the flames. The scene is described by the journalist Ward Price of the *Daily Mail*, who watched in horror from the deck of the British warship *HMS Iron Duke*:

What I see as I stand on the deck of the *Iron Duke* is an unbroken wall of fire, two miles long, in which twenty distinct volcanoes of raging flames are throwing up jagged, withering tongues to a height of a hundred feet. Against this curtain of fire, which blocks out the sky, are silhouetted the towers of the Greek churches, the domes of the mosques, and the flat square roofs of the houses. All Smyrna's warehouses, business buildings, and European residences, with others behind them, burned like furious torches. From this intensely glowing mass of yellow, orange and crimson fire pour up thick clotted coils of oily black smoke that hide the moon at its zenith. The sea glows a deep copper-red, and, worst of all, from the densely packed mob of many thousands of refugees huddled on the narrow quay, between the advancing fiery death behind and the deep water in front, comes continuously such frantic screaming in sheer terror as can be heard miles away.

Estimates of the number killed in the Turkish capture of Izmir and the ensuing fire vary widely. Admiral Mark L. Bristol, US high commissioner in Istanbul, reported that 'It is impossible to estimate the number of deaths due to killings, fire and execution, but the total probably does not exceed 2,000.' George Horton, the US consul in Izmir, estimated that 100,000 were killed in the burning of Izmir, and he wrote that 'The torch was applied to that ill-fated city and it was all systematically burned by the soldiers of Mustafa Cemal.'

Thus the *Megali Idea* ended in what the Greeks still call the *Catastrophia*, a Greek tragedy that would reach its climax with the exodus of all the Hellenes from Asia Minor, concluding a drama that began with the siege of Troy.

19

Exodus and Diaspora

After the capture of Izmir the Nationalist army headed toward the Bosphorus, the Sea of Marmara and the Dardanelles, where the Allied occupation zone was held by British, French and Italian troops. When the Nationalist forces reached the Dardanelles the French and Italian troops abandoned their positions, leaving the British alone to face the Turks. General Harington, the Allied commander in Istanbul, ordered the British troops not to fire on the Turks, and on his request the Greek fleet left the straits. The British government then forced the Greeks to withdraw beyond the Maritza (Evros) river in Thrace, which convinced Cemal to agree to negotiations for an armistice.

An armistice was signed on 11 October at Mudanya, on the Sea of Marmara. It was agreed that the Nationalists would occupy all of Thrace east of the Maritza river except for Istanbul and a zone along the straits, which would continue to be held by the British until a final peace treaty was signed.

On 1 November 1922 the Grand National Assembly in Ankara passed legislation separating the sultanate and caliphate, with the former being abolished and the latter reduced to a purely religious role subservient to the state. The Allied High Commissioners were informed that thenceforth Istanbul would be under the administration of the assembly and that Vahidettin was no longer sultan, though he retained the title of caliph. On 17 November 1922 Vahidettin left Istanbul aboard the British warship

HMS Malaya, never to return. His brother Abdül Mecit II succeeded him as caliph on 24 November 1922.

The final articles of the Treaty of Lausanne, signed on 24 July 1923, established the present boundaries of the Turkish Republic, except for the province of Hatay in south-eastern Anatolia, which was acquired after a plebiscite in 1939.

The Allied occupation of Istanbul came to an end on 2 October 1923, when the last detachment of British troops embarked from the city. Four days later a division of the Turkish Nationalist army marched into Istanbul. On 13 October the Grand National Assembly passed a law making Ankara the capital of Turkey.

Then on 29 October the assembly adopted a constitution that created the Republic of Turkey, and on that same day Cemal was elected as its first president, whereupon he chose Ismet as prime minister. Cemal subsequently took the name Atatürk, meaning 'Father of the Turks', symbolising his leadership in creating the new Turkish Republic that rose out of the ashes of the Ottoman Empire. Ismet took Inönü as his last name, in commemoration of the place where he had led the Nationalist forces to victory over the Greeks in the Turkish War of Liberation.

On 3 March 1924 the Grand National Assembly passed a law abolishing the caliphate, thus severing the last tenuous bond that linked Turkey with the Ottoman Empire. This same law deposed Abdül Mecit as caliph, stating that he and all of his family and descendants were forbidden to reside within the boundaries of the Turkish Republic. The following day Abdül Mecit left Istanbul, never to return.

And thus the Ottoman Empire finally came to an end, with the departure of the last member of the Osmanlı dynasty that had ruled in Turkey for more than 700 years. The House of Osman had fallen, and the dynasty that he had founded was sent off into exile, most of them into western Europe, which for centuries had lived in fear of the Grand Turk.

The *Catastrophia* in Asia Minor led to a revolution in Greece in which King Constantine was forced to abdicate for the second time in five years, to be succeeded by his son George II. The Revolutionary Committee established a board of enquiry to determine responsibility for the Asia Minor disaster, and after a court martial six leaders of the government and army who had presided over the *Catastrophia* were sentenced to death for high treason, including Dimitrios Gounaris. The six were executed by a firing squad on 28 November 1922 at the Averoff prison in Athens.

Meanwhile the Revolutionary Committee had appointed Venizelos to represent them in negotiations with the Allies. A separate agreement between Greece and Turkey, signed by Venizelos and Ismet Pasha at Lausanne on 30 January 1923, provided for a compulsory population exchange of their minorities, as defined in Article I of the convention:

> As from the 1st May, 1923, there shall take place a compulsory exchange of Turkish nationals of the Greek Orthodox religion established in Turkish territory, and of Greek nationals of the Moslem religion established in Greek territory. These persons shall not return to live in Turkey or Greece respectively without the authorization of the Turkish Government or of the Greek Government respectively.

Article 2 of the convention stated that the only exceptions to the exchange were the Turks of Western Thrace and the Greeks of Istanbul and the islands of Imbros and Tenedos off the Dardanelles. Article 3 noted that 'Those Greeks and Moslems who have already and since the 18th October 1912, left the territories the Greek and Turkish inhabitants of which are to be respectively exchanged, shall be considered as included in the exchange provided for in Article 1.'

Many of the Greeks left Turkey well before the formal agreement, fleeing from the war zones in Asia Minor and Eastern Thrace. Ernest Hemingway, then a young reporter for the *Toronto Star*, reported on the refugees fleeing from Eastern Thrace after the Greek army was forced to move back across the Maritza river, in a dispatch dated 20 October 1920:

> In a never-ending, staggering march the Christian population of Eastern Thrace is jamming the roads to Macedonia. The main column crossing the Maritza river at Adrianople is twenty miles long. Twenty miles of carts drawn by cows, bullocks and muddy-flanked water buffalo, with exhausted, staggering men, women and children, blankets over their heads, walking blindly along in the rain beside their worldly goods. A husband spreads a blanket over a woman in labor in one of the carts to keep off the driving rain. She is the only person making a sound. Her little daughter looks at her in horror and begins to cry. And the procession keeps moving...

The American Red Cross, which had been giving aid to the refugees, announced in March 1923 that it was withdrawing from its work in

Greece, though it emphasised that a state of emergency still existed. Dr Fridjof Nansen, the Norwegian explorer and statesman, convinced the Greek government to accept his plan for a Refugee Settlement Commission (RSC) under the auspices of the League of Nations. Henry Morgenthau, formerly US Ambassador to the Sublime Porte, was appointed chairman of the RSC. The RSC managed to obtain a loan with the assistance of the League of Nations, and so it was able to begin the great humanitarian mission that it carried on for more than seven years.

The Commission held its first meeting on 11 November 1923 in Thessalonica. Later that day Morgenthau made a tour of the port, where he witnessed the arrival of a ship carrying refugees from Asia Minor. Only then did he realise the magnitude of the problem that he faced, as he wrote in his book on the work he did with the RSC:

> A more tragic sight could hardly be imagined. I saw seven thousand people crowded in a ship that would have been taxed to capacity with two thousand. They were packed like sardines upon the deck, a squirming, writhing mass of human misery. They had been at sea for four days. There had not been a space to permit them to lie down to sleep; there had been no food to eat; there was not access to toilet facilities... They came ashore in rags, sick, covered with vermin, hollow-eyed, exuding the horrid stench of human filth – bowed with despair...
>
> A human problem! And I at the moment, above all others, pledged to redeem this throng! What an awful responsibility! How could I dare to fail them, when my failure meant a deeper misery to these people – to thousands of them, death?

The catastrophe had happened so rapidly that the refugees began pouring into Greece before any facilities had been prepared to receive them, or even to number them. When the RSC issued its first quarterly report, in April 1924, it stated that the exact number of refugees who had arrived in Greece was unknown, but that it could be estimated from a tentative census taken the previous year. According to the census, by April 1923, 786,431 refugees had arrived in Greece, 351,313 of them male and 435,118 female. The disproportionately low number of males was due to the fact that men of military age who had been captured by the Turks had been taken off to labour in Anatolia. The RSC estimated that some 200,000 more Greek refugees had arrived in Greece between April 1923 and April 1924, and they expected that another 150,000 would come through the implementation of the exchange of population programme. In addition, more than 100,000 Armenian refugees from Anatolia made their way to Greece.

Greece and Bulgaria had also agreed to an exchange of populations, signed on 27 November 1919, in which some 30,000 Greeks were expelled from Bulgaria and 53,000 Bulgarians were deported from Greece. Besides these it is estimated that there were about 16,000 Greeks who had come to Greece from Bulgaria as refugees during the First World War and now sought assistance under the exchange of populations convention.

The first accurate figures for the number of displaced people in Greece came with the 1928 census, which showed that there were 1,221,849 refugees, including 256,954 from Thrace, 626,954 from Asia Minor exclusive of the Pontus, and 182,169 from the Pontus, as well as 38,458 from Constantinople. But these figures do not take into account the refugees who died in the interim, and if this is included the total number is estimated to be as high as 1,500,000. The exchange of minorities increased the population of Greece by about a third, and at the same time it greatly altered the country's ethnological composition. Greeks represented 80.75 per cent of the population in 1920, Turks amounting to 13.91 per cent; in 1928 Greeks made up 93.85 per cent and Turks only 1.66 per cent, virtually all of the latter concentrated in Western Thrace, with smaller minorities of Bulgars, Jews, Armenians and Albanians, making Greece the most ethnically homogeneous state in south-eastern Europe.

Estimates put the number of Muslim Turks from Greece who were resettled in Turkey at about 400,000, many of them moving into the homes of Greeks who had left Eastern Thrace and Anatolia. One of the ironies of this exchange was that many of the Greeks from Anatolia spoke only Turkish, while many Turks from Greece spoke only Greek.

The Turcophone Greeks, the Karamanlides, had been the subject of discussion at the Lausanne Conference, where Lord Curzon, the British foreign secretary, thought that the population exchange should not include what he called 'the reconciled Ottoman Greeks, numbered at about 50,000 persons'. Both Ismet Pasha and Venizelos were of the same opinion about them. Ismet Pasha referred to the Karamanlides as 'Orthodox Turks [who had never] asked for treatment differing in any respect from that enjoyed by their Muslim compatriots, and it was most improbable that they would ever make such a request'. Venizelos spoke of them as the

'Turkish-speaking persons of the Orthodox faith…who would stay in any case'.

All of the Karamanlides were included in the population exchange except for a group from the village of Keskin, near Ankara, the parishioners of a Greek Orthodox priest named Papa Eftim Karahissaridis. Papa Eftim had sided with the Turkish Nationalists during the War of Independence, and as a reward he and his flock were exempted from the population exchange and moved to Istanbul.

There Papa Eftim took over the old church of the Panagia Kalafatiane in Galata, where he set himself up as the head of what he called the Turkish Orthodox Church, in which the liturgy was in Turkish.

The Ecumenical patriarch Meletios IV was at first prepared to cooperate with Eftim, proposing that the church in Galata could be 'a special ecclesiastical province, autonomous but subject to the Ecumenical Patriarchate, in which the liturgical language would be Turkish'. But Eftim broke off all relations with the Ecumenical Patriarchate, and in 1924 he convened a rump ecclesiastical council which elected him as patriarch of the Turkish Orthodox Church, after which he changed his name to Zeki Erenerol. I met with Eftim once in the early 1960s, when his parishioners were still fairly numerous, and I heard him sing the mass in resonant Turkish. After Eftim's death in 1968 the Turkish Orthodox Church was headed in turn by his sons Turgut and Selçuk, and today it is directed by his grandson Paşa Ümit, known as Papa Eftim IV, whose sister Sevgi is linked with an underground nationalist organisation called Ergenekon. Today the Turkish Orthodox Church seems to consist of only members of the Erenerol family.

Many of the Muslim refugees from Greece settled in Eastern Thrace, those from the Greek islands and Crete settling along the Aegean and Mediterranean coasts, where in the early 1960s I could still hear the older people speaking Greek. Turkish refugees from Lesbos (Mytilene) settled mainly in and around Ayvalık, many of them moving into the houses vacated by the Greeks who had moved over to Lesbos. An article in the *National Geographic* magazine in November 1922 describes the poignant scene when the Turkish refugees departed from Lesbos, where their families had lived as long as they could remember, leaving for a country that few of them had ever set foot upon.

Believers in a traditional Hellenophobia-Turkophobia would have stared at the sight of the Mytilene Greeks spreading farewell meals for their departing neighbours, and later accompanying them to the quay, where Christians and Mohammedans, who for a lifetime had been plowing adjacently and even sharing occasional backgammon games at village cafes, embraced and parted with tears. Then, seated on their heaped up baggage, with their flocks around them – the women weeping, the children hugging their pets, the gray-bearded babas all dignity, as is their wont – the Mytilene Muslims set forth for unknown Turkey.

By the end of 1930, when the RSC was finally dissolved, the Commission had permanently settled 570,156 refugees in the agricultural provinces of Greece, and the Greek government had done so for another 8,688, together amounting to about half of those who had arrived in the population exchange. During the next eight years another 167,079 were settled in farming communities, bringing the total to 668,316, most of them in Macedonia and Thrace, where many of the refugees were housed in homes that had been vacated by the exchanged Muslim and Bulgarian minorities. Sir John Campbell, vice-chairman of the RSC in the years 1924–1927, revisited Macedonia in 1930 and was struck by how much the countryside had been changed by the resettlement of the refugees, as he wrote in his report to the Commission:

The aspect of the country has entirely changed. Everywhere one sees the cheerful red roofs of the colonization settlements. Where formerly vast uncultivated plains stretched, there are now flourishing villages, full of bustling activity, and showing obvious signs of comfort, and in many cases of prosperity. The whole country-side is awake and alive with new life... The progress achieved is surprising and most gratifying... These results are due, in the first place, to the courage, the energy, the capacity for work, the receptivity to new ideas, which characterize the mass of refugees.

About half of the refugees ended up in urban areas, about sixty per cent of them in the three largest cities in Greece – Athens, Piraeus and Thessalonica – each of which received between 100,000 and 130,000 refugees. Dimitri Pentzopoulos gives a vivid explanation of why the big cities took in so many refugees:

This is explained by the fact that at the time of their arrival in 1922, these centers afforded the greatest number of convenient shelters, such as theaters, schools, churches, warehouses and requisitioned houses. Each box of the Royal Theater in Athens with its velvet upholstery and the ornate golden decorations, housed one family; each classroom of the public schools provided shelter to a number of refugees many of whom had never seen a blackboard; and in the incense-perfumed churches, in the dim light of the candles, one could see a series of straw mattresses under the icons with the severe, byzantine faces of the saints.

By the end of 1929 the RSC and the government together had constructed more than 27,000 houses for refugees in urban areas. Some of these developed into Athenian suburbs named for the places where the refugees had formerly lived, such as Nea Smyrni, Nea Philadelphia, Nea Ionia and Nea Erythrae, which even today are inhabited principally by families from Asia Minor.

Despite this effort, by 1930 there were more than 30,000 refugee families still living in shanty-towns in Athens, Piraeus and Thessalonica. The poorly housed urban refugees lived in conditions of appalling poverty, which grew much worse during the Great Depression and the German occupation of World War Two, when these communities became centres for the KKE, the Greek Communist Party. Sir Reginald Leeper, writing in 1950, describes one of the refugee quarters in Athens in December 1944, when the Communists almost seized control of the government: 'In front we looked on to some of the poorest suburbs in Athens. It was here that the Greek immigrants from Turkey had been settled... Most of the houses were wretched shacks and it was not surprising that these suburbs were Communist strongholds.'

The refugee slums in Athens preserved elements of their Anatolian culture, including *rebetika*, or Greek blues, and the songs of lament called *amanedas*, which they sang to the accompaniment of the *bouzouki* in the waterfront dives of the Piraeus and other places where the refugees found shelter in makeshift dwellings. Many of these songs, particularly the *amanedas* and those of the *rebetika* known as *Smyrnaika*, expressed the deep nostalgia (a Greek word) of the exiles for their Anatolian homeland, which for many was Smyrna and its hinterland, such as verses recorded in 1994 by Kounadis:

Cheer up, my refugee girl, forget your misfortune
and one day we shall return to our familiar haunt.
We'll build our nest in our lovely Smyrna
And you'll enjoy my sweet love and embraces.

Another song in the *Smyrnaika* tradition appears in Roderick Beaton's *Folk Poetry of Modern Greece*:

> What is it to you where I come from,
> From Karatasi, light of my life, or from Kordelio?
>
> What is to you, that you keep asking me
> What village I'm from, since you don't love me?
>
> Where I come from they know how to love,
> They know how to hide their sorrow, and how to enjoy themselves,
>
> What is it to you, that you keep asking me,
> Since you've no pity for me, light of my life, and torment me?
>
> I've come from Smyrna, to find some comfort,
> To find in this Athens of ours a loving embrace.

Many of the refugees from Asia Minor went on to the US, Canada and Australia, bringing their music and their dances and their memories with them. Sophia Bilides, a Greek-American in Boston, has preserved the songs her grandmother brought with her from Asia Minor, such as a threnody I heard her sing one day in Boston, transporting me on the wings of song to Ayvalık.

> My eyes have never seen a village like Ayvali
> Ask me about it, for I have been there.
> It has silver doors, golden keys,
> And beautiful girls as fresh as cool water.

The nostalgia of the exiles is apparent in the concept of *Romiosini*, an almost untranslatable word that epitomises the Hellenic and Byzantine spirit of the Romaioi in Anatolia, the very essence of Greekness. The word appears in the refrain of the threnody 'Smyrni', a lament written by a Samiot who calls himself Pythagoras:

> Smyrni is burning, Mother
> Our livelihood is in flames
> Our pain is untold
> Our yearning beyond words.
>
> Romiosini, Romiosini
> When will you rest?

You live in peace for just one year
And thirty amidst flames.

Smyrni is burning, Mother
Our dreams are vanishing
And those who cling on the boat sides
Are beaten back by friends.

Farewell Anatolia, *'i kath'imas Anatoli'*.

20

Ionian Elegy

Today the only Christian Greek citizens of the Turkish Republic are the 2,000 or so who live in Istanbul and the Turkish Aegean islands of Imbros (Gökçeada) and Tenedos (Bozcaada). The Turks call them *Rum* and they refer to themselves as *Romaioi*, though the empire from which they take their name vanished more than five and a half centuries ago. Besides the *Rum* there are a few thousand Muslims in the valleys of the Pontus above Trebizond who still speak Greek among themselves, though their ancestors converted to Islam after the Turkish conquest.

The external wounds of the great fire of 1922 have long since healed in Izmir. Reconstruction of the burned-out quarters of the city went very slowly at first, and when we first visited Izmir in 1962 the damage due to the fire was still evident, though by then there had been much new construction. The city has been totally transformed since then and the scars of the fire have disappeared, except in the memory of exiled Greeks.

The city has grown tremendously, its population now more than three million, the third most populous in Turkey after Istanbul and Ankara. Turkish Izmir looks toward the Aegean rather than into Anatolia, in a way fulfilling Alexander's dream that the city be part of the Western world rather than the Orient, though the vision has often led to its destruction between the opposing forces of East and West.

During the past generation Izmir has experienced a rebirth that has made it the most vibrant city in Turkey, its citizens more European in their outlook than most other Turks, its students outranking those of all other Turkish cities on the national university entrance exam. Izmir now has two public universities – Ege University, founded in 1955, and Dokuz Eylül University, established in 1982 – which between them have some 90,000 students and more than 6,000 faculty. It also has two private universities – Izmir University of Economics and Yaşar University, both founded in 2002, as well as the Izmir Institute of Technology, chartered in 1996.

The Izmir International Trade Fair, founded in 1948, is held late in August or early in September, attracting exhibitors from all over the world, with 1,500,000 visitors in 2006. The Fair is held in Kültür Parkı, a large park that was laid out on the site of the old Greek and Armenian quarters that were burned in the fire of 1922. The Izmir International Festival, founded in 1987, is held in Kültür Parkı from mid-June till mid-July, and has brought some international orchestras, ballet companies, jazz groups and individual artists to the city, with some of the performances held at the theatres in Ephesus and other ancient Ionan sites in the vicinity.

Part of Izmir's recovery has been the tremendous boom in tourism in Turkey during the past generation. Izmir is the gateway to Ionia, and many of the tourists who come to visit Ephesus and the other Graeco-Roman cities in Aegean Turkey pass through the city on their way. Some of the ancient sites in Izmir itself have been excavated in recent years, one of them, at Bayraklı, at the north-east corner of the gulf, some two miles from the city centre, revealing part of the original site of prehistoric Smyrna.

The excavations at Bayraklı were done in 1948–1951 by John M. Cook and Ekrem Akurgal. The excavations indicate that the site at Bayraklı was inhabited as early as the first half of the third millennium BC, the oldest strata of the settlement being contemporary with Troy I and II. The earliest Hellenic settlers appeared to have come to Smyrna in the tenth century BC, as evidenced by large quantities of protogeometric pottery unearthed in the site at Bayraklı. The excavations also unearthed houses dating from the ninth to the seventh century BC, as well as an archaic temple of Athena, originally built ca. 640 BC, which Professor Akurgal describes as 'the earliest and finest building of the eastern Greek world in Asia Minor'.

The supposed site of Homer's birthplace is identified as 'Diana's Baths', a spring-fed pool within the grounds of the Izmir water-supply pumping station. The spring is the source of a stream known to the Greeks as the

Meles and the Turks as Melez Çayı. This is the stream mentioned by Pausanias in his description of Smyrna: 'Smyrna has the river Meles with the finest water, and a cave with a spring where they say Homer wrote his poetry.' The name 'Diana's Baths' comes from the discovery in the pool of a statue of Artemis, the Roman Diana, as well as ancient architectural members that suggest the spring was an Artemisium. It has been suggested that this is the pool referred to in one of the Homeric Hymns to Artemis, which sings of how the divine huntress, 'having washed her horses in deep-reeded Meles, drove swiftly through Smyrna to Claros deep in vines'. An inscription in the spring, now built into the nearby Burnabat Camii, reads: 'I sing the praises of the Meles, my saviour, now that every plague and evil has ceased.' This is believed to have been the plague that ravaged Smyrna in the years AD 175–178, during the reign of Marcus Aurelius, when the curative waters of the spring were credited with ending the epidemic.

The best view of the historic centre of the city is from Kadifekale, the ancient fortress on the summit of Mount Pagos. The summit is to a large extent surrounded by the walls and towers of Kadifekale, the Velvet Castle, the bastion of the two lines of defence walls that extended down to the sea, enclosing the Hellenistic city that was built here by Lysimachus, the site revealed to Alexander through his dream on Mount Pagos. The seaward walls have vanished and all that remains is the citadel known to the Turks as Kadifekale. Even there only the foundations and a few of the lower courses date from the time of Lysimachus, with the remainder due to successive reconstructions by the Romans, Byzantines and Ottoman Turks.

The principal archaeological site remaining from Graeco-Roman Smyrna is the Agora, which is about midway between Kadifekale and the port. This market square was originally constructed in the mid-second century BC, only to be destroyed in the great earthquake of 178. Shortly afterwards it was restored by the empress Faustina II, wife of Marcus Aurelius. The Agora was destroyed in the successive Persian and Arab invasions of the early Byzantine era, after which its site was used as a cemetery, first by Christians and then by Muslims, so that it was never built upon when Izmir began to revive in the seventeenth century.

The site was first excavated by German archaeologists in the years 1932–1941. A new programme of excavation by Turkish archaeologists began in 1996, sponsored by the Greater Municipality of Izmir, and continues to the present day. The archaeological site now forms the Izmir Agora Open Air Museum.

The Agora consists of a central courtyard measuring 120 by 80 metres, surrounded on all sides by Corinthian stoas, of which only those on the north and west sides have been excavated. Beneath the north stoa there is a splendid vaulted basement, above which there was an arcade of shops that opened out into a Roman market street. The Agora was one of the monuments that made the Smyrnaians so proud of their city, which in an inscription of the third century AD they refer to as 'the First of Asia in beauty and size, and the most brilliant, ... and the ornament of Asia'.

Some of the scupltures that once adorned the Agora are now in the Izmir Archaeological Museum. The most notable of these are statues of Poseidon and Demeter, the principal figures in a beautiful and well-preserved group discovered at the beginning of the Agora excavations in 1932. These statues symbolised the two principal sources of ancient Smyrna's wealth, for Poseidon was god of the sea and Demeter goddess of agriculture.

The other exhibits in the museum are from archaeological sites in Ionia, most notably Ephesus. Ephesus is the main attraction for most of the tourists who come to Izmir, those who arrive by sea going there from the port town of Kuşadası. The archaeological site of Ephesus is outside Selçuk, the town that began to develop in the early Turkish period under the Aydınid Türkmen *beylik*, the ancient city itself then being an uninhabited area of scattered ruins, famous monuments like the temple of Artemis having virtually disappeared.

The first archaeological excavations of ancient Ephesus were begun in 1863 by the engineer John Turtle Wood in a project sponsored by the British Museum. After searching for more than six years, Wood finally unearthed part of the marble pavement of the Artemisium on the last day of 1869 at a depth of some six metres. Wood continued excavating the site until 1874, but even then he had not cleared the temple to its lowest levels. This was accomplished by D.G. Hogarth in a two-year campaign for the British Museum beginning in 1904. In the course of time he excavated the temple to its foundations, determined the several periods of its construction and recovered important architectural members. A team of Austrian archaeologists had been excavating elsewhere in Ephesus since 1895, and their successors continue to work there to the present day. These excavations have been accompanied by the restoration of many monuments ranging from the ancient Graeco-Roman age to the early Turkish era, spanning a period of nearly 2,000 years.

The archaic Artemesium was one of the Seven Wonders of the Ancient World, but now all that remains standing of the temple of Ephesian Artemis is a single column, whose drums were re-erected after they were excavated. A stork erected its nest atop the uppermost drum soon after it was put in place, and its descendants still perch there, oblivious to the hordes of tourists who photograph it as they pass the Artemesium.

The earliest shrine of Artemis discovered on this site is a protogeometric temple dating from the ninth or eighth century BC. This would have been erected soon after the founding of Ephesus, apparently on the site of an earlier shrine of the Anatolian fertility goddess Cybele, whose cult was amalgamated with that of Artemis. Then with the coming of Christianity the cult of Artemis was submerged in that of the Virgin Mary, who, according to a late tradition, spent her last years in Ephesus in the company of St John the Apostle. The first church dedicated to the Virgin at Ephesus was erected soon after Constantine the Great published a decree in 313 allowing Christians to worship together in public places. At the Third Ecumenical Council, convened at Ephesus by Theodosius II in 431, it was decreed that Mary was the Theotokos, the Mother of God, and thenceforth her cult replaced that of Artemis, whose temple had already been destroyed by a mob led by the patriarch John Chrysostom.

After its final destruction the temple of Artemis was used as a quarry for other buildings, particularly the church of St John the Theologian, built by the emperor Justinian (r. 527–565) on the Ayasuluk hill above the Artemisium. The church was destroyed during the Turkish invasions and its stones were used to build the mosque of Isa Bey, which was erected below the Ayasuluk hill in 1375. The church of St John has been splendidly restored in recent years, lacking only its superstructure. The plan is based on Justinian's long-vanished church of the Holy Apostles in Constantinople, which was also the archetype for the basilica of San Marco in Venice.

Beneath the altar is the crypt, approached by a flight of six steps. This contained the supposed tomb of St John the Theologian, the goal of the multitude of pilgrims who flocked to Ephesus during the medieval Byzantine era. Within the crypt there was a small chapel containing the grave of St John and three very precious relics: a fragment of the True Cross, a seamless garment woven by the Blessed Virgin which she wore during her last years in Ephesus, and the original manuscript of the *Book of Revelation*, written by St John the Theologian.

The site of Ephesus was virtually abandoned early in the Ottoman period by its Greek population, who moved up into the surrounding hills to a village known to the Turks as Kirkince. Kirkince is the setting for the first chapter of Dido Sotiriou's novel, *Farewell Anatolia*, which she wrote forty years after she left Smyrna as a refugee at the age of thirteen, resettling with her family in Greece. The hero of her novel, a young man named Manolis Axiotis, describes the idyllic setting of his village, which he calls Kirkica.

> If paradise really exists, Kirkica, our village, was a little corner of it. We lived close to God, high up on a hillside among forested mountains with the sea in the distance. As far as the eye could see, the fertile valley of Ephesus stretched out at our feet, thickly planted with fig and olive groves, and fields of tobacco, cotton, wheat, corn and sesame; and it is all ours... Each villager owned the land he tilled. And each had his own two-storied house, not to mention a country place with a watermelon patch, walnut and olive groves, apple, pear and cherry orchards, and bright blooming flower gardens. Gurgling streams and babbling brooks flowed year round: what more could we possibly have wished for! When the wheat and barley grew tall and ripe our fields looked like amber seas.

The villagers brought with them the traditions that their ancestors had established in Ephesus, particularly the feast day of St John in late June at the time of the summer solstice, one of several festivals that Manolis describes:

> Saint John's day was another of our great feasts. It was a celebration of manliness: gallant, strong-bodied young men girded with pistols and long knives led high-stepping stallions through their paces. But come the feast of the Holy Trinity, when the cherries hung plump and ripe from the trees, men weren't the only riders. Now tall in the saddle would be the new brides, proud and vivacious, necklaces of florins tinkling at their throats. Who could keep up with the riders of Kirkica?

> All day and long into the night the hillsides echoed with the sounds of the violin, the *oud*, the *saz* and the drum. Beaneath the trees the people danced the *karsilamas*, the *hasapikos*, the *zeybekikos*. Liberated from daily toil,

our bodies leaped skyward like flames to be kissed by the wind and carressed by the moon. Daybreak would find us still there, with barely enough time to climb into our work clothes and grab our picks and shovels.

Christmas, New Year's day, Epiphany, Carnival, Easter – could there have been a feast day we'd let pass without festivities?... And all to the accompaniment of keening songs full of love and yearning.

Manolis is caught up in the Greek–Turkish war of 1919–1922, and after the Nationalist victory he manages to escape from the flames of Smyrna to the island of Samos. There he looks back in the night toward the Anatolian shore, dreaming of the lost world in which he and his ancestors since time immemorial had lived their lives.

Across from us, on the Asia Minor shore, lanterns flickered, eyes flickered. There, across the water, we abandoned our homes, our bolted storerooms, our wedding wreaths laid atop the iconostase, our ancestors in their graveyards. We abandoned our children and parents and brothers, left our dead unburied, the living without a roof over their heads. There. Over there, until just yesterday, it has been our home...

The monotonous tinkling of bells. The broad stride of camels carrying paniers and sacks lashed across their humps, laden with raisins, figs, olives, bales of cotton and silk, jugs and demijohns of rose water and raki, brimming with the abundance of Anatolia. Gone, all of it...

So much suffering, so much tragedy. Now my mind only wanted to return to the past. If it could only all be a lie, if we could only go back to our land, to our gardens, to our forests with their songbirds, sparrows and tiny owls, to our orchards with their tangerine trees and flowering cherries, to our beautiful festivals...

The surviving Greek population of Kirkince was resettled in a village in Thessaly that they called Nea Ephesus, which we passed through for the first time in the early 1960s on our way from Istanbul to Athens. The older villagers in Nea Ephesus were still speaking Turkish, and when I spoke to some of them in the *kafenion* they expressed their nostalgia for 'i kath'imas Anatoli'.

Meanwhile Muslim Turks from Kavala were resettled in Kirkince, which has since been renamed Şirince. We first visited Şirince in the early 1960s, when all of the village elders still spoke some Greek, and they talked of how they missed their old life in Kavala.

One of the ancient Ionian cities is now part of the Greater Municipality of Izmir, namely Clazomenae, known in Turkish as Urla, a suburban town 38 kilometres west of the city. Clazomenae was the birthplace of Anaxagoras, who was born there ca. 500 BC and when he came of age he moved to Athens, where he became the teacher of Pericles and the first to theorise about the physical nature of the cosmos after the early speculations by the Milesian philosophers Thales, Anaximander and Anaximenes.

Urla produced the Greek poet George Seferis, who was born there in the seaside suburb of Skala on 29 February 1900. In 1914 he moved with his family to Athens, where he received his secondary education, after which he studied in Paris and received a degree in law. Seferis won the Nobel Prize in literature in 1963. He was the first Greek to win the prize, which was awarded to him for his role in the renaissance of modern Greek literature, for his poetry directly links ancient and modern Greece. Seferis returned to his birthplace for the first time since his youth in 1950, and some of his later poems were inspired by this journey, such as this strophe from 'Memory II', remembering a visit to Ephesus:

> I remember still:
> he was journeying to Ionian coasts, to empty shells of theatres,
> where only the lizard slithers over the dry stones,
> and I asked him: 'Will they ever be full again some day?'
> and he answered: 'Maybe at the hour of death,'
> And he ran across the orchestra howling,
> 'Let me hear my brother!'
> And the silence surrounding us was harsh,
> Leaving no trace at all on the glass of the blue.

Seferis' journal records his painful visit to the house where he was born, now abandoned and desolate along with the other old Greek dwellings in Skala:

> The panes of the ground floor windows broken, the iron door terribly rusted: it can't have been painted since we lived there. I still have the key in Athens... The shutters of the upper storey are rotted; they look as though they could never be closed. The walls were leprous. I tried to peer through to the inside of the house. I discerned the glass partition in the dining room but there wasn't enough light to see further... I strolled round, walking along the breakwater of the harbour as far as the lighthouse, now whitewashed, looking as though made of salt... There at

the sea's edge, beside the lighthouse, I suddenly turned my back to the houses, which were staring at me like sick animals. It was almost as if the little life that was left in them depended on me alone. I looked toward my islands, the sea terribly alive and the wind seeking to reunite it with the face of a dead girl. Poor Skala.

His visit to site of the Seferis house in Izmir was equally painful, as he records in his journal entries for 1–2 July 1950:

Then toward Smyrna; familiar air, familiar appearance of the countryside, and the strong aroma of herbs. Then, little by little from within, the city so well known to memory, and so strange now, returns to my mind. My God, what am I doing here!... After dinner, a few steps toward the location of our house, the <u>nothingness</u>. And still a few steps more toward the quay... The sea at dawn from my window, and the rocks known as the Two Brothers; that was all. I remembered the burial urns of Kos. Smyrna must be such an urn for me – no one can return. Smyrna has lost its shadow.

The rocky hills known as the Two Brothers are landmarks in Izmir, catching the last golden glow of sunset across the Smyrnaic Gulf, as Seferis describes them in a poem written after his return: 'The sun sets below the rock of the Two Brothers./The twilight spreads over the sky and sea like the colours of an inexhaustible love.'

The Calder and Bean *Classical Atlas of Asia Minor* lists more than 2,400 ancient Greek cities within the boundaries of modern Turkey, the preponderance of them scattered along the Aegean and Mediterranean coasts. Some are famous sites like Ephesus, where archaeologists have unearthed and restored the surviving monuments. Others are in remote areas rarely visited by travellers, such as Aegae, the only one of the ancient Aeolian cities that survives to any appreciable extent, with its ruined temples and other monuments crowning a hilltop acropolis, their moss-covered stones lying in the dappled shade of an olive grove, the only sound the resonant tinkling of belled goats in the plain below. Many of the sites have remains of monuments ranging from the archaic Greek era to the late Byzantine period, some of them with Byzantine churches built in and from the ruins of an ancient edifice, as in Miletus, where the sixth-century basilica of St Michael was erected over a classical temple of Dionysus.

These ancient Greek and medieval Byzantine monuments dot the landscape of Anatolia along with the ruins of even older civilisations, the remains of empires that rose and flourished and fell, to be succeeded by others in the ebb and flow of the tides of history. The Hellenic presence in Anatolia endured for more than three millennia, its earliest evidence being mounds like the tumulus of Achilles on the Trojan plain, where archaeologists have recently found Mycenaean burials dating back to the late Bronze Age, lending support to the historicity of Homer's epics.

I visited Troy again in the spring of 2008 and discovered that one can now drive drive directly to the tumulus. But otherwise the scene had hardly changed, for the turbaned tombstones of the old Turkish graveyard still surrounded the tumulus. Up on the Sigaeum ridge I could see the minaret of the village mosque in Yenişehir, from where the horsemen had ridden down to investigate the strangers on the plain, the oldest of them telling me of the Greek neighbours he had known there before the population exchange. But now he is gone and surely no one in Yenişehir today knows that they are living in a village whose history dates back to the Trojan War.

But the tumulus of Achilles remains, and as I stood beside it once again I recalled the lines from the last book of the *Odyssey* that had come to mind when I first saw it more than half a lifetime ago, where Agamemnon speaks to Achilles when their shades meet in the Underworld, the 'country of dreams', telling him of how the Argives had piled up a grave mound 'on a jutting promontory by the wide Hellespont, so that it could be seen afar out on the water by men now alive and those to be born in the future'.

Such were the Greeks of Anatolia, who still refer to their lost homeland as '*i kath'imas Anatoli*'.

Source Notes

(The references are to works listed in the Bibliography)

PROLOGUE – THE TROJAN PLAIN

p. xii 'The long dispute...', Wood, p. 71

p. xii 'Mound called the Tomb...', Schliemann, *Troy and its Remains*, p. 179

p. xii 'Then we the holy host...', ibid, p. 178

p. xiv 'Turkish workmen were...', ibid, p. 122

p. xiv 'It can no longer be doubted...', Blegen, p. 20

CHAPTER 1 – THE ACHAEANS IN ANATOLIA

p. 1 'we have no record...', Thucydides, 1. 3

p. 1 The best evidence..., ibid, 1.3

p. 1 'strait that surpasses...', quoted Freely, *The Bosphorus*, p. 1

p. 3 'down to a piedmont country...', Cary, *The Geographical Background of Greek and Roman History*, p. 151

pp. 4–5 'the Asian meadow...', *Iliad*, 2. 461

p. 5 'Sing, goddess, the anger...', ibid, 2. 1–7

p. 6 'It is Settlement VIIa, then,...' Blegen, p. 164

p. 6 'I can only express...', quoted, Wood, p. 244

p. 7 '*all* those excavated...' Wood, p. 134

p. 7 Now all those who... *Iliad*, p. 681–685

p. 7 '*all* those excavated have revealed Mycenaean occupation...'

p. 8 'the towns of the king...', Huxley, *Achaeans and Hittites*, p. 33

p. 8 'Tall Hektor of the...' *Iliad*, 2. 816

p. 8 'indications that the Hittite...', Latacz, p. 62

p. 9 'that the Trojan War...', Macqueen, p. 33

CHAPTER 2 – THE GREAT MIGRATION

p. 10 'the country now called Hellas…', Thucydides, 1. 2

p. 10 'the period of shifting populations…', ibid, 1. 12

p. 11 'Cyme (also known as Phriconis), Larisa,…', Herodotus 6. 46

p. 12 'The largest and best…', Strabo, VI, p. 161

p. 12 'settled near Helicon…', ibid, VI, p. 161

p. 12 'it is not agreed…', ibid, VI, p. 161

p. 13 'This men called…', *Iliad*, 2. 813–814

p. 13 'that it had an altar…', Strabo VI, p. 159

p. 13 'its most beautiful grove…', Pausanias, I, p. 61

p. 13 'given to wine…', quoted Freely, *The Western Shores of Turkey*, p. 84

p. 13 'Never on earth before…', *Iliad*, 2. 553–554

p. 14 'stay on the spot…', Strabo, VI, p. 95

p. 14 'which put pains…', *Iliad*, 1. 2

p. 15 First of all Zeus…, ibid, 20. 215–218

p. 15 'They who dwelt in…', ibid, 2. 835–836

p. 15 'set sail with his father…', Strabo, VI, p. 107

p. 15 'had the good fortune…', Herodotus, 1. 142

pp. 15–16 It is quite absurd…, ibid, 1. 146

p. 16 'it was here that…', ibid, 1. 148

p. 16 Yet in Delos…, *Hesiod, the Homeric Hymns and Homerica*, p. 335

p. 16 'The people of Smyrna…', Herodotus, 1. 150

p. 16 'the first settled…', quoted Freely, *The Western Shores of Turkey*, p. 197

p. 18 'who in earlier times…', Strabo, VI, p. 119

p. 19 'The Lycians come originally…', Herodotus, 1. 171

p. 19 'Sarpedon with unfaulted…', *Iliad*, 2. 876–877

p. 20 'There is a tradition…', Arrian, 1. 27

p. 20 'This Sidetan language…', Bean, *Turkey's Southern Shore*, p. 57

p. 20 'seem to have been…', ibid, p. 57

p. 20 Herodotus says that…, Strabo, VI, p. 325

CHAPTER 3 – THE ARCHAIC RENAISSANCE

p. 21 For with all peoples, *Odyssey*, 8. 479–481

pp. 21–2 'cannot by their language…', Dowden, p. 188

p. 22 'Whom think ye, girls…', *Hesiod, the Homeric Hymns and Homerica*, p. 337

p. 22 'But, as for Homer…', ibid, p. 567

p. 23 'Now there comes upon us…', quoted Huxley, *The Early Ionians*, p. 53

p. 23 'Once established in power...', Herodotus, 1. 14

p. 23 'They had acquired useless luxuries...', quoted Huxley, *The Early Ionians*, p. 53

p. 24 Alyattes carried on..., Herodotus, 1. 17

p. 24 'met with disaster', Herodotus, 1. 16

p. 25 'first founder', Guthrie, I, p. 40

p. 25 'the first of the Greeks,...', ibid, I, p. 72

p. 25 'solstices, times, seasons...', ibid, p. 74

p. 26 *'Panta rhei'*, Burnet, p. 46

p. 26 'Heracleitus somewhere says...', Kirk and Raven, p. 197

p. 26 'Evil witnesses are...', ibid, p. 189

p. 26 'What I understood...', Guthrie, I, p. 142

p. 27 who has gone from..., Lattimore, p. 40

p. 28 'Father Zeus...', Page, p. 226

p. 28 Tell them, Alkaios..., Burn, *The Lyric Age of Greece*, p. 240

p. 28 'the greatest work of...', Herodotus, 1. 93

p. 28 The base of this monument..., ibid, 1. 39

p. 30 When Harpagus advanced..., ibid, 1. 176

p. 31 'Megabazus marched through...', ibid, 5. 2

p. 32 The Athenians, on the contrary..., ibid, 6. 330–331

p. 32 'the first poet...', Pausanias, I, p. 70

p. 33 'Bring water, lad,...', quoted Freely, *The Western Shores of Turkey*, p. 137

p. 33 'ascribed to the gods...', ibid, I, p. 371

p. 33 'The Ethiopians say...', Kirk and Raven, p. 168

p. 33 'God is one,...', Guthrie, I, p. 374

p. 33 'Stop, do not beat...', Lloyd, *Early Greek Science: Thales to Aristotle*, p. 11

p. 33 'Three score and seven...', ibid, p. 141

p. 33 'Such things should be said...', ibid. p. 141

CHAPTER 4 – THE PERSIAN WARS

p. 34 'returned to Asia...'. Herodotus, 6. 46

pp. 34–5 'Having mastered Eretria...', Herodotus, 1. 102

p. 35 'long drawn out', ibid, 1. 102

p. 35 'his anger against...', ibid, 7. 1

p. 35 'and all Asia...', ibid, 7. 1

p. 35 'Xerxes at first...', ibid, 7. 5

p. 35 'your name will...', ibid, 7. 5

p. 35 'For the four years...', ibid, 7. 20

p. 36 At a conference of..., ibid, 7. 145

p. 36 'was indeed far greater...', ibid, 7. 21

p. 36 'Xerxes had a strong...', ibid, 7. 43

p. 36 'a throne of white marble...', ibid, 7. 44

p. 37 And when he saw..., ibid, 7. 108

p. 37 'pressing into his service...', ibid, 7. 108

p. 37 'Stranger, tell the...', quoted Hammond, *A History of Greece to 322 BC*, p. 236

p. 38 Skillfully the Greeks struck..., Aeschylus, *The Persians*, II, 422–432

p. 39 'deliberately held back...', Herodotus, 8. 85

p. 39 'My men have turned...', ibid, 8. 87

p. 39 'they accompanied him...', Strabo, VI, p. 205

p. 40 'remember freedom', Herodotus, 9. 98

p. 40 'When most of the...', ibid, 9. 106

p. 40 'Thus this day...', ibid, 9. 104

p. 40 'the future of Ionia', ibid, 9. 106

p. 41 'This done, the fleet...', ibid, 9. 106

p. 41 It was by a common..., Thucydides, 1. 18

CHAPTER 5 – BETWEEN EAST AND WEST

p. 42 So Athens took over..., Thucydides, 1. 9

p. 43 'These are the men...', *Palatine Anthology*, 7, 258

p. 44 'introduced a bill...', Plutarch, *Life of Pericles*, xvii. 1

p. 44 'urging them all...', ibid, xvii. 3

p. 45 'the demos of...', quoted Kagan, p. 118

p. 46 'uprecedented suffering for Hellas', Thucydides, 1. 23

p. 46 'greatest action that we know...', ibid, 7. 88

p. 47 Some people spoke..., Xenophon, *Hellenica*, II. 2. 22–23

p. 49 'be handed over to...', Cambridge Ancient History, Vol. 6, p. 117

p. 49 Nearly the whole of Greece..., Xenophon, *Hellenica*, VII, 27

p. 50 'Nothing occurs at random,...', Kirk and Raven, p. 413

p. 50 'We must suppose...', ibid, p. 378

p. 50 'The sun, the moon...', ibid, p. 391

p. 51 But the man who most..., Plutarch, *Life of Pericles*, iv: 4

p. 51 'a little before the...', *Oxford Classical Dictionary*, p. 507

p. 51 'Herodotus of Halicarnassus here displays...', Herodotus, 1. 1

CHAPTER 6 – ALEXANDER'S DREAM

p. 53 'Philip and his descendants', Hammond, *History of Greece*, p. 572

p. 54 'He upbraided his son...', Plutarch, *Alexander*, 10. 3

p. 56 'not much more...', Arrian, i. 11

p. 56 'the first of all...', *Iliad*, 2. 702

p. 56 'to ensure better luck...', Arrian, 1. 11

p. 56 'offered sacrifice to...', ibid, 1. 11

p. 56 'One account says...', ibid, 1. 12

p. 57 'Arsites escaped to...', ibid, 1. 16

p. 57 'he recalled everyone...', ibid, 1. 18

p. 58 Alexander founded the..., Pausanias, 1, p. 240

p. 58 'was to make...', ibid, 1, p. 236

p. 59 'King Alexander presented...', Freely, *The Aegean Coast of Turkey*, p. 241

p. 59 'all the cities...', Diodorus, 17. 24, 1–3

p. 60 'made the boy head...', quoted Freely, *The Western Mediterranean Coast of Turkey*, p. 71

p. 61 'from then on...', Arrian, 1. 26

p. 61 'a fortified town...', ibid, 1. 27

p. 61 'Alexander then proceeded...', ibid, 1. 29

p. 62 'destined to be...', ibid, 2. 3

p. 62 For Alexander, then,..., ibid, 2. 3

p. 63 'he received the submission...', ibid, 2. 4

p. 65 'Successive delegations from Greece...', ibid, 7. 23

p. 65 'I put them down...', ibid, 7. 27

p. 65 It is my belief..., ibid, 7. 30

p. 65 'No admission to...', Freely, *The Aegean Coast of Turkey*, p. 244

CHAPTER 7 – ALEXANDER'S SUCCESSORS

p. 68 'in a kingdom reduced...', Polybius, *The Histories*,1.1.1

p. 69 'how, and under what...', ibid, 1. 1.

p. 70 'friends and allies ...', quoted Shipley, p. 396

p. 71 'He took ninety...', Plutarch, quoted by Freely, *The Companion Guide to Turkey*, p. 342

p. 71 '*Veni, vidi, vici!*...', Freely, *The Companion Guide to Turkey*, p. 401

p. 73 He founded cities..., quoted Cohen, p. 66

p. 74 'it was thought to...', Strabo, Vol. VI, p. 53

p. 75 'was adorned with costly...' Vol. VI, p. 297

p. 78 'Without Chrysippus no Stoa', Sarton, Vol. 1, p. 161

p. 80 'in the harmony and skill...', Strabo, 14. 1. 40

p. 80 'he suspects that the length...', Strabo, 2. 3. 7

CHAPTER 8 – ROMAN RULE AND REVELATION

p. 81 'Zeus, the Earth, the...', Magie, Vol. 1, p. 465

p. 83 'friend and ally', Magie, Vol. 1, p. 443

p. 84 'violent and overbearing,...', Mommsen, Vol. 1, p. 577

p. 85 'aided the cities, both...', Dio Cassius, lxix 5, 2f

p. 85 'the largest and most beautiful...', Magie, Vol. 1, p. 614

p. 85 'Olympian Zeus... Saviour of the whole...', Cadoux, p. 257

p. 85 'no longer are the cities...', Magie, Vol 1, p. 629

p. 86 'the worst excesses...', Goodman, p. 75

p. 88 'the first and greatest...', Cadoux, p. 291

p. 88 'the First of Asia...', ibid, p. 291

p. 88 'the utility of geography...', Strabo, 1. 1. 1

p. 91 'they were to live together...', *Acts*, 11: 26

p. 91 'Men of Israel...', ibid, 13: 17

p. 91 'assembled to hear...', ibid, 13: 44

p. 91 'they spoke so effectively...', ibid, 14: 1

p. 91 'sailed for Antioch,...', ibid, 14: 26

p. 91 I now feel sure..., ibid, 20: 17–38

pp. 91–2 'Last of all, John,...', *Jerusalem Bible, The New Testament*, p. 112

p. 92 My name is John..., *Revelation*, 1: 1–11

p. 92 'used to describe...', Cadoux, p. 353

p. 92 'an angel announces...', *Revelation*, 18: 21–24

CHAPTER 9 – NEW ROME

p. 96 'seeking after a city...', Zosimus, II, 30

p. 97 'homes for certain Senators...', ibid, II, 31

p. 98 'Now I know...', quoted Freely, *Istanbul, The Imperial City*, p. 44

p. 100 'the Emperor Theodosius entered...', Zosimus, IV, 33

p. 100 'The Bishop of Constantinople...', quoted Mitchell, *A History of the Later Roman Empire*, pp. 247–248

p. 102 'renowned Constantine, the...', Bury, *History of the Later Roman Empire*, Vol. 1, p. 232

p. 103 'No one is to call Mary...', Theophanes, 88

p. 105 'as probably the greatest...', Cameron, *The Later Roman Empire*, p. 13

p. 105 'the emperor's speedy death...', quoted Jones, *The Decline of the Ancient World*, p. 351

p. 105 'He was a man...', Ammianus, XXV, 4. 1

p. 105 'and if you would...', Bowersock, pp. 13–14

p. 106 Tell the king on earth..., Bury, *History of the Later Roman Empire*, Vol. 1, p. 370

CHAPTER 10 – THE AGE OF JUSTINIAN

p. 107 Though I am a Hellene..., quoted Freely, *Istanbul: The Imperial City*, p. 78

p. 109 'We have good hopes...', quoted Bury, *History of the Later Roman Empire*, Vol. II, p. 26

p. 109 'the last great historian...', Mitchell, *A History of the Later Roman Empire*, p. 26

p. 110 'infected with the madness...', quoted Bury, *History of the Later Roman Empire*, Vol. II, p. 367

pp. 110–11 'the Emperor, disregarding...', Procopius, *Edifices*, I, 1. 20

p. 112 'Thus died this prince,...', quoted Freely, *Istanbul: The Imperial City*, p. 89

p. 113 'who apply mathematical...', Procopius, *Edifices*, I, i, 24

p. 113 'suspended from Heaven', ibid, I. 1. 47

p. 114 'He does not guide...', quoted Baynes and Moss, p. 243

CHAPTER 11 – MEDIEVAL BYZANTIUM

p. 118 'In this year the emperor...', Theophanes, 347

p. 122 'and so unite...', ibid, 475

p. 125 'Although he could...', Psellus, p. 127

p. 125 'consul of philosophers', Ostrogorsky, p. 328

p. 125 'guardian of law', ibid, p. 328

p. 125 I met some of the experts..., ibid, p. 127

CHAPTER 12 – SELJUK TURKS AND CRUSADERS

p. 128 'a woman of great spirit...', Psellus, p. 255

p. 132 'he was the crowning...', Choniates, 47

p. 133 'The accursed Latins...', quoted Freely, *The Imperial City*, p. 140

p. 137 There were lamentations..., ibid, pp. 574–575, 586

CHAPTER 13 – THE LATIN OCCUPATION

p. 142 'Sultan of the Two Seas', Freely, *Storm on Horseback*, p. 69

p. 142 'No eye remained...', quoted, ibid, p. 76

p. 144 Around the lovely..., Gardner, p. 303

p. 145 'thorns replaced the rose...', quoted Freely, *Storm on Horseback*, p. 98

p. 146 'like smoked out bees', quoted Freely, *The Imperial City*, p. 152

p. 147 The emperor entered..., quoted ibid, p. 152

CHAPTER 14 – THE SONS OF OSMAN

p. 149 'troubles confused the Emperor...', quoted Freely, *Storm on Horseback*, p. 102

p. 150 'the region of the Maeander', quoted, ibid, p. 102

p. 150 'to uncoordinated attacks...', quoted, ibid, p. 102

p. 150 'uprooting vineyards, destroying...', quoted ibid, p. 103

p. 150 'the surrounding population...', quoted ibid, p. 103

p. 151 'When the emperor...', quoted ibid, p. 112

p. 152 'received a great army...', quoted ibid, p. 114

p. 153 'an impious alliance', quoted ibid, p. 165

p. 155 'a great Christian prince...', quoted ibid, p. 168

p. 156 'had the heads collected...', quoted Imber, p. 119

p. 157 'with such mournings...', quoted ibid, p. 169

p. 158 'knew that Belgrade...', quoted Imber, p. 119

p. 158 'many men and lords...', quoted ibid, p. 119

p. 159 'I have given...', quoted ibid, p. 129

p. 161 When he became heir..., Kritoboulos, pp. 13–14

p. 161 'This man, who just...', Sphrantzes, p. 59

CHAPTER 15 – THE FALL OF BYZANTIUM

p. 162 'to build a strong...', Kritoboulos, pp. 15–16

p. 162 'moved with a great...' quoted Freely, *The Grand Turk*, pp. 34–35

p. 163 'Spare us, O Lord,...', Doukas, p. 221

p. 163 'asked to be forgiven...', Sphrantzes, pp. 124–125

p. 163 After this the Sultan..., Kritoboulos. pp. 76–77

p. 166 'The spider is the...', Freely, *Istanbul: The Imperial City*, pp. 43–44

p. 166 'appointed some of the youths...', Kritoboulos, pp. 85–86

p. 166 'of the horrible...' quoted Setton, Vol. 1, p. 139

p. 166 'shame of Christendom.', quoted Setton, Vol. 1, p. 140

p. 166 'to his vezirs and...', Inalcık, 'The Policy of Mehmet II...', p. 233

p. 166 'a most intelligent...' Kritoboulos, p. 85

p. 167 He sent an order..., Kritoboulos, pp. 93, 105

p. 167 'He issued orders...', Sphrantzes, p. 134

p. 168 'that no one should...', Babinger, p. 104

p. 168 'the finest and best...', Kritoboulos, p. 93

p. 168 'ordered the construction...', ibid, p. 93

p. 168 'command... to all able...', ibid, p. 140

p. 168 'also commanded them...', ibid, p. 140

p. 160 'He saw it and was...', ibid, p. 136

p. 170 'marched straight into...', Sphrantzes, p. 80

p. 172 'Sultan of the two...', Necipoğlu, p. 34

CHAPTER 16 – THE TIDE OF CONQUEST TURNS

p. 173 'inquired about the tombs...', Kritoboulos, p. 181

p. 174 'glory and splendor...' Babinger, p. 284

p. 174 'All Venice is in the grip...', Babinger, p. 284

p. 176 'The enemy is at...', quoted ibid, p. 358

p. 177 'at the twenty-second...', quoted Imber, p. 252

p. 177 'Beside the gracious gift...', quoted ibid, p. 252

p. 180 'Selim the Grim died...', quoted Freely, *Jem Sultan*, p. 304

p. 180 'He is said to be...', quoted Freely, *Istanbul: The Imperial City*, p. 194

p. 181 'to be master...', quoted Freely, *Jem Sultan*, p. 306

p. 183 'all the Christians would...', quoted Freely, *Inside the Seraglio*, p. 171

p. 185 'to respect the...' Freely, *The Grand Turk*, p. 207

CHAPTER 17 – *TOURKOKRATEIA* AND THE *RHOMAIOI*

p. 189 'we are now bereft...', Vacalopoulos, p. 110

pp. 189–90 'For if our nation...', ibid, p. 116

p. 190 'to regain their mother tongue...', Augustinos, p. 170

p. 190 'Greek brothers who had...', ibid, pp. 170–171

p. 190 'by a pure and unadulterated...', ibid, p. 171

p. 190 'They have not the tie...', Ramsay, 'Intermixture of Races', pp. 240–241

pp. 190-1 Throughout Turkey the power..., ibid, pp. 403–404

p. 191 'pitiable remnants of the once...', Augustinos, p. 32

p. 191 When the Greeks recovered..., ibid, p. 261

pp. 192-3 When we first came..., Bryer, IX, p. 31

p. 193 'living secretly', Vacalopoulos, p. 251

p. 194 'as shall resort hither...', Freely, *The Aegean Coast of Turkey*, p. 88

p. 194 'for commerce, Smyrna is...', Augustinos, p. 38

p. 194 'the taverns were open...', *Music in the Aegean*, p. 46

p. 194 'The factors, and other...', Chandler, p. 60

pp. 194-5 The conflux at Smyrna..., ibid, p. 60

p. 195 'Girls of inferior rank...', ibid, p. 61

p. 195 'We now saw a level...', ibid, pp, 13–15

p. 195 'a Greek village, so miserable,...', ibid, p. 35

p. 195 'The Ephesians are now...', ibid, p. 87

p. 195 'We now seek in vain...', ibid, p. 93

p. 195 'a very mean place', ibid, p. 97

p. 196 A small bier, prettily..., ibid, p. 159

p. 196 'We were assured...', ibid, p. 198

p. 197 'New Miletus, metropolis...', Clogg, *I Kath'mas Anatoli*, p. 137

p. 197 'a free republic...', ibid, p. 137

p. 197 'Ayvalık was for half a century...', ibid, p. 137

p. 197 'the first piece of free...', ibid, p. 137

p. 198 has resulted in the..., Augustinos, p. 29

p. 198 'A number of factories...', Llewellyn Smith, pp. 25–26

p. 199 Greek scholars incline..., Clogg, *Anatolica*, p. 66

p. 199 'It would seem...', Vryonis, p. 457

p. 200 'the divine language...', Clogg, *Anatolica*, III, p. 81

p. 200 'of the foreign usages,...', ibid, III, p. 81

pp. 200-1 During the early years..., ibid, III, p.85

p. 201 'As many as wish...', Bryer, XVII, p. 13

p. 201 'I have seldom seen...', Hamilton, Vol 1, p. 170

p. 202 'most earnestly Christian', Bryer, XVII, p. 20

p. 202 'These people felt...', ibid, XVII, p. 20

p. 202 Then, when I went..., Dawkins, p. 261

CHAPTER 18 – *MEGALI IDEA* AND *CATASTROPHIA*

p. 203 The Kingdom of Greece..., Llewellyn Smith, pp. 2–3
p. 204 Do not think that..., Clogg, *Anatolica*, IV, p. 253
p. 204 'In the large commercial cities...', ibid, II, p. 196
p. 205 'The terror attacked...', Toynbee, p. 140
p. 205 'he would be unable...', Akçam, p. 105
p. 206 'Couldn't we just throw...', ibid, p. 105
p. 206 'The number of persons dispatched...', quoted ibid, p. 106
pp. 206–7 It is true that..., quoted Llewellyn Smith, p. 53
p. 209 'the Turkish national sentiment...', quoted ibid, p. 112
p. 213 What I see as I stand..., quoted ibid, p. 310
p. 213 'It is impossible to estimate...', quoted Dobkin Housepian, p. 201
p. 213 'The torch was applied...', quoted ibid, p. 229

CHAPTER 19 – EXODUS AND DIASPORA

p. 216 As from the 1st May, 1923,..., Pentzopoulos, Appendix I, p. 17
p. 216 'Those Greeks and Moslems...', ibid, Appendix I, p. 17
p. 216 In a never-ending,..., quoted Freely, *Turkey Around the Marmara*, p. 24
p. 217 A more tragic sight..., Pentzopoulos, p. 96
p. 218 'the reconciled Ottoman Greeks,...', quoted Clogg, *Anatolica*, III, p. 65
p. 218 'Orthodox Turks [who had never]...', quoted Pentzopoulos, p. 65
p. 219 'Turkish-speaking persons...', quoted ibid, p. 65
p. 219 'a special ecclesiastical province...', quoted ibid, p. 82
p. 220 Believers in a traditional..., quoted Clark, p. 217
p. 220 The aspect of the country..., quoted Pentzopoulos, p. 111
pp. 220–1 This is explained by..., ibid, pp. 112–113
p. 221 'In front we looked on...', ibid, p. 193
p. 221 Cheer up, my refugee girl,..., Hirschon, *Crossing the Aegean*, p. 252
p. 222 What is it to you..., Beaton, p. 195
p. 222 My eyes have never seen..., Freely, *The Western Shores of Turkey*, p. 67
pp. 222–3 translated for the author by Eirene Bamias

CHAPTER 20 – IONIAN ELEGY

p. 225 'the earliest and finest...', quoted Freely, *The Aegean Coast of Turkey*,
     p. 81

p. 226 'Smyrna has the river Meles...', Pausanias, I, p. 244

p. 226 'having washed her horses...', Freely, *The Aegean Coast of Turkey*, p. 85

p. 226 'I sing the praises...', ibid, p. 85

p. 227 'the First of Asia...', Cadoux, p. 172

p. 229 If paradise really..., Sotiriou, pp. 15–16

pp. 229–30 Saint John's Day was..., ibid, pp. 17–18

p. 230 Across from us,..., ibid, pp. 297–298

p. 231 I remember still:..., Seferis, *Collected Poems*, p. 188

pp. 231–2 The panes of the..., Seferis, *A Poet's Journal*, pp. 167–168

p. 232 Then toward Smyrna;..., ibid, pp. 164–165

p. 233 'On a jutting promontory...', *Odyssey*, XXIV, 80–85

Bibliography

Aeschylus, *The Persians*, tran. Herbert Weir Smith, Cambridge, Mass., 1959–63

Akçam, Taner, *A Shameful Act: The Armenian Genocide and the Question of Turkish Responsibility*, New York, 2006

Akurgal, Ekrem, *Ancient Civilizations and Ruins of Turkey: From Prehistoric Times to the End of the Roman Empire*, tran. John Whybrow, 6th edn, Istanbul, 1985

Alexandris, Alexis, *The Greek Minority of Istanbul in Greek-Turkish Relations, 1918–1971*, Athens, 1992

Allen, Susan Heuck, *Finding the Walls of Troy: Frank Calvert and Heinrich Schliemann at Hisarlik*, Berkeley, 1999

Ammianus Marcellinus, *Res Gestae*, 3 vols, tran. John C. Rolfe, Cambridge, Mass., 1939

Anderson, Sonia, *An English Consul in Turkey, Paul Rycaut at Smyrna, 1667–1678*, Oxford and New York, 1989

Angold, Michael, *A Byzantine Government in Exile: Government and Society Under the Laskarids of Nicaea (1204–1261)*, London, 1975

———, *The Byzantine Empire 1025–1204: A Political History*, London and New York, 1984

Anna Comnena, *The Alexiad*, tran. E. R. A. Sewter, London, 1969

Arrian, *The Campaigns of Alexander*, tran. Aubrey de Sélincourt, Harmondsworth, 1958

Augustinos, Gerasimos, *The Greeks of Asia Minor: Confession, Community and Ethnicity in the Nineteenth Century*, Kent, Ohio, 1992

Austin, M. M., *The Hellenistic World from Alexander to the Roman Conquest: A Selection of Ancient Sources in Translation*, Cambridge, 1981

Babinger, Franz, *Mehmed the Conqueror and his Time*, tran. Ralph Manheim, ed. William C. Hickman, Princeton, 1978

Barbaro, Nicolo, *Diary of the Siege of Constantinople*, tran. J. P. Jones, New York, 1969

Baynes, Norman H. and H. St. L. B. Moss (ed.), *Byzantium: An Introduction to East Roman Civilization*, Oxford, 1949

Bean, George, *Aegean Turkey, An Archaeological Guide*, London, 1966

———, *Turkey's Southern Shore*, London, 1968

———, *Turkey Beyond the Maeander*, London, 1971

———, *Lycia*, London, 1978

Beaton, Roderick, *Folk Poetry of Modern Greece*, Cambridge, 1980

Benson, E. F., *The Life of Alcibiades: The Idol of Athens*, London, 1928

Bible, *The Jerusalem*, Popular Edition, London, 1966

Blegen, Carl W., *Troy and the Trojans*, New York, 1995

Boardman, John, *The Greeks Overseas*, Baltimore, 1964

Bowersock, G. W., *Julian the Apostate*, Cambridge, Mass., 1978

Braude, Benjamin and Bernard Lewis (eds), *Christians and Jews in the Ottoman Empire: The Founding of a Plural Society*, 2 vols, New York, 1981

Brewer, David, *The Greek War of Independence: The Struggle for Freedom from Ottoman Oppression and the Birth of the Modern Greek Nation*, New York, 2001

Brown, Peter, *The World of Late Antiquity*, London, 1971

Bryce, Trevor, *The Trojans and Their Neighbours*, London and New York, 2006

Bryer, Anthony, *Peoples and Settlement in Anatolia and the Caucasus, 800–1900*, London, 1998

Burn, Andrew Robert, *The Lyric Age of Greece*, London, 1960

———, *Persia and the Greeks: The Defence of the West, c. 546–478 BC*, London, 1962

———, *The Pelican History of Greece*, Harmondsworth, 1965

Burnet, John, *Greek Philosophy: Thales to Plato*, London, 1981

Bury, J. B., *History of the Later Roman Empire, from the death of Theodosius I to the death of Justinian*, 2 vols, New York, 1958

———, *A History of Greece to the Death of Alexander the Great*, 3rd edn, London, 1966

Cadoux, Cecil John, *Ancient Smyrna: A History of the City from the Earliest Times to 324 AD*, Oxford, 1938

Cahen, Claude, *Pre-Ottoman Turkey*, London, 1968

———, *The Formation of Turkey: The Seljukid Sultanate of Rum, Eleventh to Fourteenth Century*, tran. and ed. P. M. Holt, Harlow, Essex, 2001

Cambridge Ancient History, 3rd edn, Vol. II, Part 1, *History of the Middle East and the Aegean Region c. 1800–1380 BC*, ed. I. E. S. Edwards et al, Cambridge, 1973

———, Vol. VI, *The Fourth Century BC*, 2nd edn, ed. D. M. Lewis et al, Cambridge, 1994

Cambridge History of Islam, The, 2 vols, ed. P. M. Holt, Ann K. S. Lambton and Bernard Lewis, Cambridge, 1970

Cameron, Averil, *The Later Roman Empire AD, 284–430*, London, 1993

Cary, M., *The Geographical Background of Greek and Roman History*, Oxford, 1949

————, *A History of the Greek World from 323 to 146 BC*, London, 1951

————, *A History of Rome Down to the Reign of Constantine*, London, 1954

Chadwick, John, *The Mycenaean World*, Cambridge, 1976

Chamoux, François, *Hellenistic Civilization*, tran. Michael Roussel, Oxford, 2003

Chandler, Richard, *Travels in Asia Minor 1764–1765*, ed. and abridged by Edith Clay, London, 1971

Choniates, Nicetas, tran. H. Magoulias as *O City of Byzantium*, Detroit, 1984

Clagett, Marshall, *Greek Science in Antiquity*, London, 2001

Clark, Bruce, *Twice a Stranger: How Mass Expulsion Forged Modern Greece and Turkey*, London, 2006

Clogg, Richard (ed.), *Anatolica, Studies in the Greek East in the 18th and 19th Centuries*, Aldershot, Hampshire, 1996

————, *I Kath'imas Anatoli: Studies in Ottoman Greek History*, Istanbul, 2004

Cohen, Getzel M., *The Hellenistic Settlements in Europe, the Islands, and Asia Minor*, Berkeley and Los Angeles, 1995

Cook, J. M., *The Greeks in Ionia and the East*, London, 1962

————, *The Troad: An Archaeological and Topographical Study*, Oxford, 1973

————, *The Persian Empire*, New York, 1983

Cook, Michael A., *Population Pressure in Rural Anatolia, 1450–1600*, London, 1962

Croke, Brian, *Count Marcellinus and his Chronicle*, Oxford, 2001

Crossland, R. A. and Ann Birchall (ed.), *Bronze Age Migrations in the Aegean: Archaeological and Linguistic Problems in Greek Prehistory*, Park Ridge, New Jersey, 1976

Dakin, Douglas, *The Unification of Greece 1770–1923*, London, 1975

Dawkins, R. M., 'The Crypto-Christians of Turkey', *Byzantion* VIII (1933), 247–275

Desborough, V. R. d'A., *The Greek Dark Ages*, New York, 1972

————, *The Last Mycenaeans and their Successors: An Archaeological Survey c. 1200 – c. 1000 BC*, Oxford, 1994

Deuel, Leo, *Memoirs of Heinrich Schliemann: A Documentary Portrait Drawn from His Autobiographical Writings, Letters, and Excavation Reports*, New York, 1977

Dio Cassius, *Dio's Roman History*, 3 vols, tran. Earnest Cary, London, 1914–17

Diodorus Siculus, tran. C. H. Oldfather et al, London, 1933–1967

Dobkin Housepian, Marjorie, *Smyrna, 1922: The Destruction of a City*, Kent, Ohio, ca. 1990

Doukas, *Decline and Fall of Byzantium to the Ottoman Turks*, tran. Harry J. Magoulias, Detroit, 1975

Dowden, Ken, 'The Epic Tradition in Greece', in Robert Fowler (ed.), *The Cambridge Companion to Homer*, pp. 188–205

Drews, Robert, *The Coming of the Greeks: Indo-European Conquests in the Aegean and the Near East*, Princeton, 1988

_____, *The End of the Bronze Age: Changes in Warfare and the Catastrophe ca. 1200 BC*, Princeton, 1993

Dunbabin, T. J., *The Greeks and their Near Eastern Neighbours*, London, 1957

Erskine, Andrew (ed.), *A Companion to the Hellenistic World*, Oxford, 2003

Eusebius, *The History of the Church (Ecclesiastical History)*, tran. G. A. Williamson, New York, 1965

Finkel, Caroline, *Osman's Dream: The Story of the Ottoman Empire 1300–1923*, London, 2005

Finkelberg, Margalit, *Greeks and Pre-Greeks: Aegean Prehistory and Greek Historic Tradition*, Cambridge, 2005

Finley, M. I., *The World of Odysseus*, Harmondsworth, 1954

Fisher, Sydney Nettleton, *The Foreign Relations of Turkey, 1481–1513*, Urbana, Illinois, 1948

Foss, Clive, *Byzantine and Turkish Sardis*, Cambridge, Mass., 1976

_____, *Ephesus After Antiquity*, Cambridge, 1979

Fowler, Robert (ed.), *The Cambridge Companion to Homer*, Cambridge, 2004

Fox, Robin Lane, *Alexander the Great*, Harmondsworth, 1973

_____, *Pagans and Christians*, New York, 1987

Fraser, P. M and George Bean, *The Rhodian Peraea and Islands*, London, 1954

Freely, John, *Classical Turkey*, London, 1991

_____, *The Bosphorus*, Istanbul, 1993

_____, *The Companion Guide to Turkey*, 2nd edn, London, 1993

_____, *The Aegean Coast of Turkey*, Istanbul, 1996

_____, *The Black Sea Coast of Turkey*, Istanbul, 1996

_____, *Istanbul: The Imperial City*, London, 1996

_____, *The Western Mediterranean Coast of Turkey*, Istanbul, 1997

_____, *The Eastern Mediterranean Coast of Turkey*, Istanbul, 1998

_____, *Turkey Around the Marmara*, Istanbul, 1998

_____, *The Western Interior of Turkey*, Istanbul, 1998

_____, *Inside the Seraglio, Private Lives of the Sultans in Istanbul* London, 1999

_____, *The Lost Messiah*, London, 2001

_____, *Jem Sultan: The Adventures of a Captive Turkish Prince in Renaissance Europe*, London, 2004

_____, *The Western Shores of Turkey*, London, 2004

_____, *Storm on Horseback: The Seljuk Warriors of Turkey*, London, 2008

_____, *The Grand Turk: Sultan Mehmet II – Conqueror of Constantinople, Master of an Empire and Lord of Two Seas*, London, 2009

Gardner, Alice, *The Lascarids of Nicaea: The Story of an Empire in Exile*, London, 1912

Gibbons, Herbert Adams, *The Foundation of the Ottoman Empire: A History of The Osmanlis up to the Death of Bayazid I (1300–1403)*, Oxford, 1916

Goffman, Daniel, *Izmir and the Levantine World, 1550–1650*, Seattle, 1990

_____, *The Ottoman Empire and Early Modern Europe*, Cambridge, 2002

Gondicas, Dimitri and Charles Issawi (ed.), *Ottoman Greeks in the Age of Nationalism: Politics, Economy and Nationalism in the Nineteenth Century* Princeton, 1999

Goodman, Martin, with the assistance of Jane Sherwood, *The Roman World, 44 BC – AD 180*, London, 1997

Grant, Michael, *The Rise of the Greeks*, London, 1987

Green, Peter, *Alexander of Macedon, 356–323 BC: A Historical Biography*, Berkeley, 1991

Gurney, O. R., *The Hittites*, London, 1954

Guthrie, William K. C., *A History of Greek Philosophy*, 6 vols, Cambridge, 1962–1981

Hall, Jonathan, *Hellenicity: Between Ethnicity and Culture*, Chicago and London, 2002

Hamilton, William J., *Researches in Asia Minor, Pontus and Armenia*, 2 vols, London, 1842

Hammond, N. G. L., *A History of Greece to 322 BC*, Oxford, 1959

_____, *Philip of Macedon*, London, 1994

Hansen, Esther V., *The Attalids of Pergamum*, 2nd edn, Ithaca, New York, 1971

Hasluck, F. W., *Christianity and Islam Under the Sultans*, Oxford, 1929

_____, 'The Crypto-Christians of Trebizond', *Journal of Hellenic Studies* 41 (1921), 199–202

Herodotus, *The Histories*, tran. Aubrey de Sélincourt, new edition, rev. John Marincola, London, 1972

Hesiod, the Homeric Hymns and Homerica, tran. Hugh G. Evelyn-White, Cambridge, Mass., 1914

Hesiod, Theogony and Works and Days, tran. Dorothea Wender, New York, 1973

Hignett, C., *Xerxes' Invasion of Greece*, Oxford, 1963

Hirschon, Renée, *Heirs to the Greek Catastrophe: The Social Life of Asia Minor Refugees in Piraeus*, New York, 1989

————, (ed.), *Crossing the Aegean: An Appraisal of the 1923 Compulsory Population Exchange Between Greece and Turkey*, New York and Oxford, 2003

Homer, *The Iliad*, tran. Richmond Lattimore, Chicago, 1951

The Odyssey, tran. Richmond Lattimore, New York, 1965

Hooker, J. T., *Mycenaean Greece*, London and Boston, 1976

Hornblower, Simon, *The Greek World, 479–323 BC*, rev. edn, London and New York, 1991

Huxley, G. L., *Achaeans and Hittites*, Oxford, 1969

————, *The Early Ionians*, London, 1966

Imber, Colin, *The Ottoman Empire, 1300–1481*, Istanbul, 1990

Inalcık, Halil, *The Ottoman Empire: The Classical Age*, Oxford, 1959–1962

————, 'The Policy of Mehmet II Toward the Greek Population of Istanbul and the Byzantine Buildings of the City', *Dumbarton Oaks Papers* 23–24 (1969–1970)

Irbie-Massie, Georgia L. and Paul T. Keyser, *Greek Science of the Hellenistic Era: A Sourcebook*, London and New York, 2002

Janin, R., *The Separated Eastern Churches*, London, 1933

Jeffrey, L. H., *Archaic Greece: The City-States c. 700–500 BC*, New York, 1976

Jenkins, Romilly, *Byzantium: The Imperial Centuries AD 610–1071*, Toronto, 1987

Jones, A. H. M., *Cities of the Eastern Roman Province*, Oxford, 1937

————, *The Later Roman Empire, 284–602*, 4 vols, Oxford, 1964

————, *The Decline of the Ancient World*, New York, 1966

Kafadar, Cemal, *Between Two Worlds: The Construction of the Ottoman State*, Berkeley, 1995

Kagan, Donald, *The Outbreak of the Peloponnesian War*, Ithaca and London, 1969

Kazhdan, A. P. (ed.), *The Oxford Dictionary of Byzantium*, 3 vols, Oxford, 1991

Kinross, Patrick Balfour, Baron, *Atatürk: The Rebirth of a Nation*, London, 1964

Kirk, G. S. and J. E. Raven, *The Presocratic Philosophers*, Cambridge, 1962

Korfmann, Manfred and Dietrich Mannsberger, *Homer, the Iliad and After*, Istanbul, ca. 1992

————, *A Guide to Troia*, Istanbul, 2001

Kritoboulos of Imbros, *History of Mehmed the Conqueror*, tran. Charles T. Riggs, Princeton, 1954

Latacz, Joachim, *Troy and Homer: Towards a Solution of an old Mystery*, tran. Windle and Rosh Ireland, Oxford, 2004

Lattimore, Richmond (tran.), *Greek Lyrics*, 2nd edn, Chicago, 1960

Leaf, Walter, *Troy a Study in Homeric Geography*, London, 1912

Lefkowitz, Mary R., *The Lives of the Greek Poets*, London, 1981

Llewellyn Smith, Michael, *Ionian Vision: Greece in Asia Minor, 1919–1922*, London, 1996

Lloyd, G. E. R., *Early Greek Science: Thales to Aristotle*, New York, 1970

_____, *Greek Science After Aristotle*, New York, 1973

Lloyd, Seton, *Early Anatolia*, Harmondsworth, 1956

_____, *Early Highland Peoples of Anatolia*, London, 1967

_____, *Ancient Turkey*, London, 1989

Lowry, Heath W., *The Nature of the Early Ottoman State*, Albany, 2003

_____, *Ottoman Bursa in Travel Accounts*, Bloomington, Indiana, 2003

Macqueen, J. G., *The Hittites and their Contemporaries in Asia Minor*, revised edn, London, 1986

Magie, D., *Roman Rule in Asia Minor*, 3 vols, Princeton, 1950

Mallory, J. P., *In Search of the Indo-Europeans: Language, Archaeology and Myth*, London, 1989

Mansfield, Peter, 'Letter from Tere-Sapunadzi', *Times Literary Supplement* 21 April 2000, pp. 15–16

McCarthy, Justin, *Muslims and Minorities: The Population of Ottoman Anatolia and the End of the Empire*, New York, 1983

Meiggs, Russell, *The Athenian Empire*, Oxford, 1972

Meinardus, Otto F. A., *St Paul in Ephesus and the Cities of Galatia and Cyprus*, Athens, 1973

_____, *St John of Patmos and the Seven Churches of the Apocalypse*, Athens, 1974

Mellaart, James, *Earliest Civilizations of the Near East*, London, 1965

_____, *The Neolithic of the Near East*, New York, 1975

Miller, William, *Trebizond: The Last Greek Empire of the Byzantine Era, 1204–1461*, Chicago, 1969

Mitchell, Stephen, *Anatolia, Land, Men and Gods in Asia Minor*, 2 vols, Oxford, 1995

_____, *A History of the Later Roman Empire AD 284–641*, Oxford, 2007

Mommsen, Theodor, *The Provinces of the Roman Empire, from Caesar to Diocletian*, tran. William P. Dickson, 2 vols in 1, 1909, repr. New York, 1996

Music in the Aegean, Greek Ministry of Culture – Ministry of the Aegean, Athens, 1987

Nagy, Gregory, *Homeric Questions*, Austin, Texas, 1966

Necipoğlu, Gülrü, *Architecture, Ceremonial and Power: The Topkapı Palace in the Fifteenth and Sixteenth Centuries*, Cambridge, Mass., 1991

Nicol, Donald M., *The Last Centuries of Byzantium 1261–1453*, 2nd edn, Cambridge, 1993

Ostrogorsky, George, *History of the Byzantine State*, tran. Joan Hussey, Oxford, 1968

Oxford Classical Dictionary, ed. N. G. L. Hammond and H. H. Scullard, Oxford, 1970

Page, Denys, *Sappho and Alcaeus, An Introduction to the Study of Ancient Lesbian Poetry*, Oxford, 1955

_____, *History and the Homeric Iliad*, Berkeley and Los Angeles, 1959

Palatine Anthology, tran. as the *Greek Anthology* by W.R. Paton, London 1916–18

Pallis, A. A., *Greece's Anatolian Venture – and After: A Survey of the Diplomatic and Political Aspects of the Greek Expedition to Asia Minor (1915–1922)*, London, 1937

Pastor, Ludwig, *The History of the Popes, from the close of the Middle Ages: Drawn from the Secret Archives of the Vatican and other Original Sources*, 5th edn, 10 vols, tran. from the German, London, 1950

Pausanias, *Description of Greece*, 2 vols, tran. Peter Levi, Harmondsworth, 1985

Pentzopoulos, Dimitri, *The Balkan Exchange of Minorities and its Impact on Greece*, new impression, London, 2002

Peters, F. E., *The Harvest of Hellenism: A History of the Near East from Alexander the Great to the Triumph of Christianity*, New York, 1970

Petropoulos, Elias, *Songs of the Greek Underworld: The Rebetika Tradition*, tran. and intro. Ed Emery, London, 2000

Plutarch, *Parallel Lives*, 11 vols, tran. Bernadotte Perrin, London and Cambridge, Mass., 1958–1959

Polybius, *The Histories*, 6 vols, tran. W.B. Paton, London, 1922–1927

Procopius of Caesarea, *Works*, 7 vols, tran. H. B. Dewing, London, 1914– 1940

Psellus, Michael, *The Chronographia*, tran. E. R. A. Sewter, New Haven, 1953

Ramsay, William, *Impressions of Turkey During Twelve Years' Wanderings*, London, 1897

_____, *Letters to the Seven Churches*, London, 1901

_____, 'The Intermixture of Races in Asia Minor: Some of its Causes and Effects', Proceedings of the British Academy 7 (1915–1916), 359–422

_____, *Asianic Elements in Greek Civilization*, London, 1928

_____, *The Historical Geography of Asia Minor*, New York, 1972

Rice, Tamara Talbot, *The Seljuks in Asia Minor*, London, 1961

Ricks, David and Paul Magdalino (eds), *Byzantium and the Modern Greek Identity*, Ashgate, Hampshire 1998

Rostovtzeff, M., *The Social and Economic History of the Hellenistic World*, 3 vols, Oxford, 1941

Runciman, Steven, *The Fall of Constantinople, 1453*, Cambridge, 1965

_____, *The Great Church in Captivity: A Study of the Patriarchate of Constantinople from the Eve of the Turkish Conquest to the Greek War of Independence*, Cambridge, 1985

Rycaut, Paul, *The Present State of the Ottoman Empire*, London, 1668, reprint, London, 1972

Sandars, N. K., *The Sea Peoples: Warriors of the Ancient Mediterranean 1250–1150 BC*, London, 1978

Sarınay, Yusuf, Hamit Pehlivanlı and Abdullah Saydam, *The Pontus Issue and the Policy of Greece*, Ankara, 2000

Sarton, George, *A History of Science*, 2 vols, Cambridge, Mass., 1952, 1959

Schliemann, Heinrich, *Troy and its Remains: A Narrative of Researches and Discoveries On the Site of Ilium and in the Trojan Plain*, London, 1875, reprint New York, 1976

_____, *Ilios: The city and country of the Trojans, the results of researches and Discoveries on the Site of Troy and Throughout the Troad in the Years 1871, 72, 73, 78, 79. Including an Autobiography of the Author*, London, 1881, reprint, New York, 1996

Schwoebel, R., *The Shadow of the Crescent: The Renaissance Image of the Turk, 1454–1517*, New York, 1967

Sealey, Raphael, *A History of the Greek City States ca. 700–338 BC*, Berkeley, 1976

Seferis, George, *Complete Poems*, tran. and ed. Edmund Keeley and Philip Sherrard, London, 1995

_____, *A Poet's Journal: Days of 1941–1955*, tran. Athan Anagnostopoulos, Cambridge, Mass., 1974

Sélincourt, Aubrey de, *The World of Herodotus*, Boston, 1966

Setton, Kenneth M., *The Papacy and the Levant (1204–1571)*, 4 vols, Philadelphia, 1976

Shaw, Stanford J., *History of the Ottoman Empire and Modern Turkey*, Vol. 1, *Empire of the Gazis: The Rise and Decline of the Ottoman Empire 1280–1808*, Cambridge, 1977

Shaw, Stanford and Ezel Kural Shaw, *History of the Ottoman Empire and Modern Turkey*, Vol. 2, *Reform, Revolution and Republic: The Rise of Modern Turkey 1808–1975*, Cambridge, 1977

Shipley, Graham, *The Greek World After Alexander 323–330 BC*, London and New York, 2000

Sinasos in Cappadocia, Athens, 1986

Smith, John Sharwood, *Greece and the Persians*, Bristol, 1990

Snodgrass, A. M., *The Dark Age of Greece: An Archaeological Study of the Eleventh to Eighth Century BC*, Edinburgh, 1971

Sotiriou, Dido, *Farewell Anatolia*, tran. Fred A. Reed, Athens, 1991

Sphrantzes, George, *The Fall of the Byzantine Empire*, tran. M. Philippides, Amherst, 1980

Starr, Chester G., *The Origins of Greek Civilization*, New York, 1962

Strabo, *The Geography*, 8 vols, tran. Horace Leonard Jones, Cambridge, Mass., 1969

Tatsios, Theodore George, *The Megali Idea and the Greek-Turkish War of 1897: The Impact of the Cretan Problem on Greek Irredentism, 1866–1897*, New York, 1984

Theophanes Confessor, *The Chronicle of Theophanes Confessor*, tran. Cyril Mango and Roger Scott, Oxford, 1997

Thucydides, *History of the Peloponnesian War*, tran. Rex Warner, Harmondsworth, 1987

Toynbee, Arnold J., *The Western Question in Greece and Turkey: A Study in the Contrast of Civilisations*, Boston, 1922

Traill, David A., *Schliemann of Troy, Treasure and Deceit*, London, 1995

Treadgold, Warren, *A History of the Byzantine State and Society*, Stanford, California, 1997

———, *The Early Byzantine Historians*, New York, 2007

Tursun Beg, *The History of Mehmet the Conqueror*, tran. Halil Inalcık and Rhoads Murphey, Minneapolis, 1978

Ülker, Necmi, *The Rise of Izmir, 1688–1740*, Ann Arbor, Michigan, 1971

Vacalopoulos, Apostolos, *The Greek Nation, 1453–1669: The Cultural and Economic Background of Modern Greek Society*, tran. Ian and Phania Moles, New Brunswick, New Jersey, 1971

Van Dam, Raymond, *Kingdom of Snow, Roman Rule and Greek Culture in Cappadocia*, Philadelphia, 2002

Vitruvius, *The Ten Books on Architecture,* tran. Morriss Hicky Morgan, New York, 1980

Vryonis, Speros, Jr., *The Decline of Medieval Hellenism in Asia Minor and the Process of Islamization from the Eleventh through the Fifteenth Century*, Berkeley, 1971

Wilson, N. G., *Scholars of Byzantium*, Baltimore, Maryland, 1983

Wittek, Paul, *The Rise of the Ottoman Empire*, London, 1938

Wolff, Robert Lee, *Studies in the Latin Empire of Constantinople*, London, 1976

Wood, Michael, *In Search of the Trojan War*, New York, 1983

Woodhouse, C. M., *Modern Greece: A Short History*, 4th edn, London, 1968

Xenophon, *The Persian Expedition*, tran. Rex Warner, Harmondsworth, 1959

_____, *Hellenica (A History of My Times)*, tran. Rex Warner, Harmondsworth, 1966

Zosimus, *Historia Nova*, tran. J. J. Buchanan and H. T. Davis, San Antonio, Texas, 1967

Index